THE BUTTON BOX

Lifting the Lid on Women's Lives

Lynn Knight

Chatto & Windus

LONDON

1 3 5 7 9 10 8 6 4 2

Chatto & Windus, an imprint of Vintage,
20 Vauxhall Bridge Road,
London SW1V 2SA

Chatto & Windus is part of the Penguin Random House
group of companies whose addresses can be found at
global.penguinrandomhouse.com

Penguin
Random House
UK

First published by Chatto & Windus in 2016

Illustrations by Willa Gebbie.

www.vintage-books.co.uk

A CIP catalogue record for this book is available from the British Library

ISBN 9780701188917

Typeset by Palimpsest Book Production Ltd, Falkirk, Stirlingshire

Printed and bound in Great Britain by Clays Ltd, St Ives plc

Penguin Random House is committed to a sustainable future for our
business, our readers and our planet. This book is made from Forest
Stewardship Council® certified paper.

MIX
Paper from
responsible sources
FSC
www.fsc.org   FSC® C018179

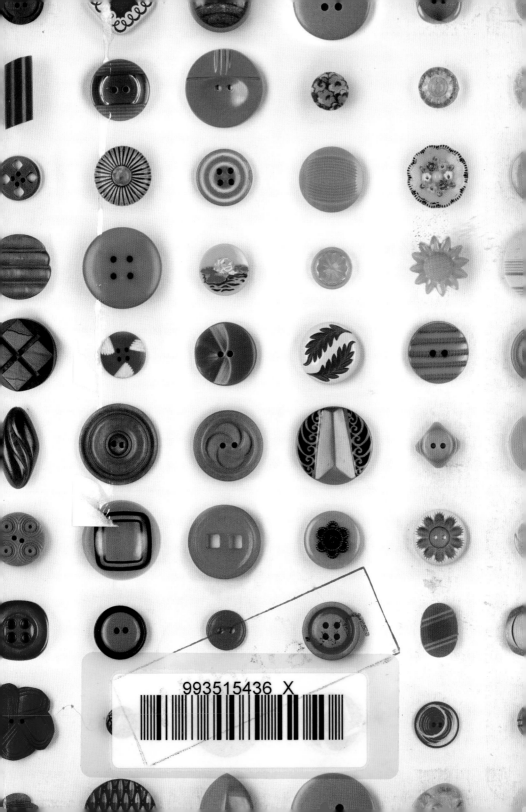

993515436 X

THE BUTTON BOX

I used to love the rattle and whoosh of my grandma's buttons as they scattered from their Quality Street tin.

An inlaid wooden box holds the buttons of three generations of women in Lynn Knight's family: a scarlet ladybird from her own childhood, chunky turquoise buttons that fastened her mother's sixties-era suit, a sky-blue buckle from a dress her grandmother wore. Every button tells a story.

'They change our view of the world and the world's view of us', said Virginia Woolf of clothes. *The Button Box* explores their role as emblems of security, identity and independence. From the jet button of Victorian mourning, to the short skirts of the 1960s, taking in suffragettes, bachelor girls, little dressmakers and madam shops, Biba and the hankering for vintage, *The Button Box* examines women's lives with elegance and wit.

ALSO BY LYNN KNIGHT

Clarice Cliff

Lemon Sherbet and Dolly Blue:
The Story of an Accidental Family

For my mother

CONTENTS

Preface: Family Buttons and Vintage Finds   **1**

1   **The Jet Button:** From Mourning to Glamour   **5**

2   **The Blackcurrant Button:** Elementary Sewing and the White-Blouse Revolution   **14**

'The Lasses' Resolution to Follow the Fashion'   **28**

3   **Girls Rule OK:** The Purple, White and Green   **29**

4   **The Silver Thimble:** The First World War and Munitionettes   **35**

5   **The Shoe Button:** Bachelor Girls Stride Ahead   **42**

Independent Living in the 1920s   **54**

6   **The Mackintosh Button:** Derring-Do and Fantasy Photographs   **55**

7   **The Linen Button:** Small Miracles on Small Means   **64**

A 1930s Button-Making Machine   **72**

8   **The Baby's Button:** 'Pray Let partiuclare care be taken'en off this Child'   **73**

9   **Eva's Glove Button:** Model Gowns and Inexpensive Dress   **81**

10 **The Interwar Fashion Button:** Tennis and Afternoon Tea   **93**

11 **The Edge-to-Edge Clasp:** Kissproof Lipstick and Ginger Rogers Frocks   **101**

Instructions from Miss Towsey, Draper   **113**

12 **The Twinkling Button:** Stitch in the Chic   **115**

13 **The Blue Slide Buckle:** A Paintbox of Summer Colour   **128**

Buttons and How to Make Them   **134**

14 **The Silver-and-Blue Button:** Good Little Suits in Wartime   **135**

The Women's Land Army: Uniform   **145**

15 **The Land Army Button:** Uniforms Not Uniformity   **146**

16 **The Velvet Flowers:** Hats   **160**

17 **The Coat Button:** Post-War and the New Look   **167**

Woman's Clothing Budget   **174**

18 **The Small, Drab Button:** Office Life in the 1950s   **175**

19 **The 'Perfect' Button:** The Etiquette of Dress   **185**

20 **The Doll's-House Doorknob:** Homemaking Large and Small   **192**

21 **The Ladybird Button:** Childhood   **202**

22 **Suspenders:** Corsetry, Scanties (& Sex)   **213**

23 **The Apron Button:** Domesticity   **223**

Buttonholes Step-by-Step   **235**

24 **The Diamanté Clasp:** A Little Razzle Dazzle   **236**

25 **The Toggle:** God, This Modern Youth!   **242**

26 **The Turquoise Button:** The New Kind of Woman   **253**

27 **The Statement Button:** Biba and the Hankering for Vintage   **261**

Clothing Prices: 1970–79   **268**

28 **Pearl Buttons:** Full Circle   **269**

Notes   **275**

Bibliography   **295**

Acknowledgements   **307**

THE BUTTON BOX

PREFACE: FAMILY BUTTONS AND VINTAGE FINDS

I reach into the button box to find the spangled mother-of-pearl criss-crossed with lines and the smaller pearl buttons with serrated edges I remember from my childhood. Here too are workaday reds, blues and greens; flats, domes and globes, diminutive glass flowers and glinting diamantés.

I used to love the rattle and whoosh of my grandma's buttons as they scattered from their Quality Street tin, but the tin has done its duty: my own button box is a Victorian writing case with zig-zag bands of marquetry and inlaid mother of pearl. I no longer hear the delicious sound of buttons striking metal but it is still a pleasure to delve for the button whose fish-eye holes, cut diagonally for thread, transform a simple square into diamond-shaped glamour.

As a very small child, I spent Friday afternoons at the house my grandma Annie shared with my great-aunt Eva. The Quality Street tin lodged on a window sill beside the one for Blue Bird Toffees which held my grandma's cotton reels. Buttons stood in for both sweets and currency in the games of shop the three of us played; their kitchen steps were my counter, askew in the pantry doorway. These afternoons also meant Jacobean-print curtains, lemon-scented geraniums and a stained-glass bureau whose individual panes I could trace with my fingertips; there was a rag rug before the hearth and a radio but no television. When my mum came to collect me, straight from town, in her nail polish and belted trench coat, she brought the 1960s into their sitting room.

My grandma's buttons reached back into the past with metal-shanked beauties from the nineteenth century and came forward into my childhood with the pale blue waterlily buttons and lady-birds she stitched on to the clothes she made for me. These buttons now sit among others I have amassed and some of my mother's too. (She, having a mother who at one time sewed for a living, has made it her business to do as little sewing as possible.) I cannot see their buttons without conjuring up the garments they fastened; the eye-popping turquoise buttons from my mum's sixties suit so very different in their message from the jet buttons of yesteryear, and the jet buttons themselves, different again from one another, whether fastening ankle-length Edwardian coats that just about swished clear of grimy pavements, or twinkling in a suggestion of upholstered, prickly bodices stiff with beads. I can hardly grasp the tiny buttons that fastened 1920s shoes; no wonder my great-aunt Eva's handbags from that time always held a buttonhook. Octagonal buttons recall a trim jacket of hers from the 1940s, that era of morale-boosting suits; a silk-covered button comes from the Chinese-style jacket my mum wore in the late 1950s, while expecting me. A *Times* leader rightly described button boxes as 'an epitome of family history'.

My grandma Annie was born in 1892, the decade of the New Woman. Times were changing and this working-class girl was photographed standing proudly with the bicycle that took her to grammar school. My great-aunt Eva was born in 1901 on the day of Queen Victoria's funeral. Not one for formal lessons, Eva left school as soon as she could and joined my great-grandma Betsy behind the counter of the family's corner shop on the outskirts of Chesterfield, Derbyshire.

My great-grandfather's name was above the door but, like many men in the district, he was engaged in industrial work of one kind or another; the shop was run by my great-grandma. This small shop served a straggle of terraced houses with basic foodstuffs, animal feed and occasional fripperies; linen buttons too, for sewing on to working men's shirts: the majority of customers in this tight small community were the wives of the colliery and foundry men who worked nearby and relied on the shop for groceries and more besides.

There was an Edwardian fastidiousness about my grandma Annie, whereas Eva was as sprightly as the 1920s, the decade when she came of age. My great-aunt was a good playmate when my brother and I were small; if anyone was likely to lead you into mischief it was Eva. More than the many games we played, I remember my delight when, as a teenager in the early 1970s, I discovered clothes my grandma and great-aunt had worn years earlier and had carefully put away: floor-length ribboned night-gowns with lacework bodices, a black silk dress buttoned with tiny glass flowers; a shimmering art-deco scarf. Old was becoming modern and, in some circles at least, vintage was newly chic (though, back in the day, 'vintage' was plain 'second-hand'). The magazines I read, *19* and *Honey*, showed young women who, when not reclining in Biba-like sophisticated poses, wore crêpe-de-Chine frocks set off with little leather handbags or beaded purses like the ones I found upstairs at Annie and Eva's. Around this time, my grandma's buttons acquired new meanings. I started raiding her button box for interesting finds to sew on home-made smocks and saw how glacé mint buttons and tiny pearl flowers complemented vintage clothes. Further discoveries awaited me in my own home: clothes worn by my mum as a younger woman, including a red tiered chiffon dress that shouted the 1960s.

Even now I can recall the thrill of those discoveries, see the jazzily patterned runner on the upstairs landing in Annie and Eva's house, recapture the shiver of silk and the shock of that red chiffon. Many of the clothes have long disappeared but the buttons remain. The button that makes a play on geometry was Annie's; best-dressed days saw Eva wearing buttoned gauntlets outlined in caramel-coloured leather – my grandma and great-aunt were no different from all the other women wanting to add a touch of glamour to their lives. Writer Jenifer Wayne lovingly recalls a purple dress that signified her becoming a woman; my own equivalent was a crêpe-de-Chine suit now remembered by a single button. 'They change our view of the world and the world's view of us', said Virginia Woolf of clothes. *The Button Box* explores their role as emblems of security, identity and independence, and the key part they play in keeping up appearances. Favourite dresses, best coats, everyday overalls, children's clothes: their buttons reach across the generations and the large and small stories of women's lives.

1 **THE JET BUTTON:** FROM MOURNING TO GLAMOUR

Buttons, beading, jewellery: jet was everywhere in the late nine-teenth and early twentieth centuries, scattered across fabrics and dripping from bosoms and shawls. Children's author Alison Uttley recalled the jet buttons in her mother's button box, 'shining like new coal, cut into facets, flat and pointed and angular'. She could rub jet buttons to electrify them and make paper men rise up and dance.

Multifaceted and twinkling, or resembling the large, flat Pontefract cakes that were my great-aunt Eva's favourite sweets, several jet buttons glitter in my own button box. The daintiest, with tiny metal shanks that fastened them on to nineteenth-century clothing, spangle with impressed flowers; the heaviest, a sturdy quarter-inch thick, for more robust garments, are well worn and chipped, while smoothly polished buttons of a later vintage await a little black dress. Buttons like these throw out an invitation to scintillate and sparkle, but their origins place them within the realm of mourning. What is more, the majority are impostors: most of the buttons we describe as 'jet' are actually pressed glass.

All things jet complemented the black clothing associated with bereavement. When George IV's daughter Charlotte died in 1817 at the age of twenty-one, the fashionable showed their respect by wearing jet girdles with long pendants. The national mourning ordered by Queen Victoria on the death of William IV in 1837 led to its use in increasingly elaborate ways, but it was Victoria's own prolonged mourning for her husband Prince Albert, from 1861 until her own death forty years later, that provides a vivid folk memory and led to her being recalled as a little woman in black.

Queen Victoria's buttons were honed from Whitby jet, a form of fossilised wood that can take a high polish. Rare today and expensive in the nineteenth century, jet has been worn and worked since the Stone Age, with examples found in mainland Europe as well as Britain. The Romans used jet, but it was not until it became a fashionable symbol of mourning that jet transformed the fortunes of the Yorkshire coastal town, and the Whitby jet industry expanded from employing a handful of workers in 1822, to some 1,400 men and boys in the 1870s when the fashion was at its peak.

Victoria set the standard for jet, but it was the dour provincial industrialists, with their civic dignity and non-conformist sobriety, who cemented the look. Plain dress and plain speaking going hand in hand, they wanted to see their wives in dark colours, and as their fortunes were founded on coal – be they mill owners, button makers, silversmiths, potters, engineers, all relied on the dark, black stuff – it seems entirely appropriate that their wives glittered with it. Black clothing was practical too, among those dark satanic mills, hence its popularity as working dress.

Those who could not afford jet buttons and beading could nonetheless enjoy its effect. Buttons replicating jet were made in large quantities, the majority produced from glass manufac-tured in Venice, Bohemia and Austria, although a number of

American firms also adopted European methods. Pressed glass was easier and cheaper to mass-produce, it was also more enduring: jet easily chips and flakes. Horn, vegetable-ivory and papier-mâché buttons were also substituted, as were lignite and ebonite. Ebonite looks the same but, on closer inspection, gives off a whiff of sulphur. Of all the imitators, glass was best. It is hard to distinguish from the real thing and sparkles every bit as brightly on a black dress.

High mortality rates within the population as a whole provided all too many personal occasions on which black could be worn. Nineteenth- and early-twentieth-century mourning was an elaborate affair, subject to strict conventions and its etiquette, moving from full into half mourning and shading from deepest black into grey and mauve, was explained in numerous manuals. Deep mourning draped widows in a dull black gauze called crape, but though the fabric was sombre, the actual clothing needed not be. Even the smallest draper's shops sold mourning fabrics, while drapers of any size and department stores had their own mourning departments; some provided undertaking too, conveniently addressing all the practicalities of bereavement under one roof. The Peter Robinson store kept a mourning brougham outside, together with two female fitters dressed in black and ready to be dispatched with sympathy, scissors and pins. All dressmakers and drapers' assistants knew 'the correct scale of lamentation by trimming'. There was money to be made from the solicitous attention to death.

John Lewis sold fifty different kinds of crêpe. The mourning department of the Army and Navy Stores which, in addition to supplying the living and breathing middle classes with all and sundry, were 'agents for the principal cemeteries and churchyards throughout the country', offered multiple fabrics, including alpaca, cashmere, crape, crêpe de Chine, grenadines, poplins, paramatta, serges, voiles and worsted twills, plus more than a dozen black silks and satins. And then came the black mantles, ribbons and gloves; the silk neckerchiefs and scarves; the fischus, bows and jabots, the widow's collars and cuffs, handkerchiefs and jewellery. Grief was a thriving business.

Grief had its fashions too, as pilloried in this irresistible mid-nineteenth-century skit. A lady is shown a widow's silk – 'Watered, you perceive, to match the sentiment. It is called "Inconsolable", and is very much in vogue in Paris for matrimonial bereavements. And we have several new fabrics introduced this season to meet the demand for fashionable tribulation', including a 'splendid black' velvet called 'The Luxury of Woe'. The mourner is reassured that there is something to suit every sentiment, 'from a grief *prononcé* to the slightest *nuance* of regret'.

Buttons added to the ornamentation of beaded and bejetted clothing. Flowers, like the delicate ones on my handful of small 'jet' buttons, provided incised decoration; birds, too. Like other buttons of their type, and jewellery, they achieve their effect by combining matt and polished decoration; gold or silver lustre added an even more ornate finish. Some jet buttons imitated the fabrics on to which they were sewn, recreating a taffeta sheen or the hazy shimmer of watered silk.

The Victorian predilection for mourning gave rise to unusual and occasionally ghoulish jewellery; some chilling buttons, too. In the early nineteenth century, single eyes were reproduced on paper, ivory or enamel and worn as mementos. Unlike a braided lock of hair fastened in a brooch, the single eye looks outwards, as if building a protective wall about the mourner and ensuring the supremacy of the dead. An example in London's Victoria and Albert Museum, a widow's brooch circa 1790–1810, a watercolour on ivory circled in pearls, weeps delicate diamond tears. A set of buttons in a private collection, each one a single staring eye, must have been all the more disconcerting when faced in a vertical row.

Elizabeth Gaskell described the large number of brooches 'like small picture-frames with mausoleums and weeping-willows neatly executed in hair inside' worn by the women of *Cranford*. My great-grandma Betsy had a crude version depicting a jet gravestone saying 'My Dear Father', with a space before the pin for a lock of hair. This example of the jewellery sold at the cheaper end of the market may have belonged to her mother; Betsy's father died after the fashion for such displays had passed. Brooches, black-edged paper, mourning cards, In Memoriam verses – anyone who could afford to observe mourning rituals did so. More attractive family brooches also survive: a moon decorated with flowers, a shiny French jet pin, a small black heart as dark as the broken heart it surely represented – and are worn by me with barely a nod to their origins. The choice of jet for mourning jewellery continued into the Second World War: when my grandfather died, my grandma wore a pair of jet-black clips on her jacket; my mum, a black floral brooch.

Within weeks of the outbreak of the First World War, the *Manchester Guardian* advised the fashionable to add a black gown or at least a black tunic to their wardrobe for eveningwear. A black tunic could be worn over a white satin underdress, it suggested, reviving a fashion first seen almost 200 years earlier, during the period of national mourning that followed Queen Caroline's death. Flexibility was key: 'opportunities for sudden transformations are well to keep in mind at present', its journalist warned, having no idea how long 'at present' would last. 'Black, black, black everywhere,' was one woman's recollection of the 1914–18 war. 'Everyone seemed to be wearing black.' Ostentatious display ceased, however. One etiquette manual reported that 'quite a strong feeling has arisen against wearing black for relatives who have died on active service; a black band on the left arm is often the only intimation given.'

It was hard to strike a balance between respect and practicalities for those with few changes of clothing to begin with. The narrator of Barbara Comyns's semi-autobiographical novel, *Sisters by a River*, describes how, when their father died in the 1900s, she and her sisters had 'not a shred of black between them', and their mother made do with a semi-evening frock which 'looked all wrong in the sunshine'. In *A London Childhood*, her account of the 1930s, Angela Rodaway recalls how her mother frequently dyed the family's faded clothes to give them a new lease of life, but her spirit failed after the death of her sister-in-law when it came to dyeing her one and only coat. On this occasion, she let the drycleaner do the job; drycleaners offered an especially quick service for mourning. Formal mourning held sway until the stringencies of wartime rationing finally made it less practicable.

Many Victorians who went into mourning spent the rest of their lives in black; others of that generation adopted black for general dress. One of my mother's early childhood memories is of meeting Betsy's stepmother, a diminutive mid-Victorian, then in her late seventies (a distinctly late age in the 1930s). Her resemblance to Queen Victoria was striking. She swished into the corner shop in a rustle of coal black and, in true Victorian style, presented my mum with a pressed-glass dish inscribed: 'For a Good Child'. My great-grandma favoured her own 'ample severity of black'. Although she liked strong colour in blouses, Betsy's outdoor coats and skirts were always the deepest black. The two garments of hers that survive, a black satin skirt with fancy trimming and a coat with an equally dense black sheen – unfinished examples of home-dressmaking – are quintessentially late Victorian, although they were begun much later. A day at the seaside in the early 1930s saw my great-grandma sitting in a deckchair, minding my mother. My mum played in the sand in a sleeveless sundress; Betsy did not remove her black toque and overcoat.

The velvet that became fashionable in the 1840s added its own shimmer to jet and was matched by the popularity of the cheaper velveteen, the mainstay of Lewis's Manchester and Liverpool stores from the late nineteenth century until the eve of the First World War. With all its best-dress associations, velvet required considerable stamina to produce. Irene Burton's mother worked at a fustian mill during the 1920s and Irene recalled sitting beneath a long line of cloth as a very small child, watching her mother at work. She and other women with their own long lines of cloth, walked 'the velvet runs', lifting tiny threads with a knife-like implement which raised the nap to form velvet. The women reckoned that they covered the equivalent of the distance from Stoke-on-Trent to Manchester and back during the course of each working week. 'They walked and walked . . . down one side and up the other . . . So minute the tiny stitches.' The women wore clogs, and a piece of white cloth pinned to their right hip protected the velvet they brushed against while walking. Irene's mother walked until her feet bled, and continued walking. From time to time, she paused to sharpen her knife. If the tip broke and interrupted her work further, she was fined.

A strip of jetted brocade and a black beaded panel from the 1920s are among the stray items that came to me when my grandma died. The long thin canes known as bugle beads were cut by machine; in the nineteenth and early twentieth centuries beadwork trimmings were done by hand, often by home workers, adding a further skill to the long list of seamstresses' sweated labour. The beaded garments worn by Edwardian ladies were elaborate confections; by the 1920s, beading was used differently, though in a manner demanding equal skill. Dressmaker Esther Rothstein recalled that the fringed and beaded dresses of that era took a week or a fortnight to make: bead upon bead, and thousands of them. The beaded panel (given to Annie, I suspect, for her to make use of the beads) is a surprising weight. It slinks and swings and would have scintillated during the Charleston, but the original dress must have been heavy to wear. Beaded gowns worn by a wealthy Liverpool woman Emily Tinne in the 1930s swirl in expensive homage to geometry; gowns like hers are museum quality, but beaded cocktail jackets and sequined and bejetted frocks from all eras form the basis of the party wardrobes of many with a liking for vintage, mine included.

In the 1920s black was considered, mourning excepted, too old a colour for anyone under the age of thirty to wear; by the 1930s it was a mark of metropolitan chic. All the same, the novelist Penelope Mortimer startled her wedding guests by choosing to marry in black. Though black was the colour of 1950s cocktail dresses – 'Black is right if you like a sophisticated look,' Christian Dior advised – it could also be a sign of non-conformity. Black has long had the power to disconcert.

The black dress is a blank canvas, capable of expressing everything from grief to sophistication and seduction, taking in decorum, respectability and servility. Never has one garment contained more meanings, depending on the occasion and the manner in which it is worn. A black dress can look 'nothing' until it is put on, and then, stunning. A little black dress can be safely relied on (and, in the 1960s, was derided by Mary Quant for that reason). A black dress transforms and emboldens the fictional Miss Pettigrew when she visits a nightclub, is worn by Olivia in *The Weather in the Streets* for her first assignation with Rollo at the start of their love affair; and was the uniform worn by Lyons' Nippies and parlourmaids, and by old-fashioned shop assistants on whom the colour conferred anonymity as well as turning them into 'a good background . . . if they [were] holding up a most beautiful gown'. In my childhood, black dresses belong to the women who served high tea in Cole Brothers and the Odeon Tea Room, memories which themselves exist in black and white, with a glint of silver: acres of starched linen tablecloths, quiet black frocks and heavy EPNS cutlery (plus thinly sliced bread and butter and cups of over-strong tea).

The last word on all things jet black belongs to E. M. Delafield's Provincial Lady who, after agonising over what to wear for a literary soirée, finally settles on her Blue, and sets out for a fashionable address. 'Sloane Street achieved . . . Am shown into empty drawing-room, where I meditate in silence on unpleasant, but all-too-applicable, maxim that It is Provincial to Arrive too Early. Presently strange woman in black, with colossal emerald brooch pinned in expensive-looking frills of lace, is shown in . . . Two more strange women in black appear, and I feel that my Blue is becoming conspicuous . . . Three more guests arrive – black two-piece, black coat-and-skirt, and black crêpe-de-Chine with orange-varnished nails. (My Blue now definitely revealed as inferior imitation of Joseph's coat, no less, and of very nearly equal antiquity.)' On the next occasion the Provincial Lady ventures out, she knows exactly what to wear: black crêpe-de-Chine (minus the orange nails).

2 **THE BLACKCURRANT BUTTON:** ELEMENTARY SEWING AND THE WHITE-BLOUSE REVOLUTION

The blackcurrant button takes me straight back to childhood. It fastened a blouse my grandma often wore. This small glass button is a twinkling, iridescent mix of black, blue, green and purple, but I called it blackcurrant because it always reminded me of a fruit gum. My grandma read to me, played school with me, but the lesson I really learned with her was sewing (although, through my own neglect, I have forgotten much of what I was taught). My grandma's Singer sewing machine had a sturdy black frame with gold decoration and a handle that gave a satisfying click when it slotted into place. Maintaining a rhythm was important; gaining speed took practice and I never attained the fluency of Annie's professional days, when my mum recalls her Singer racing across seams, keeping pace with Dick Barton's theme tune on the wireless.

Angela Rodaway danced to the sound of her mother's sewing machine; she danced while her mother chopped vegetables but sewing was even better, 'slower and more dignified . . . and, after a while, bright scraps of material and ends of cotton would appear

on the floor and I would stop dancing to gather these "flowers".'
She also loved her mother's rag-bag: 'All the remains of past
sewing were there, beautiful pieces from years and years ago.'
My grandma also kept a rag-bag; it supplied the materials for my
early lessons in sewing.

Sewing belonged to Sunday afternoons at Annie and Eva's
when I was about eight years old, after the last strains of Jimmy
Clitheroe had faded from the radio and before 'Greetings, pop
pickers' alerted us to evening. The first thing we sewed was a
man's handkerchief, a gift for my dad, and having mastered four
straight lines and four corners, I progressed to an apron for my
mum. How very Janet and John. It took greater skill to gather
fabric on to a narrow band and trim the apron-front and its
small pocket with braid. This was not a serious apron, but the
kind of pinny women wore when guests came for afternoon tea
which, in our household, was not an everyday occurrence. At
some stage, I made a peg bag, an intermediate task, intended,
I suspect, to teach me to sew neat curves. An apron and a peg
bag: my poor mother; lessons in domesticity for us both. My
brother, briefly 'doing' pottery at school – perhaps while the girls
in his class were busy sewing – chose to make and decorate an
ashtray, a far more appropriate gift for a Swinging Sixties mum.
Next came an A-line dress with a small white collar, the collar
a further stage in the seamstress's vocabulary, being carefully
curved and very much on show. The dress was sleeveless – one
dressmaker said that an ability to fit sleeves well separates the
professional from the amateur (although those who know the
complex leg-of-mutton sleeves home-dressmakers grappled with
in the 1890s, may disagree).

My grandma's structured teaching, from straight lines to curves
and collars, stemmed from her years as a teacher in elementary
schools. Needlework was one of half a dozen subjects she taught

in the years immediately before and during the First World War. The majority of teachers entering elementary schools at this time came into classrooms via the pupil-teacher system and Annie was no different. In 1909, she embarked on a three-year apprenticeship during which she divided her time between teaching infants and studying at a nearby Pupil-Teacher Centre. The Staveley Netherthorpe Centre, and others like it, enabled working- and lower-middle-class young men and women to attain a professional qualification and status without embarking on costly full-time study. Although they were less well trained than their college-educated colleagues and had fewer prospects, teaching provided young women like Annie with a dignified and well-respected occupation.

My great-grandparents were enthusiastic supporters of Annie's continuing education and her decision to teach. And parental support was needed: pupil-teachers were still studying while their friends and neighbours were bringing in a wage; and there were books and stationery to pay for, and appropriate clothing to find. Pupil-teachers were expected to look the part.

An advertisement in *The Lady* for the Cameron Safety Self-Filler Fountain Pen – 'The Pen for Every Lady' was illustrated by six scenes: a woman signs for a parcel delivered to her door; another writes a letter at home. The third drawing takes us into the world of work, with a woman – a headmistress, perhaps – interviewing a female member of staff who stands before her in a white blouse, suit and floppy tie, her hands clasped behind her back; a further young woman takes dictation; two clerical workers sit side-by-side at a steeply sloping desk. Finally, a schoolgirl in a Panama hat marches forth with her briefcase. How busy women are, this advertisement suggests; although, on closer inspection, there are few types of worker represented.

My grandma and those busy workers were part of an expanding

professional class. Between 1881 and 1911, the numbers employed in teaching, nursing, retail and office work increased by 161 per cent, compared with a rise of only 24 per cent in domestic service and manufacturing. Teaching and nursing were the two professions that actively welcomed women, although the uncertain hours and stamina nursing required made that a less attractive prospect. The office work available was in low grades – the secretary and ledger-writers of the advertisement – and these women faced opposition from those who objected to '*Miss*printed' texts; the small number of civil-service posts were fiercely contested, with extra tuition needed to pass the entrance exams.

Some young women were initially drawn to teaching because of the ladylike appearance and manner of the women who taught them. A ladylike appearance was no hardship for Annie – it was always said that, like the girl in the nursery rhyme, she was meant to 'sit on a cushion and sew a fine seam'; friends described her as a lady, the highest praise for a young woman then. A photograph shows Annie and her fellow pupil-teachers in the familiar clothes of their calling. Several wear the high necklines that look authoritative but were simply fashionable dress, worn by leisured Edwardian women as well as workers. One or two wear the necktie some educated women favoured; another has a large, soft bow at her throat. All look the part: hair swept back from their faces (some in the exaggerated puffed-out styles of the day); well-polished boots or shoes peep from beneath long skirts. The effect is neat and tidy, undemonstrative.

Only one of their number is in any way decoratively dressed. On top of her blouse she wears a short-sleeved coatee jacket, edged with velvet. Three horizontal strips of velvet decorate her skirt, a button defining the edge of each strip. Coatees were 'in' in 1912, the probable date of the photograph, as were decorative buttons, and quantities of them, descending from throats and rising from hemlines. Chesterfield's premier draper and costumier, John Turner, sold costumes (suits) and dresses festooned with buttons; the *Derbyshire Times* advertised paper patterns showing buttoned skirts women could make at home.

The advent of the sewing machine had transformed life for home-dressmakers as well as for professional seamstresses. From the mid-nineteenth century, when Isaac Merritt Singer patented his sewing machine, and other manufacturers followed suit, many more women sewed at home and newspapers and magazines began offering paper patterns on a regular basis. At least one home-dressmaker knew that for the price of a card of buttons, she could reproduce a fashionable theme. That woman was my grandma, the young woman in the coatee suit, although I am surprised to see a schoolteacher so fashionably dressed. Annie may have chosen to dress more elaborately for the photograph, although none of her classmates did. Even when I was a child she had a knack for adding trimmings and interesting flourishes to the clothes she made. Evidently, this was a skill acquired early.

Annie's Netherthorpe tutor, Miss Lockhart, dressed like the young women she taught. The daughter of a Wesleyan minister, Miss Lockhart hailed from Yorkshire and was a former pupil-teacher herself. One of the growing band for whom no work meant no dinner, Miss Lockhart lodged nearby. Then in her mid-twenties, she was popular with her charges, who included a farmer's daughter and the sons and daughters of colliery men – labourers as well as a colliery deputy. Staveley Netherthorpe's admissions register gives my great-grandfather's occupation as 'Artisan, civil engineer'. 'Civil engineer' sounds like an upgrading to me, although around this time he was a foreman presiding over the construction of one of Chesterfield's reservoirs. The children of artisans and tradesmen were precisely the types drawn to the pupil-teacher scheme. Teaching was a way to better yourself and move upwards and out of your social class. This was illustrated by Mabel Doughty, the headmistress of the infant school where Annie spent her apprenticeship. Miss Doughty, a woman in her thirties, was also an ex-pupil-teacher; she and a younger sister both taught, having trained locally. Their two older sisters were dressmakers, the choices made by the different generations reflecting the changing landscape.

Copperplate writing on my grandma's gilt-framed certificate states that, in 1912, she satisfied the Oxford Senior Local examiners in Arithmetic, History, English Language and Literature including Composition, Geography and Needlework. 'If she carries out the promise of her work here,' Miss Doughty concluded, when writing a reference for her, 'I am sure she will make a good teacher.' And so Miss Nash was launched into the world.

Within the elementary-school curriculum needlework usually meant plain sewing. Proficiency in this subject was regarded as a badge of femininity, and its importance was underlined. A female London School Board examiner of the 1890s thought all other subjects of secondary importance for girls. Spelling could be learned, she asserted, by copying words such as 'herringbone' or 'cross-stitch'. Sewing drills were introduced: one elementary school Scheme of Work included sewing, thimble *and* knitting drills, thimble drill requiring girls to put on and take off a thimble numerous times, a test of no discernible value, except to instil obedience to go with the 3 Rs. The girls were instructed to produce six to ten stitches to the inch when hemming and twelve when sewing a seam, and to demonstrate these skills by joining two pieces of calico five inches in length (thereby accomplishing sixty perfect stitches in a row). Dictatorial stitching; no damp, crumpled rags or cobbled seams, and why *five* inches of calico?

A Board of Education's *Suggestion for the Teaching of Needlework* in 1909 asserted that needlework appealed 'directly to the natural instincts of the girls'. The seeming impossibility of separating entrenched notions of femininity from the skills involved made sewing a penance for many, including those with a better and more refined education. Some middle-class teachers, themselves constrained by hours of decorous stitching – *Must* we sit and sew? – paid scant attention to needlework. Plain sewing has its uses, however, especially for those embarking on independent lives, and could also forestall criticism by those who feared educated girls becoming uppity. When, in the 1880s, M. V. Hughes sat the entrance exam for North London Collegiate, a school established by pioneering educationalist Frances Mary Buss, she was amazed to discover that a written paper alone was insufficient: 'Now, dear, just make a buttonhole before you go,' the officiating mistress told her. 'I confessed that I hadn't the faintest idea how to set about it, and thought that buttonholes just "came". Up went Miss Begbie's hands in shocked surprise. "What! A girl of sixteen not know how to make a buttonhole!"' One week of practising later, assisted by lessons from her mother (who, having hated needlework herself had not inflicted it on her daughter), Molly applied herself to the task, with the aid of a needlecase specially made by her mother to show that Molly meant business. 'It was a rule of the school that no girl should enter who couldn't make a buttonhole.' M. V. Hughes went on to set up the teacher training department at Bedford College; later, she became a school inspector.

Around the time I started sewing with my grandma, I also learned hemming at school. The junior-school mistress who taught me was a teacher of the old guard and made clear her displeasure at our feeble attempts to sew. Like our nineteenth-century fore-bears, we too were given short strips of white cotton. I can see mine now, damp and quickly greying, with its mishmash of stumpy stitches, the occasional upright standing amidst others leaning at all angles. My failure did not disturb me unduly, although I was interested to see the other girls' more proficient work, like the sly description of the sister in Barbara Comyns's *Sisters by a River*, 'who sometimes sewed us things . . . with tiny stitches, but never completely finished, pinifores [*sic*] without buttons and button-holes, peticoats [*sic*] with the tucks only tacked . . . All the same it was nice to look at the small stitches, like a good example.'

I attained some competence later. Domestic Science required another apron – a full pinafore this time, something for me to make and then wear while baking raspberry buns. I made a smock there too, with a floral pattern and short capped sleeves. For a while, until I discovered that a mixture of beaks and ears was impossible to fasten, the smock's blue buttons were replaced by a set of animal buttons that came free with *Petticoat* (this being the era when childish things seeped into adolescent and grown-up clothes). By then, I was tackling facings and (briefly) tailor's chalk. Soon I was sewing at home. Having escaped the view that sewing would define me, I made other hippyish smocks, plus printed cotton maxi skirts, in between doing my homework.

The question of educated women was a vexed one in my grandma's day. While Annie was a pupil-teacher, the *Derbyshire Times*'s 'Home' columnist, 'Domestica', advised her female readers how to care for their 'crowning glory' and reminded them that 'excessive mental activity . . . certainly tells upon the hair'. Adopting a more elevated tone (though a no more enlightened attitude), *The Lady* asked, 'Do Men like Highly Educated Wives?': 'Girls who are inclined to be bookish, women who are regular dragons at mathematics, fair ladies who are never so happy as when swimming in seas of science, take themselves so dreadfully seriously. They don't seem to carry their learning as easily as men do . . . It oozes out of them in season and out of season. Nothing bores a man so much as the pedantic woman.' The journalist clearly cared nothing for the battles fought to counter what Virginia Woolf called 'Arthur's Education Fund', whereby sons were educated but not daughters.

My grandma made no claim to be highly educated, but she was evidently troubled by similar schoolmarm accusations. Pasted into her commonplace book is a newspaper article advising that 'the stuck-up school teacher is not the best kind of wife, and she fails lamentably as a mother'. (With marriage bars less rigorously enforced in teaching before the 1920s, women of Annie's generation might anticipate continuing work after marriage, if their local authority approved.) The article concluded that the teacher 'who realises she does not know everything' but 'takes the trouble to really learn' would make 'a splendid wife'.

Unsurprisingly, not every young woman seeking a profession wanted to teach. The increasing feminisation of clerical work made it a tempting prospect, despite opposition from those who felt that women should be crocheting at home and not in spare moments at the office. Others, including employers looking for lower-paid workers, sought to attract women into the workplace. A late-nineteenth-century Pitman's manual reassured those entering the profession that 'the type-writing involves no hard labour, and no more skills than playing the piano'. The fact that the word 'typist' came to refer to a woman shows how much things changed over time. The 6,420 women employed as clerks in Britain in 1881 represented 2.7 per cent of all clerks; by 1911, 124,843 women were employed, 18.1 per cent of the total. Their growing numbers gave rise to the term 'the white-blouse revolution', thanks to their uniform dress.

One such clerical worker was Edith James, a railwayman's daughter born in 1893, the year after my grandma. A scholarship pupil – indeed, the first girl from Wellingborough awarded a high-school scholarship – Edith was offered a pupil-teacher bursary on leaving school, but declined it in favour of commercial work. (From 1907, high schools were required to keep some free places available so that poorer students could remain at school until seventeen and then proceed to training college with the aid of bursaries. However, the take-up was relatively low.) Edith's family had no additional funds with which to support her, but her father eked out her scholarship money – £20 a year, for two years – so successfully that there remained just enough to train her in shorthand and typing, provided she learn quickly, and Edith did. When she passed her exams, the whole college was granted a day's holiday in recognition of her speedy progress.

In 1908 Edith James found work with a local firm of leather dressers and manufacturers of boot and shoe uppers, leggings and gaiters. Throughout her employment, she spent her winter evenings studying shorthand at the Technical Institute, and took classes in French to assist her in translating letters for the export side of the firm. (Beyond this, Edith relied on schoolgirl French and German and dictionaries, and was amused to think of the hilarity with which the recipients must have greeted the results.) The method by which copies were made of the documents she typed will surprise today's computer users: after signing, letters were copied into large bound books by placing each one on top of a sheet of tissue paper overlaying a wet rag. The book was then shut, put into a large iron press and screwed down for a few minutes. The moisture took sufficient ink from the type to make a copy on the tissue, but the letters were usually too damp to put into envelopes straightaway, and so had to be laid out until dry. Much clerical work was equally laborious.

Professional women like my grandma and Edith James had to be well turned out. Their white blouses required meticulous laundering to look their best and were easier to buy than to make.

Though ready-to-wear garments were a godsend to busy professional women, their quality was frequently disparaged. In 1910, the dressmaking magazine *Fashions for All* described them as 'one example of how money may be wasted. They are certainly cheap . . . but for the girl who has to make sixpence do the work of a shilling they are a snare and a delusion. Washed, the material becomes coarse, the lace tears, and the whole blouse loses its shape. A blouse made at home, by clever fingers, of good muslin simply tucked, will look well to the last day of its life.' There was a moral dimension too, as demonstrated by *Home Notes*: 'To some, [ready-made clothing] is a sign of greater wisdom on the part of the women of to-day, who refuse to be the slaves of the needle,' but, the article explained, ready-made clothes were often of poor quality and, what is more, were 'a gross extravagance when their purchase means only increased opportunity for idleness, or a waste of time worse than idleness'. Women workers beware: after a long day in the office or schoolroom, they should go home to their sewing machines.

The professional women grateful for ready-made clothing probably gave little thought to the seamstresses behind the white-blouse revolution who made their blouses and a great deal else besides. A turn-of-the-century American journalist talked to London seamstresses who much preferred the liberty and independence of dressmaking to the 'cap and apron life' of domestic service. Many, however, found it a considerable struggle. In 1908, the year before my grandma became a pupil-teacher and began to require a great many white blouses of her own, an investigation was conducted into the conditions of women's work in the London tailoring, dressmaking and underclothing trades. The ensuing report, which contributed to the ongoing debate about 'sweated' labour, followed an exhibition of 'sweated' goods organised by the *Daily News* two years earlier, and the formation of the National

Anti-Sweating League with the intention of establishing a minimum wage.

Sweated labour had been discussed since the 1840s; Fabian socialist Beatrice Webb later undertook sweated work as one of Charles Booth's investigators. In her diary for 19 October 1887 she described her first morning 'learning how to sweat' in a backroom workshop in London's East End:

> Coats turned out at 1s 2d each, trimmings and thread supplied by the sweater [the 'sweater' was the middleman or woman who put the workers to work] . . . Mistress said the women by working very hard could earn 10s a week, with 2s deducted for silk. Evidently these people worked tremendously hard; a woman working from eight to ten without looking round, and master working up to two o'clock, and often beginning at five the next morning. The mistress was too busy to give me much information; and I did nothing but sew on buttons and fell sleeves.

Buttonholes, at 4½d a dozen, were made by an outside worker.

Beatrice Webb's description is not unlike those detailed in the 1908 investigation and a further report published in 1915 which looked at married women's work countrywide. Both questioned factory and home workers. They included women like Miss S. who made blouses in Japanese silk with elaborate latticework blouse-fronts, tucks and rows of insertion; the backs, collars and cuffs were similarly elaborate and the sleeves tucked throughout their length. Even when working hard, Miss S. could only make three such blouses a day – the wonder is that she completed any – for which she was paid 4s a dozen. (Another worker said that the four-shilling blouses took her so long to make that she could not estimate the length of time involved.) Similar blouses in finely tucked Japanese silk, with an embroidered turn-down collar, were

advertised by the Army and Navy Stores in 1913 and retailed at
£1 8s 9d.

Alpaca blouses required less work. For these Miss S. received
3s a dozen and could make six a day. Plain shirts paid 1s 2d a
dozen, but even with a sewing machine, she could not make that
number in one day. Each week, Miss S. had to pay 2d for use of
the kitchen, and if she earned as much as 10s, a further 3d for
power. She supplied her own cotton at 4½d in every 8s or 9s.
Miss S. was one of many for whom 'a necessary reel of cotton
mean[t] the price of a loaf'.

Investigators found that although there was no marked difference between the pay of home and factory workers, the higher-paid
tended to be among the factory employees. One machinist
received 5d for each plain blouse, which she could make by the
hour; 1s 8d for a handkerchief blouse, of which she could make
two a day; and 2s or 2s 6d for lace blouses, of which she could
make only one. She was more fortunate than some in that all
materials were provided by her employer; she was also fortunate
in averaging 15s a week. The best-paid workers in her factory
were the time workers (paid by the hour rather than per garment)
who received 21s and worked 'very hard for it'.

It was almost impossible to estimate how much work was done
for a shilling by each worker and for each employer, but the
investigators concluded that the figures did not meet a living
wage. At the same time, however, it acknowledged that 'scattered
over London' were women 'earning something like a living' by
making blouses for individual customers. One seamstress made
blouses almost entirely for teachers in local elementary schools.
'Thus are the various threads of life interwoven; the Education
Acts and the duty recognised by all instructors of setting an
example to youth, combine to keep comfortable a certain household in an out-of-the-way street of a dull neighbourhood.'

Sewing in workshops and little back rooms in dull neighbour-hoods is centuries old and has its part in my own family story, but sewing – for whatever purpose – was a world other women already disdained. Education was their escape. Alison Uttley was one example. Uttley read physics at Manchester University and, in 1906, became its second female honours graduate. Brought up in rural Derbyshire, she travelled to school in the market town of Bakewell: 'Four apprentice dressmakers travelled each morning on my school train . . . we noted their little baskets with lids on top . . . their books of patterns, their pale faces. We were sorry for them starting a life of sewing when there were so many inter-esting things to do. Nobody wanted to sew, we were delivered from the fetters of our mothers, who had made samplers and who sewed with tiny stitches. Our stitches were large and indi-vidual, and we despised such feminine arts as stitchery, when we had a science laboratory in which to experiment.'

'THE LASSES' RESOLUTION TO FOLLOW THE FASHION' (*c.*1870)

Good people, come listen awhile, now,
A sketch of the times I lay down,
Concerning the rigs and the fashions
That are now carried on in each town;
The lasses they have such a spirit,
They will imitate the new pride,
With bustles to wear on their hips, boys,
To make them look buxom beside.

. . . Stuff slippers and white cotton stockings,
These lasses they mostly do wear,
With a dimity corduroy petticoat,
It is whiter than snow, I declare;
With a fringe or a flounce round the bottom
These lasses they will have beside,
And a sash, for to go round their middle
And to tie up in bunches behind.

. . . The servant girls follow the fashions
As well as the best in the place;
They'll dress up their heads like an owl, boys,
And will think it no shame or disgrace.
They will bind up their heads with fine ribbands,
And a large bag of hair hangs behind;
And when they do walk through the streets, boys,
No peacock can touch them for pride.

A Touch on the Times: Songs of Social Change,
1770–1914, Roy Palmer, ed. (1974)

3 **GIRLS RULE OK:** THE PURPLE, WHITE AND GREEN

'Girls rule OK' is the message on a button badge a colleague gave me in the early 1980s. I had joined the publishing house Virago and we had recently moved to the attics of the Oxford University Press building in London's Dover Street. A lift with a rickety folding metal gate took us up to a vestibule with a tiny loo and a butler's sink that doubled up as somewhere to wash cups. Ahead, beyond stacked boxes and cardboard, was the door to the actual offices where a suffragette flag and a suffragette poster hung on the walls. Some of the furniture was painted green or purple, the most practical of the suffragettes' three colours (the third being an impractical white).

By the time I joined Virago in 1980 the second wave of feminism was already engaged in uncovering the first wave and the story of the suffrage movement, including their own use of button badges for sloganeering. Edwardian supporters of women's suffrage could choose from a wide selection, including one depicting Emmeline Pankhurst and another proclaiming 'Votes for Women'; Boadicea cost 3*s* 6*d*. Badges could also be purchased in the suffragette colours, the colour scheme created in 1908 by

Emmeline Pethick-Lawrence, treasurer and co-editor of *Votes for Women*, the weekly newspaper published by the Women's Social and Political Union (WSPU).

The decision to adopt purple, white and green was an astute exercise in branding. Mrs Pethick-Lawrence explained the symbolism: 'Purple . . . stands for the royal blood that flows in the veins of every suffragette, the instinct of freedom and dignity . . . white stands for purity in private and public life . . . green is the colour of hope and the emblem of spring.' White or cream should predominate, with purple and green introduced as additions. All those white blouses stitched in little back rooms acquired new meaning: the 'white-blouse revolution' was given a new twist. 'If every individual in this union would do her part,' Mrs Pethick-Lawrence told supporters, 'the colours would become the reigning fashion, and strange as it may seem, nothing would so help to popularise the WSPU.' Politics and fashion joined forces.

Women were encouraged to wear the colours at public events and especially for major processions, such as the WSPU Women's Sunday rally in Hyde Park on 21 June 1908, attended by 250,000 people. Other suffrage organisations adopted their own colour schemes. The National Union of Women's Suffrage Societies took up red, white and green; the Women's Freedom League, a WSPU breakaway group, chose green, white and gold to complement its slogan: 'Dare to Be Free'. Courage and daring were needed – whether marching in a procession for the first time, addressing a public meeting, or rushing the Houses of Parliament, knowing that prison awaited. One supporter's evening gown revealed the words 'Votes for Women' in glitter across her bare back. Picture the scene when she lets her wrap fall from her shoulders and slowly turns around. Subversion and the struggle to be heard took many forms.

Women – and men – had been organising for women's suffrage since the nineteenth century, but the movement gained new impetus with the founding of the WSPU by the Pankhursts in Manchester in 1903. Before that date, the main suffrage organisation was the NUWSS, established in 1897 by Millicent Garrett Fawcett. Whereas the NUWSS were suffragists or constitutionists, the WSPU favoured direct action; their motto was 'Deeds Not Words'. Derided as 'suffragettes' by the *Daily Mail* in 1906, the WSPU adopted the term as their own (just as, seventy years later, Virago turned a pejorative noun into a positive statement).

By July 1909, *Votes for Women* was pleased to report that 'almost every draper of any standing now stocks dresses, hats, ties, hosiery, etc, in the purple, white and green'. Sunshades in the colours could be purchased to greet the summer months; Derry & Toms offered tricolour kid shoes, while those wishing to display their allegiance when disrobing might buy specially dyed bedroom slippers in velvet and quilted satin from Lilley and Skinner. No detail that could be harnessed to the Cause was overlooked: cakes were iced in the colours; purple, white and green sweet peas filled gardens with the fragrant promise of equality. (Even jam-making had a political purpose – and a nice line in dry wit: in December 1909 the Kensington WSPU advertised 'Militant Jam With Stones' or 'Stoneless Variety, the stones extracted for other purposes'.)

Retailers large and small recognised the value of advertising in *Votes for Women*. On 9 June 1911 Derry & Toms took a full-page advertisement, promising that 'During the next few days we shall be exhibiting in one of our windows hats and toques made in the colours of the various organisations in connection with the Women's Suffrage movement.' Readers were encouraged to patronise dressmakers and costumiers who were themselves suffrage supporters, but not everyone could afford a winter coat

advertised at 19*s* 9*d*, let alone one priced 59*s* 6*d*, nor the lifestyle
suggested by motoring scarves and croquet hats. An advertisement
advocating Fels-Naptha laundry soap – 'ranks with the sewing
machine as the greatest time-saver and labour-lightener ever
invented for womankind' – was clearly not pitched at the woman
buying her golfing jacket from Jaeger and wearing hand-sewn
glacé leather house shoes. Mme Rebecca Gordon's London Atelier
satisfied all comers, being 'not merely a place where beautiful
gowns and hats may be purchased', but 'a model work room,
where good wages [were] paid and everything possible done for
the well-being of the employees'. An advertisement placed in
February 1909, 'Wanted a Good Plain Cook', conjures up an
interesting household where both mistress and cook read a suffragette paper.

Sewing machines were themselves partisan. The 'unrivalled
"Defiance" Lockstitch Sewing Machine', worked by hand or
treadle, cost 39*s* 6*d* (or was 'sent to any part of the country on
easy terms', 5*s* a month). Any clothing so defiantly stitched
might fasten with Smart's Invisible Hooks and Eyes, the
'patented invention and property of two members and supporters
of the WSPU', or with hand-embroidered buttons bearing the
WSPU insignia. Women marched beneath beautifully embroidered banners; the Holloway Prison Banner, carried in June
1910, featured the embroidered signatures of eighty suffragette
hunger strikers who had 'faced death without flinching' – a use
for neat stitches far exceeding anything their mothers could
have envisaged.

As militant activity grew in the face of political intransigence
and hostility, suffragette caricatures became so extreme that law
enforcers and organisers of public meetings, on the lookout for
the creatures so derided in newspapers and *Punch* cartoons, could
be misled by women not fitting the stereotype. Evelyn Sharp used

this as the basis of one of her short stories. In 'Shaking Hands with the Middle Ages', from *Rebel Women* (1910), a woman dressed in black and a fellow suffragette, demure in grey, are able to disrupt a political meeting precisely because the stewards expect 'dreadful women' who look 'like nothing on earth'. (Those who met Emmeline Pankhurst were often surprised by her slight frame and a gentility that concealed a will of steel.)

Similar misconceptions came in useful on the evening of 1 March 1912 when the WSPU took their campaign into the very heart of London's retail sector. Shortly before six o'clock, the *Daily Mail* reported, 'From every part of the crowded and brilliantly lighted streets came the crash of splintered glass. Scared shop assistants came running out to the pavements; traffic stopped; policemen sprang this way and that . . . Any unaccompanied lady in sight, especially if she carried a handbag, became an object of menacing suspicion.' Women who were window shoppers one minute became window breakers the next. Mary Richardson, who smashed a window at the Liberty store, was one of many who evaded arrest by posing as a shopper; Richardson insisted she was 'only admiring the carpets'.

Retail supporters of the Cause were stunned that even they were targeted, but a WSPU leaflet explained that 'The Suffragettes bear no grudge against you personally . . . On the contrary, the women are good friends to you, and without them and their support what would become of that flourishing business of yours?' The decorous woman might not only carry a hammer or a stone in her handbag, she might also withdraw her custom if store owners did not continue in their support. At least one unexpected sale came of it: Lady Rhondda's Aunt Janetta felt so guilty about her own involvement that she returned to the shop the next day and purchased a five-guinea hat. Good relations between the WSPU and department stores were gradually restored, with

Christabel Pankhurst even claiming that 'those whose windows were not broken were a little piqued at being so neglected'.

My home town had its own suffrage meetings and the suffragette Winifred Jones. Winifred and her sister Gladys were both involved in the movement. Winifred was imprisoned twice and on the last occasion, in November 1910, sent to Holloway for throwing a stone through the window of 10 Downing Street. Winifred Jones was a solicitor's daughter, one of many ordinary women compelled into action by a firm belief in the righteousness of the Cause, and appalled by the repeated obduracy of parliamentarians. Evelyn Sharp wrote of her own conversion to militancy that she 'travelled the road to Holloway . . . because, when the call came, no alternative seemed possible . . . Reforms can always wait a little longer, but freedom, directly you discover you haven't got it, will not wait another minute.'

4 **THE SILVER THIMBLE:** THE FIRST WORLD WAR AND MUNITIONETTES

My grandma was twenty-one when war was declared in 1914. Her Singer sewing machine was a twenty-first birthday gift and one of its tasks was making the blackout blinds wartime regulations demanded for the family's corner shop. The silver thimble dates from around this time and was worn by her until it became too small and was transferred to the button box. I remember seeing it there during my childhood, something to delve for among all the buttons. Later, my grandma gave the thimble to me.

The Singer sewing machine has a decorative silver panel, an intricate pattern of flowers, fit for a special gift. Some Edwardian young women received silver buttons on coming of age but Annie's present was more down to earth, as was her silver thimble. Though circled, petal to petal, with tiny daisies, its elegance is diminished, I discover, on closer inspection, by the blunt words 'Payne, Jeweller, The Moor, Sheffield', although, as a shopkeeper's daughter, my grandma perhaps appreciated the need for a jeweller to advertise his wares.

The idea of blackout blinds would have been unthinkable even days before war was declared but the need for them soon felt real enough. The Yorkshire coastal town of Scarborough was bombarded in December 1914; in January 1916 bombs fell in Derby some thirty miles away from the shop. Sewing acquired other new uses during the Great War: as a young journalist, Rebecca West visited a cordite factory in 1916, where she watched 'a great circle of women sitting at sewing-machines, making covers for [explosive] charges out of the fine cambric that is used for expensive baby-frocks, and turning gleaming sheets of Japanese silk into sachets, for gun-cotton'.

Some of Chesterfield's factories found their own new roles in the production of munitions. My grandma's neighbour and close friend Ethel leapt at the chance for war work – far better than her job in a nearby factory washing and stacking bottles. Ethel had an abundance of spirit and could fettle with the best of them; it was what women like her did. The majority of munitionettes, as the press called them, were working class but some middle-class and even titled women volunteered for the task and stuck at it. ('Say, young Doll, see that there lydy on the end machine? They do say as 'ow she's a Dook.')

The women worked alongside one another affably enough, for the most part, and gained mutual respect, but their separate status was maintained, as the writer Sylvia Townsend Warner discovered. She responded to a 1915 article in *The Times* promoting a volunteer scheme whereby 'educated women of the leisured classes' would undergo three weeks' training at Vickers' factory and then undertake relief work to enable the regular women working extremely long shifts to benefit from weekend breaks. Before setting out for her training, the writer received a list advising her to bring 'short skirts, thick gloves and boots with low heels'. A final recommendation was appended: 'evening dress [will] not be necessary'. That such advice was needed is just a small indicator of the vast chasm between the social classes. Even Sylvia Townsend Warner, that most democratic of writers (a Communist during the thirties and a delegate at the Congress of Madrid), wrote of 'girls' and 'lady-workers'. This was the climate in which both lived. 'Leisured' women like herself, who joined the Vickers scheme, were known among the general workforce as 'the Miaows', thanks to their strangulated vowels.

Long-sleeved gowns, trousers with matching tunics that buttoned at the shoulder, or overalls in khaki, blue or even white identified munitions workers. No metal was allowed on sites manufacturing explosives; a worker at the Woolwich Arsenal recalled the instruction: no hairpins and no clothes with hooks and eyes. No corsets either, thanks to the metal in them: 'Oh Annie,' my grandma's friend Ethel told her, 'the blessed relief.'

Munitions workers attracted particular interest from the outset. Unlike the Voluntary Aid Detachment nurse (VAD) demonstrating her exquisitely feminine skills, these women were angels of death. Initial reluctance to employ women at munitions work was, like so much else during the early years of the war, fuelled by anxieties about their capabilities and assumptions about what was 'appropriate'. In fact, and as other industries also discovered, women were not only capable of taking over male roles, they soon exceeded all expectations. One factory manager echoed the views of others when he told Rebecca West how four women in his employ, 'who have been at work for only a few months, produce a larger output than four men who have been trained to this process for six years'. Gratitude at female efficiency only went so far: a worker at a different factory noted how any suggestions for improvements that might make machinery more efficient invariably met with the response that the men operating the machines before them had found they worked perfectly well.

Between July 1914 and November 1918 the number of women

employed in munitions and related industries rose from 212,000 to 947,000. Many were escaping from domestic service and welcomed the better pay and relative freedom of fixed hours, however long and exhausting. Some factories worked eight-hour shifts, but twelve hours was common. With workers drawn from all over the country and many factories placed at a distance from town centres, few women lived at home. Some were billeted in barracks or bleak hostels, others stayed in lodgings, which could be equally bleak, and paid over the odds for the privilege.

Munitions wages were famously said to be high, but varied considerably. Thirty shillings a week was quoted by one source; £5 (a sum that presumably included bonuses) by another, but Sylvia Townsend Warner wrote that the '£1 1s and something' she received could not have sustained her had she needed to survive on that wage, a view which gains greater force when upheld by a working-class woman who said she could not live on the 25s she was paid. Perhaps the most telling comment comes from the munitionette who said that while everyone heard about high wages, they were nearly always being paid to a 'friend's sister's niece'. However, it was generally agreed that the women were better off than they had been as domestic servants: 'Years back I wore tatters, / Now – silk stockings mi friend!'

Kathleen Gilbert, who was 'put out to service' at the age of fourteen, was one of many thousands who made the switch. She started her munitions work on shell cases, shaving the brass casing to produce a smooth finish (and was still finding scraps of brass in her hands fifty years later). At her next factory, she filled shells with TNT, dressed in a white overall and cap. Hats were essential: horrific injuries were caused by hair becoming tangled in machinery, and those working with TNT would have otherwise seen their hair turn green. (Faces turned yellow for the same reason, hence the munitionettes' nickname, 'canaries'.) Some workers wore mob caps, like old-fashioned servants, but even the most basic hat could be adjusted to give a glimpse of individuality, as an observer of the Woolwich Arsenal noted: 'The caps . . . which were simply a circular piece of material with a string round the edge (rather like a pudding cloth) could be arranged so skilfully that it seemed as though a dozen different headgears had been issued by the authorities.'

Equally inventive were the ways women personalised their uniforms: 'The first fashion touch was a posy pinned to the gown, each shop having its own flower emblem; but as these were confiscated during working hours, someone got the idea of substituting brightly coloured ribbon for the government shoe laces. First the "cap shop" girls strutted proudly with emerald green . . . the "new fuse" girls followed with yellow, and soon the whole Arsenal was in the fashion.' Sylvia Townsend Warner and her fellows wore their blue overalls with pride: 'No one else seemed to see . . . anything but a uniform: we knew them, secretly, as a vestment.'

Working conditions varied, depending on whether women were making or finishing shells, dealing with cordite, lyddite, TNT or other explosives, and at what stage of production. Some workshops were almost silent; others a nightmare of noise. Nearly all mimicked domestic tasks: Kathleen Gilbert polished her shell cases 'to look like glass'; Ballasite resembled Lux soap flakes, but was brown; cordite looked like macaroni. High explosives were weighed on scales, pressed through wire sieves, stirred in giant vats, set as jellies or made into cakes. Few of the young women who had got to grips with Brasso in someone's back kitchen or learned to make soufflés or desserts could have envisaged their domestic skills coming to this.

Anything that could vivify the day was much appreciated. At

Vickers, a shell casing stood in for a vase at the end of a work-shop bench and was daily replenished with dahlias, coarse daisies and chrysanthemums. The illusion of normality was further heightened by the geographical position of some munitions sites. One factory was set among trees and running water, with 'a sweet night smell coming up from the long wet meadow grass . . . But the trees had been planted to check the course of explosions; the water ran yellow from the lyddite shops [and] the sweet night smell was dispersed by puffs of thick-scented steam'. Many things were contradictory during wartime.

The women whom Rebecca West saw wearing scarlet and khaki and looking 'very young in their pretty, childish dresses', were engaged in lethal work and their bright Robin-Hood-type hats were fireproofed to protect them in the event of an explosion, explosions being occupational hazards. A few days before her visit, two munitions huts had been gutted and the women had needed to escape through the flames. One lost a hand on that occasion. The loss of hands, feet or eyes was not uncommon; there were also fatalities. Overall, explosions killed seventy-one British women; sixty-one were poisoned through handling toxic chemicals, and a further eighty-one died in other fatal accidents.

Colourful ribbon laces and a delight in blue overalls were not inconsiderable pleasures when set against dangerous work which frequently involved heavy lifting, was exceedingly monotonous, and yet required efficiency and speed. Cheered for their productivity and the 'passionate diligence' they brought to the role, munitionettes were also admonished for their immorality, spending and general swagger. Munitionette Mary Brough-Robertson recalled that '[we] were just about the lowest form of life in the eyes of the general public . . . they called us all sorts of things, even shouted things after us'. A thick skin helped, as did courage, youth and bravado and a firm belief in the righteousness of their task.

Of course, foot soldiers did not necessarily thank them. Munitionettes came under attack in Siegfried Sassoon's coruscating poem 'Glory of Women'. 'You make us shells,' he hurled at them in a phrase that calls to mind the knitted mufflers women also made for their menfolk. Soldiers sitting in trenches or, more likely, biding their time before going up the line, honed and polished spent bullets and turned them into handles for buttonhooks. Were they domesticating the lethal or returning the bullets to the women who had sent them out there in the first place? It seems an odd souvenir to give to a loved one, but many soldiers brought back military items – buttons, medals, German helmets – and made them into trophies or tamed them in some way, making the abhorrent manageable. My grandfather brought a shell case from the Middle East and stood it on the hearth to house the poker. He also kept his tin hat, which he painted with a ring of forget-me-nots. My grandfather was fortunate, of course. Some soldiers did not return.

5 **THE SHOE BUTTON:** BACHELOR GIRLS STRIDE AHEAD

'How narrow women had grown lately! . . . like stalks of corn,' Virginia Woolf wrote in *Orlando*, evoking the 1920s and the sheath-like dresses that came into vogue in the middle of that decade. The freedom of movement they represented was a real emancipation. Hemlines had never dared so high. Shorter skirts seemed to reflect freedoms women were beginning to experience in other aspects of their lives.

My great-aunt came of age in 1922. She wore dropped-waist frocks, long dangling beads and dashed about – Eva never did anything slowly – in the one-bar buttoned shoes of the time. The button box contains three pairs of tiny buttons which fastened shoes like hers. Of course, where there were buttoned shoes, there were also buttonhooks; Eva's nestled in the little handbags she carried and later passed on to me, and which also speak so eloquently of that era.

Couturier 'Lucile', described the sheath-like style as a response to post-war stringencies. Wealthy women had less money to spend: there could be no more elaborate 'picture dresses' and so the 'boyish woman' was born. Paris fashions percolated down to the high street and were seized by women who wanted looser, freer clothing and 'little hats which can go under umbrellas', a phrase which immediately conjures up modern women going about their busy lives.

Eileen Whiteing, the daughter of a City businessman, recalled being a slave to 'whatever current trend was in vogue . . . the craze for knitted silk jumpers, ultra-low waists, cloche hats and two-tone shoes', but it was not only the middle and upper classes who paid close attention to fashion. The new styles could be mass-produced cheaply and were relatively easy to replicate at home. For the first time, modernity was quickly and affordably within reach.

Sisters Flora and Edith Hodson ran a shop from their front room in Willenhall, near Birmingham, selling clothes and haber-dashery to working women, many of them factory workers. The shop's ready-to-wear clothing reveals a knowledge of fashion equal to that of department-store buyers, and styles as elaborate as those seen in women's magazines. Dresses ranged from striped 'tub' frocks in coarse cotton, to patterned artificial 'art' silks and crêpes, and were decorated with as many panels, buttons, buckles and trimmings as modish women could want. The sisters' stock also included the chic jersey suits of the period: the look created by couturiers Chanel and Jean Patou not only filtered down to the high street, it also found its way, via city wholesalers, to a little house-shop.

The new shorter styles drew attention to women's legs; they also drew attention to their feet in one-bar buttoned shoes. How petite these shoes look if you come upon them in a vintage shop; and what fabrics: glacé and kid leather, satin, patterned brocade, metallic sheens. A touch of the exotic was popular: polished python was said to be a new craze; you could also purchase sealskin shoes trimmed with lizard. An unwanted consequence of these narrow shoes was the agonies women suffered with corns. Country-house occupant Lesley Lewis recalled how most women took a sharp intake of breath if you came anywhere near their feet.

By the late 1920s, the modern woman could complement her shoes with stockings in bluebell, chrome yellow, scarlet, cyclamen and every shade of green; vivid colours decorated clothing too, reflecting the increasing thirst for colour in all things. Metropolitan and bohemian circles had swooned to the dramatic statements of colour created for Diaghilev's Ballets Russes before the First World War, but mainstream and provincial tastes were slower to catch on. Startling shades and exuberant patterns were not widespread until much later. Once they were, colour was a shorthand for modernity. Painter and textile designer Sonia Delaunay declared, 'If painting has become part of our lives, it is because women have been wearing it.'

The flapper of popular mythology was a further manifestation of the modern. Garter buttons decorated with the flapper's stylised face – a wide-eyed Betty Boop-like creature – suggest that life is nothing but fizz and bubble; the wearing of a garter was pretty dizzying in itself. Schoolgirl Angela Rodaway was fascinated by older girls who 'wore light stockings and high-heeled shoes. Their skirts were short, nearly up to their knees and, most exciting of all, they wore long silk knickers and fancy garters.' A 'rollocking young flapper', with her 'merry pranks and harmless mischief' formed the basis of a 1920 *My Weekly* serial, 'Sally, Sport-of-a-Girl'.

The flapper also gave her name to the so-called 'flapper vote', the extension of the franchise in 1928 to women aged twenty-one, following the partial enfranchisement ten years earlier of women aged thirty and over, with a household qualification. This denigratory phrase infuriated Dame Millicent Fawcett, founder member of the National Union of Women's Suffrage Societies. 'Why call them flappers?' she asked in the *Evening Standard*. 'Why call them girls?' (a question that could have been asked many times since). 'They are young women . . . On the whole I am a great admirer of the modern young woman. She is far more capable, sensible and has a broader outlook on life than ever she had.' So many column inches were expended on the 'flapper vote' that even the manufacturer of Abdullah cigarettes joined in: a 1929 advertisement featured 'Our New Electorate' with a poem about 'Miss Infatuation' who decides to vote Communist after sitting next to 'Bert Hunks at a Bolshevik Tea'.

Women of all ages and social classes displayed their party allegiances at the general election in May 1929. Socialist factory workers wore red; an elderly voter decorated her bath chair in Tory blue; mill girls polled early in large numbers; one woman flew from Manchester to Blackpool to register her vote, while women on the Yorkshire moors were conveyed to the polls by a young men's 'flying squad' of motorcyclists. Many of the cars transporting voters were driven by 'girls who dashed along the streets behind windscreens and bonnets gaily decorated with party colours'. Women seemed to be zooming ahead.

The achievement of universal suffrage marked a decade of legislative progress. There were now fourteen women MPs; female magistrates and jurors sat in court; divorce law reform finally accorded women equal status while, thanks to the Sex Disqualification (Removal) Act of 1919, the first woman was called to the Bar (and told what to wear beneath her robe). Small numbers of professional women were making real gains but, by 1920, almost two-thirds of the women who entered the workforce during the First World War had left it again, a movement begun almost before the ink dried on the Armistice; still others gave up work on marriage or at first pregnancy. For most young women, work was an interlude between school and marriage, and often a harsh interlude at that.

The mixed messages of the period are apparent in a magazine like *Good Housekeeping* which, on its launch in 1922, announced 'we are on the threshold of a great feminine awakening'. This magazine was directed at middle-class readers, most of them homemakers, but its contributors also addressed the question of professional work (appealing to the higher echelons of the workforce, not the young clerical workers dashing off for a sixpenny lunch): 'A Career for Women – H. M. Inspector of Taxes by a Civil Servant' (April 1925); 'Why Are There Not More Superwomen In Business?' pioneering lawyer, Helena Normanton asked (November 1926). Too few opportunities, could have been the swift answer. In 1938 only 4 per cent of salaried women earned more than £250 a year, compared with over 50 per cent of men, while the marriage bars in teaching, nursing, medicine and the civil service, together with the stigma attached to married women working, ensured that the professional woman was likely to be single. 'There is still in many quarters . . . much resistance, or at least very half-hearted support, to the idea of women having serious jobs', Margaret Cole wrote in 1936, when advising young women on professional life.

For all the legislative gains, a strong domestic ethos prevailed, with commentators quick to remind women of all social classes that marriage was their best career. In 1931 *Woman's Life* reported that

business, if accepted in the right spirit, can be an invaluable training . . . The girl who learns to look after her employer's interests will look after her husband's. She will also learn to be subservient to rightful authority, which will teach her, later on, to respect the authority of her husband. This may seem old-fashioned when people are never tired of talking about women's new freedom and equality. But it is common sense, just the same.

The young working woman of the period was frequently char-acterised as a business girl or bachelor girl, a term giving a more attractive gloss to independent singledom than the word 'spinster' ever could, but emphasising the working woman's immaturity. Bachelor girls were often office workers. By 1921 there were nearly 600,000, representing 46.1 per cent of all clerks, more than double the number of those 'white-blouse' workers of 1911. These were the young women Agnes M. Miall advised to 'try to forget that you are a woman' when working alongside men. Her *Bachelor Girl's Guide to Everything* included a step-by-step guide to typewriting, 'a generally useful accomplishment to the woman wage-earner in the business world'. Advertising executive Florence Sangster would have approved. Advertising held no barriers for the ambitious young woman, she reported, 'but let her first learn to do one thing well, be it only typewriting so that she can knock at the door of her first employer with something useful to offer,' suggesting that all too often young women lacked the skills they needed to get on.

Then, as now, 'business' clothes accounted for a significant proportion of a working woman's wardrobe; Miall offered budget-ary advice. Women earning 25s a week, or less, should allow approximately £12 a year for clothes, while those earning from 27s to £3 should allocate £15 to £20. Miall's *Guide* appeared in 1916, but the office worker's needs and dilemmas had not changed and Miall's somewhat over-generous estimation of wages was now more realistic. In 1935 *Good Housekeeping* suggested that an eighteen-year-old provincial typist might earn 25 shillings a week, while an experienced London secretary in her thirties could command £4. Some women were earning considerably less, however; among them the retail workers who might earn as little as 10s selling dresses to other business girls. Independent adviser Gladys Burlton informed shop workers, whose own numbers were increasing – by 1931, there were over 394,000 shop assistants, with women outnumbering men three to one – that a 'business girl cannot dress as a private character'. Burlton advocated that those earning £3 a week should spend a third on dress, while those earning more could afford to spend a little less. However, a 1934 study showed that few working women could spend anything like a third of their income on clothes and that some shop workers could barely clothe themselves. The following year, Gladys Burlton was interviewed by the *Sunday Express* for a series on 'Women Who Make Money'. Therein lies the rub: women made money, whereas bachelor girls struggled to make ends meet. The difficulty was not confined to the lowliest ranks. Virginia Woolf based part of her argument in *Three Guineas* on an appeal made by professional women for clothing. A further difficulty lay in laundering the few clothes women owned and in keeping themselves clean in those pre-deodorant days when 'not to smell [was] an expensive thing'. One anxious young woman who wrote to *Home Chat*'s 'Mrs Jim' was advised to 'dust the armpits with a mixture of boracic powder, bicarbonate of soda, and starch, in equal parts'.

The bachelor girl's salary would go further if she made her own cotton frocks, blouses and underwear, and trimmed her own hats, Miall advised, though two of the 'Simple Designs for Home or Office' *Woman's Life* recommended for home-dressmakers look far from simple to achieve. *How to Dress Well* advocated buying an unlined jersey suit and tailored blouses or a 'one-piece, slip-on dress' which could be dry-cleaned and 'reappear as fresh as . . . new' – provided the business girl could afford the dry-cleaning bill. Whatever her circumstances, the working woman needed to put her best foot forward. 'Remember that appearances reveal more than they hide,' *Miss Modern* reminded her, 'and that a lost button may mean a lost job . . . Wear a costume that fits you, and look trim and spruce . . . Match your stockings with an eye to your hat, your blouse, your gloves. There is still an almost superstitious faith in shoes and gloves as marking a woman's standard of refinement.'

Miss Modern was on the business girl's side. Its launch issue included 'Pity the Pretty Girl in Business', 'Look Smart at the Office', and 'That First Interview', though a feature on 'Bachelor Girl Cookery' proposed a four-course meal few could have managed to rustle up. An entertaining squib in a later issue describes junior shorthand typist Miss Geranium Jones, who attracts the attention of unarticled clerk Marmaduke Youngman, when she starts work with solicitors Messrs Haggle and Sharpe. 'Our ambitious Geranium had not only got on – she had got off.' Women exceeded men by 1.75 million, but most young working women hoped their 'bachelor' status would be short-lived.

Meanwhile, unless she still lived at home, much of her salary disappeared on board and lodgings. Bachelor flats – as novelist Dodie Smith pointed out, there is no such thing as a spinster flat – could leave a lot to be desired; life at a boarding house or as a paying guest had its drawbacks, and hostel living, though cheap, was regimented and often primitive. Barbara Comyns's *A Touch of Mistletoe* fictionalises the downsides of singledom: tiny hostel cubicles, poky bed-sitting rooms, poor diet – rotting cabbage (and boils).

How the business girl must have longed for Virginia Woolf's room of her own. *Modern Home* conjured one up for her. Along with the 'Modernist' (all stripes and angles and 'severe chic'), the 'Country Cottage' and the 'Bride', a 1930 feature described the 'Bachelor Girl' which, combining 'the comforts of a bedroom with the dignity of the study', was decorated in biscuit and fuchsia, with a picture of a greyhound 'done in linen' on the wall – something for the business girl to stitch in her spare time, perhaps, when she had finished trimming her hats and making her frocks and blouses. (Though less sophisticated than the borzois which stride across art-deco bronzes, the greyhound was nonetheless a symbol of all things modern and a fitting companion for slender young women: a greyhound's head was the logo of a ready-to-wear wholesaler which supplied the Willenhall shop run by the Hodson sisters.)

In advertisements of the period, bachelor girls are positive, exuberant young creatures – diving into the water to swim (unlike their Victorian grandmothers), or seeking a loan to set themselves up in business. They exist more quietly in the small ads: seeking help to run kennels, offering typewriting services, or, quieter still, seeking posts as companions. A business girl is the subject of Dod Procter's painting *Lunch Hour*. The young woman reading at a cafe table may have smuggled in a surreptitious sandwich to accompany her cup of tea – the bachelor girl who could rarely spend more than fourpence or sixpence on a meal was often hungry – but it is the young woman herself, with her shiny bobbed hair and ginger-coloured coat and dress, who holds our interest. She appears to be reading, but is resting her head in her hand and could just as easily have fallen asleep. The bachelor girl is also the subject of Thomas C. Dugdale's painting *Underground*, exhibited at the Royal Academy in 1932, in which a weary-looking woman, staring blankly ahead, is strap-hanging on a busy Tube train. The *Illustrated London News* found the painting 'relentless in its realism'. As women had known all along, there was nothing girlish about independence. A *My Home* serial acknowledged this with an almost histrionic strap-line: 'For the Women of Today There are No Sheltered Places . . . They Must Go Out to Battle and Take Life as they Find It. This is Modern Youth!'

In a period with much to forget as well as celebrate, many sought distraction on the dance floor. Museum-collection gold and rosebud-patterned buttoned shoes, circa 1925, and a pair in gold lamé decorated with metallic fringing and a Sphinx's head (a product of the Egyptomania which followed the opening of Tutankhamen's tomb) were surely meant for dancing. Tango teas had been part of bohemian culture since before the First World War, but by the 1920s, all segments of society and all parts of the British Isles had caught up. Newspapers and magazines printed steps by 'famous London dancing masters', lyrics for the latest foxtrots and hesitation waltzes and features on the dos and don'ts of dancing. London's Dickens and Jones was one of the first department stores to introduce a *thé dansant*; Brown's of Chester ('the Harrods of the North') included a dance floor in its 1926 refurbishment; while in Edinburgh it was reported that 'jazz reigns supreme and the shimmy is coming into its own'. By the end of the decade most provincial towns had dance halls.

'The dance craze is, no doubt, greatly responsible for the headdress fashion', the *Ladies Field* reported; in a like vein, the *Daily Mail* described 'a demi-turban of silver gauze with a wisp of monkey fur falling almost to the shoulders'. Cartoonists had fun – and no wonder – with some fashionable styles, especially the backless evening gown. So much flesh on display was startling and daringly new. Dancing was not just about skimpy glamour, however (and certainly not in chilly provincial halls). In no time at all, dance music piped through the wireless was increasing productivity in factories; one young Staffordshire pottery worker and keen dancer, employed as a lathe treader, practised her steps while she worked.

The 1920s saw skirt lengths rise only to fall again; by the end of that decade sleek boyish lines changed into a softer silhouette, with waist and bust returning. Commentators spoke of a more feminine look, and remarks about a more feminine look are usually accompanied by prescriptive assumptions about female behaviour. The freedom shorter skirts demonstrated now seemed to be under threat. *Guardian* readers corresponded on the subject: were women to be hobbled once again?

The question of dress was becoming complicated in ways that are still recognisable. The long skirt and white blouse had provided a uniform for the educated Edwardian, but how was the interwar woman to dress now that a greater choice of practical and attractive clothing was available? Must she disdain fashion and sacrifice style as a badge of her intelligence? 'The date is passing when frumpiness counts as cleverness,' one journalist insisted. Vera Brittain also felt strongly on the subject and vented her feelings in her diary: 'Why, why must social reform and political intelligence . . . be associated with shiny noses & unwashed hair?' Brittain loved clothes and, years earlier, not yet acquainted with the educated 'look', had startled the Principal of Somerville by arriving for an evening interview wearing a flimsy gown, 'modish' satin cloak and high-heeled white suede shoes.

In 1927 writer Winifred Holtby attended a conference at which she saw 'line after line of dark velour coats with dreary rabbitskin collars, line after line of unbecoming hats . . . line after line of heads with rather untidy hair, of sallow complexions and listless unlovely figures.' Passing a mirror in the entrance hall, she saw a similarly dressed woman who 'gave a general impression of dowdiness, lethargy and neglect', and realised she was looking at herself. 'Since then I have been thinking hard about the problem . . . Ought we to abandon an interest in our clothes?' Reflecting on the subject, Holtby concluded: 'We want clothes in which we can dress ourselves quickly and comfortably, and which we can wear all day if necessary without feeling awkward . . . And we want to feel that in them we appear as charming, as chic and more entitled to self-respect than the [leisured fashionable women] whose photographs today we admire so wistfully in the illustrated papers.' One academic of the period evidently resolved the situation to her own satisfaction, and with great panache: each time Eileen Power, Professor of Medieval History at the London School of Economics, had an article published she travelled to Croydon, boarded a flight to Paris, and bought herself a new dress.

INDEPENDENT LIVING IN THE 1920S

Our bed-sitting room was in a large Victorian house in a quite a pleasant square with a garden in the centre where lime trees grew. Our room was on gthe hall floor and was painted a brilliant orange and blue, even the cheap china was orange and blue. The divan cover was a large damask tablecloth dyed black. We thought it a wonderful room with its gas fire and ring with a little tin kettle on it. There were even a few books on a shelf. The toilet arrangemengts were crude, consisting of an enamel basin and jug standing on a painted packing case behind a curtain, and water had to be fetched from the bathroom. The room had been advertised on a card in a shop window as 'a complete home in miniature' and it was in a way, except that it depended on what you meant by home . . . Although we were not as poor as we were to become later on, we had to shop very carefully. We used to buy grim little oranges for two a penny, which must have been dyed because the inside of the peel was almost the same colour as the outside, and there were broken biscuits that only cost 4d a pound . . . The only meat or fish we bought were sausages and kippers, which were easy to cook on a gas ring, and sometimes we shared ready-cooked Scotch egg . . .

Living in a blue and orange 'complete home in miniature' began to affect us in various ways . . . It also got into our clothes. We bought some vivid blue and orange shantung amd I made an orange dress trimmed with blue and Blanche a blue dress trimmed with orange. We cut the necks too large and the collars would not sit properly. We wore these shinning dresses for the first time on a sunny spring day . . . and they were so bright they seemed to be beating. We were wearing the same blue and orange dresses when we engaged a bedroom for Mother in a small Bloomsbury hotel and the startled landlady asked us if we were wearing out national costume. We wore them in bed as nightdresses after that.

Barbara Comyns, *A Touch of Mistletoe* (1967)

6 THE MACKINTOSH BUTTON: DERRING-DO AND FANTASY PHOTOGRAPHS

'If you are going to drive alone in the highways and byways', Miss Dorothy Levitt told women in 1902, 'it might be advisable to carry a small revolver. I have an automatic "Colt", and find it very easy to handle as there is practically no recoil – a great consideration to a woman.' For less challenging encounters while driving, Miss Levitt explained that 'a little drawer beneath the seat is the secret of the dainty motoriste. In its recesses put clean gloves, veil and handkerchief, powderpuff, pins, hairpins and a hand mirror. Some chocolates are very soothing sometimes.' A second vanity mirror was recommended so that vehicles approaching from the rear could be seen. Lesley Lewis's country-house family added cologne and smelling salts to their list, for those dicey four-wheeled moments.

A first consideration was clothing, no minor decision when cars lacked windscreens as well as mirrors, and drivers sat atop rather than inside them. Drivers and passengers alike had need of a gabardine, mackintosh or dust coat. The Edwardian woman might choose the Cyprus waterproof, in Art Shades of Cashmere for 42*s* 9*d*, though some took inspiration from the 'Swift' overcoat, complete with a windshield and storm cuffs. This retailed at 48*s*; the higher-grade Featherweight Double weighed in at 57*s* 3*d*. In clothing, as in all vehicular matters, Miss Levitt no doubt chose wisely. No faint-hearted driver, as has already been seen, she established a woman's world record of 91 mph in 1906 and thought nothing of motoring from Warwick to London and back for Sunday lunch. She also thought nothing of the 12 mph speed limit, and 'before she had been driving eight months' was twice fined for exceeding it.

My own gabardine, with its marbled grey buttons, has led a rather more pedestrian life than those worn by early motorists. Belted, grey, with a leather-covered buckle, back-buttoned flap and a nifty inside pocket, plus shoulder buttons for epaulettes, the gabardine is, I was told, army surplus. It keeps out the wind and rain and would, I am sure, have withstood innumerable hours of square-bashing, though I doubt it would have been protection enough for the Edwardian driver.

I found the gabardine on a lone stall near London's Berwick Street Market. This stall, stuffed with khaki bags and camouflage clothing, was a miniature version of London's Laurence Corner which, in turn, reminded me of Wakefield's, the Chesterfield store which, during the sixties and early seventies, when army surplus was in vogue, was sought out by those who would not have dreamed of embarking on military life. Wakefield's was the source of the 'grandad' vests my brother and I tie-dyed, as well as scratchy woollen sailor trousers; it may even have yielded grey gabardines like mine.

Come the First World War, daredevils fastened their gabardines to drive ambulances in France. They included Muriel Thompson, winner of the unfortunately named Ladies' Bracelet

Handicap at the Brooklands motor circuit in 1908. Thompson joined the Women's Transport Service, served on the Western Front from 1915 to 1918, and was awarded medals for bravery under fire. After the war, some young women put their gabardines and wartime skills to enterprising use. Miss Doris Winter, for example, ex-driver for the Australian Headquarters, established a hire company, driving her own landaulet, while, after their demobilisation, the Misses Ellington, Mayo and Parbury opened a garage in Kensington, taking responsibility for all repairs.

By the late 1920s, magazines and newspapers regularly thrilled with tales of women flying aeroplanes or racing cars and motorcycles. Even pillion riders were part of the story: 'Pillion Girls Want Speed', the *Daily Mail* reported from the 1927 Cycle and Motor Cycle Show. The boldest took to the skies. The best known British pilot of my grandma's day was Amy Johnson, 'Amy, wonderful Amy', as the bandleader Jack Hylton crooned, following her first solo flight. On 31 May 1930, the *Illustrated London News* devoted its front page to Amy Johnson's photograph and the caption 'The First Woman Pilot to Fly Alone to Australia, and the Only Woman Ground Engineer Certified by the Air Ministry.'

Swept up as a celebrity, Amy Johnson was in demand; stories of her achievements were everywhere. Harry Gordon Selfridge, well attuned to the value of publicity and to seizing the initiative, was quick to negotiate the rights to display her green de Havilland Moth, first in Oxford Street and then at his key provincial store: Cole Brothers, Sheffield (I do hope my great-aunt Eva saw that). Quick to capitalise on this mood, *Punch* observed the British achievement of universal female suffrage in June 1928 with a cartoon of an aviatrix. Resisting offers of assistance, this 'Free and Independent' woman makes a beeline for her plane. The cartoon's message is abundantly clear: from now on, women will be piloting their own lives.

Amy Johnson had dreamed of flying since she first saw aeroplanes at the cinema; that dream persisted and, while living near a private aerodrome in London's Maida Vale, she watched planes fly overhead: 'I envied those pilots. I longed for the freedom and detachment it seemed they must enjoy . . . I had always, subconsciously, wanted freedom and adventure.' For a young woman earning £3 a week in a solicitor's office, flying lessons seemed out of the question, but, 'drawn irresistibly by those tiny darting planes', she took a bus to the aerodrome and, summoning up her courage, asked how much lessons cost: 'Two pounds an hour for instruction. Thirty shillings an hour solo. Three guineas entrance fee and three guineas subscription. Takes from eight to twelve hours to learn.' Amy Johnson was twenty-three years old; that conversation changed her life.

The thrill of flying had existed since pilots first mastered the air in the early twentieth century; in no time at all flying in one form or another became a feature of local shows and fetes. Those visiting Chesterfield's Shopping Festival in the spring of 1914 could watch 'famous British airman' B. C. Hucks give a demonstration of upside-down flying, including 'Looping the Loop', and later that evening repair to the town's Corporation Theatre to watch the 'Aeroplane Ladies', an acrobatic troupe, 'whirl the whirl'.

B. C. Hucks was the festival's star attraction. The *Derbyshire Times* produced advance reports and a diagram of the feats he would perform, plus a rather deflating account of the occasion when Hucks and his plane found themselves bunkered on the town's golf course. A few months later, the nation's planes and pilots would have less entertaining feats to perform, but with the First World War still unimaginable, Hucks offered a glimpse of an exciting future; the adventurous could apply in advance for a passenger flight.

Joy rides increased in popularity after 1918. Nellie Taylor, holidaying in Margate, was captured by society photographer Bassano while awaiting her turn, dressed in her gabardine, goggles and balaclava. 'In England almost every holiday resort will be the scene of "joy rides",' the *Lady's Pictorial* announced in June 1920, encouraging 'all those who have not flown to take the first opportunity of a joy ride. It will be well worth the [guinea] fee.'

From 1919 the *Lady's Pictorial* published an occasional column, 'Woman on the Wing', with the drawing of sylph-like figure as its colophon and advice for the would-be aviatrix. 'Clothes for the Airwoman' was an early theme: 'A closely-woven material, like gabardine, wool or fur-lined, is the best for a flying costume,' a wing adjutant advised.

Plain, warm, windproof clothes are necessities, and anything which flutters or is liable to come loose or tangle in the wire and fittings of the aeroplane must be avoided . . . The woman aviator must not be heartbroken if she finds smears of grease or oil on her newly bought aviation costume . . . For general utility leather is too heavy . . . Wool-lined boots and thick foot coverings are necessary. Silk stockings and thin shoes are not suited for flying. Gloves must also be warm, preferably with a slit in the palm, through which the naked hand may be thrust if necessary . . . Good leather, stretching well up to the elbow, with a fur back and lined with lambs'-wool, gives ample protection from the cold. Headgear exists in many varieties. The helmet should be lightly made of chamois leather, lined with fur where it touches the ears, cheeks, and forehead, to prevent frostbite. The type which fastens with a buckle under the chin is best, as it does not come loose in the wind, a disadvantage of those types which are fastened with a ribbon. Goggles should be spring-sided Triplex.

The article was illustrated by a photograph showing a row of aviators in their flying gear. 'Which is Which?' the caption asked. 'Men and woman will be dressed exactly alike when they go flying, and it will often be difficult to distinguish between them.' The new world was a challenging place.

The aviatrix was not alone in being advised and patronised in the same breath; women's magazines, including the *Lady's Pictorial*, ran similar columns for the woman driver. She too was advised against unsuitable clothing, especially fox fur or anything else with 'waving paws and fluttering tails' that might obstruct the driver. Patronising assumptions aside, advice about sensible clothing was rooted in common sense. Isadora Duncan's death in 1927, when her silk scarf became tangled in the rear wheel of the car she was driving, was an all too modern reminder that fashion and safety may not mix.

One speed-loving sportswoman insisted on wearing whatever she liked. Mildred Bruce (the Honourable Mrs Victor Bruce) combined a passion for aviation with an equal enthusiasm for fast cars and fast boats. Bruce, who drove a Bentley at 90 mph for twenty-four hours and later pioneered UK air-to-air refuelling, went on to hold seventeen world records for her achievements in all three fields. Her bold approach to all things was demonstrated by the way she took up flying in the first place. She bought her first plane, it is said, while out shopping for a dress. The dress did not fit and so Bruce returned to examine a Blackburn Bluebird she had seen earlier in a car showroom, priced £550. 'Could one fly round the world in this?' she asked. 'Of course . . . easily!' came the reply. Eleven weeks later, after only forty flying hours, this brand-new pilot left Croydon for Tokyo on a 20,000 mile solo flight. Mildred Bruce was the kind of woman for whom the words 'pep' and 'verve' might have been invented. Immensely fashion-conscious, she refused to race her car wearing the usual overalls, preferring instead a skirt and blouse, and paired her leather flying coat and goggles with a fur stole and string of pearls.

Clothes figured in many adventurers' stories. The women racing in the Ladies' Bracelet Handicap fastened their long skirts with rope so they would not become tangled in the machinery or catch the wind and expose their legs; Lady Mary Heath, who flew from Cape Town to London in 1928, 'the first solo flight from an Overseas Dominion to the Mother Country', packed evening gowns in her luggage. Mildred Bruce paraded her femininity, along with her courage and skill. We can do it, and wear silk stockings and pearls, these women told naysayers. Amy Johnson opted for designer chic.

By 1936, and her flight from Gravesend to Cape Town which established a new flight record, Amy Johnson was dressed by Elsa Schiaparelli. For the first leg of the journey she wore Schiaparelli's signature press-clippings blouse and a mist-proof blue woollen suit whose divided skirt enabled her to reach the controls; the outfit also included a matching three-quarter-length coat. During a refuelling stop on the northern edge of the Sahara, Johnson changed into lighter cream silk toile, again with a divided skirt, and a blouse printed with a pattern of postage stamps; a chenille snood covered her head. For evenings, the feted pilot wore a high-waisted gown in heavy white crêpe embroidered with black sequins and a full-length black moiré cape.

The lives of most women were very different from those of aviatrices and racing drivers; even ordinary cars were the privilege of a relative few. Though car ownership increased between the wars and manufacturers directed their advertisements at women, the majority led bus or tram lives and stood in queues with mud-splattered stockings. My grandma was practically a married woman before she even sat in a car; neither she nor my great-aunt ever learned to drive; a car would have been too expensive to run. Most women of the period were as likely to fly a plane as to own their own car. For the majority, even the Aviation Cocktail was just a dream.

Those who could not drive, nor pluck up courage for a joy ride, could still enjoy the idea. Travellers who journeyed only in their imagination need look no further than their local photo-graphic studio on the high street. As a young woman, my mum, who had no camera, regularly took herself to 'Arthur's Studio' to be snapped; it was a way of keeping a record, and of sending cards to friends. Anyone could have their picture taken and reproduced on card for not much more than a penny. Supplementary hand-tinting cost extra, though, statistically, 'Penny Plain was much preferred to Tuppence Coloured.'

All that was needed for a fantasy journey was a painted back-drop and a cut-out plane, motorcycle or car. Some photographic studios ran to actual vehicles, but whether composed of vulner-able cardboard or sturdier metal, all these machines were stationary. Sepia or black-and-white postcards show friends and sweethearts posing behind the wheel or leaning away from the camera as if cresting the wind. Mostly, they are smiling, enjoying a bit of a lark or a holiday caper; sometimes they seem embar-rassed by their fantasy role. Some young women posed solo, rather than with friends, and perhaps because they felt less self-conscious when photographed alone, their make-believe looks real. Elsie Fitton, a young Derby railway clerk, was photographed astride a motorbike whose numberplate reads '1929'. She was one of many young women who did not travel far, but sought speed and adventure via painted country roads, her gabardine buttoned up to her throat. For an eternal moment, the open road stands before her.

7 **THE LINEN BUTTON:** SMALL MIRACLES ON SMALL MEANS

The linen button is the lowliest button of all, produced in vast quantities since the mid-nineteenth century and used, in different sizes, to fasten poorer-quality underwear, some babies' clothing and working men's shirts. During my mother's childhood, labouring men fastened their collars with linen buttons whereas collar-and-tie chaps, like my great-grandfather, had the benefit of mother-of-pearl.

Linen buttons numbered among the items sold at the family's corner shop. Like all corner shops, my great-grandma's was a repository of many things, from starch and string to pig powders, pickles and broken biscuits. Aside from a dazzle of cheap dress rings – the shop's one concession to glamour – linen buttons were the sole items relating to dress. Rings may seem inexplicable in a shop servicing a poor industrial neighbourhood where money was scarce and many goods retailed in quantities of two ounces, but, well into the twentieth century, corner shops sold some attractive tat along with essential goods. I remember similar rings from my own childhood – an expandable band that had to be wrestled from an elasticated card and turned your ring finger green, but whose stone shone every bit as brightly as a Woolworth's gem. Unlike dress rings, linen-covered buttons were decidedly mundane, the linen stretched across stiff metal, with holes stamped in them for thread. The button box contains three linen shirt buttons, attached to scraps of their original cards. Men wore these buttons, but it was nearly always women who sewed them on to husbands' and sons' shirts. My great-grandma Betsy sold no female equivalent, perhaps because no one female button was so ubiquitous.

In addition to being cheap, the linen button had another great virtue. Unlike more expensive buttons, these survived the mangle, that essential part of the weekly wash. 'Will not break in mangling' was a virtue not to be underestimated for those with little money to spare for buttons or very much else. Worn by men doing filthy, heavy work, linen buttons needed to be robust. Much working-class life in the early years of the twentieth century required robustness of one sort or another, especially for those, like my great-grandma's immediate neighbours, at the poorer end of the scale.

The wives of colliery and foundry men accounted for most of Betsy's customers; the poorest among them strayed not much further than the corner shop itself, which was the place to catch up with neighbours as well as purchase groceries. The struggles they faced included clothing themselves and their large families – despite a general fall in the birth rate, the poorest families still had six or seven children apiece well into the 1930s – the tyranny of wash day and the many difficulties arising from insufficient funds, poor housing and consequent ill-health.

My great-grandparents took on the tenancy of the corner shop around 1905 and were there until their deaths in 1951. (Although my great-grandfather's name stood above the door, he never stood behind the counter; the shop was run by Betsy and, later, Betsy and Eva.) Surprisingly few changes took place throughout that time, although the neighbourhood acquired a greyhound track and the illustrations on condiments and biscuit tins switched from depicting Edwardian women astride bicycles to athletic-looking young things dashing to the tennis courts or strapping on roller skates.

My great-grandma seems to have been well regarded locally, a view derived from multiple family stories and the fact that in all the years my mother played with the children who lived round about and who knew the corner shop well, no child spoke against my great-grandparents or great-aunt – and children are usually less concerned with neighbourly politesse. My great-grandma could not read or write but she could reckon, and she made a good fist of the shop; neighbours came to her for advice as well as groceries. In the 1930s two local newspaper vendors regularly vied for her attention and an invitation into the house; the one delivering the morning paper fared best as, arriving in time for breakfast, he was often invited to pull up a chair, whereas the other, arriving mid-afternoon, only managed a cup of tea.

Not all corner-shopkeepers were viewed in a positive light. Journalist Leonora Eyles described the difficulties they could make for the women dependent on their goods, deciding who was eligible for tick and over-charging those with little choice about where to shop. Helen Forrester, whose family descended into extreme poverty in Liverpool during the Depression, described a shopkeeper who sold bread by the slice as a 'skinflint harridan'. I wonder what Helen Forrester would have made of my great-grandma who did the same when people could not afford the whole or half a loaf.

For many working-class families, low wages, variable shifts and intermittent industrial action meant that household budgeting was a fine art. In 1922 a Derbyshire woman, Mrs Blackwell, was awarded first prize in a Women's Institute competition for the way she managed hers. The wife of a 'working man' in the village of Baslow, part of the Chatsworth estate, she received a weekly housekeeping allowance of £2 5s (a sum echoed in a contemporary advertisement for Rowntree's Cocoa) and managed her expenditure down to the last halfpenny – a halfpenny went further than one might think. Half of her weekly income was allocated to 'food and stores', one quarter spent on 'rent, rates, insurance, food and light' and the remainder divided between 'boots, clothes and sundries', and a 'reserve for emergencies'. Fruit and vegetables were not listed, but garden seeds and manure formed part of the emergency contingency, 'emergency' reserves being required to provide for irregular but necessary purchases in many a household budget. Everything was pared down to basics. The winner of a 1930 WI competition (prize: one pig, to add to her smallholding) grew a wide variety of fruit and vegetables, as well as herbs, and listed a substantial number of bottled, pickled and cured foodstuffs. Her home was a picture of self-sufficiency. Managing and getting by could be a full-time job.

Linen buttons probably accounted for a few of the pennies Mrs Blackwell allocated for haberdashery, along with sewing thread. Mrs Blackwell bought ready-made clothes, but could not escape the task of mending, that essential domestic chore which, in some people's eyes, constituted female leisure (especially for domestic servants expected to tackle piles of darning on their afternoons off). For house-bound women, mending was an opportunity to sit down, although there was little respite in replacing buttons, repairing frayed collars and cuffs and turning sheets sides to middle. Mending acquired an additional, unexpected role. In the days when reliable contraception was hard to come by, a pile of mending might come in useful. Even in the 1930s, the decade that saw the Family Planning Association established, and some fifteen years after Marie Stopes's *Married Love* was published, contraception was still almost unmentionable; some married women who consulted their doctors for advice were merely told to 'behave' themselves. Margaret Forster's mother was not the only woman to say, in effect, 'I'll be up in a minute,' hoping that by the time she had finished sewing, her husband would have fallen asleep.

Winifred Foley, born in 1914, divided her Forest of Dean village into the 'feckless, filthy and friendly' at one end, and the 'prim, prudish and prosperous' at the other. Though neither prim nor prudish, my great-grandparents were better off than many in the vicinity, and, as shopkeepers' daughters, Annie and Eva fared better than their neighbours. Their ribbon-threaded nightgowns, hair slides, Dorothy bags, necklaces, lockets and brooches, not to mention silk parasols with crochet-hook curled handles, demonstrated that money could be found for extras as well as necessities.

Wherever you stood on the working-class scale, clothing was an expense. For the very poorest, clothing was 'frankly, a mystery', in the words of the Fabian Women's Group who examined life for those who lived on approximately a pound a week in the London borough of Lambeth from 1909 to 1913. 'In the poorer budgets items for clothes appear at extraordinarily distant intervals, when, it is to be supposed, they can no longer be done without. "Boots mended" in the weekly budget means less food for that week.' Boots were always a problem. During periods of especial hardship, such as industrial strikes, some head teachers administered boot funds along with hand-outs of food. Photographs from Annie and Eva's childhoods show ragamuffin youngsters sitting alongside those from 'better' homes, broken-soled shoes lined up beside polished button boots. Equally striking are the starched white pinafores worn by the majority of the girls, despite the fact that many – including Annie and Eva – came from houses with no hot water and only one cold tap. Clean clothes were a triumphant achievement on their mothers' part.

In 1913 Rebecca West introduced readers of the *Clarion* to 'Mary Brown', who appealed to that newspaper's readers for cast-off clothing. 'I want to go out to work to help my family, as things cannot go on as they are.' She told how her three young boys and daughter were 'so badly off for clothes that I am ashamed to look at them, and it breaks my heart to send them to school.' When her husband's fares and their rent of 6s 6d were subtracted from his weekly wage of 24s or less, there was not enough left for food. 'If any of your readers can help me with some old garments for my children and myself I will go out to work. I can put my baby girl in the day nursery for 3d a day. I must go and do something to help, for we cannot live on 10s or 11s a week, which is what it amounts to.' Rebecca West deftly linked Mrs Brown's plight to a discussion of the clothes worn by theatrical performer Gaby Deslys at a time when the Bishop of Kensington and others were getting hot under the collar about Deslys's 'indecent' scanty dress. What *was* immoral, West insisted, was the scanty clothing Mary Brown and her children were forced to wear. 'Now, is that not indecent?' she asked, in a typically astringent piece.

For the very poorest little changed over the next twenty years. Helen Forrester, kept from school in the 1930s to mind her younger siblings, quickly learned that the one who did not have to leave the house would be clothed last, and fed last too. Her coat, hat and shoes were passed to her sister; by their second winter in Liverpool, Helen was dressed in rags and had no shoes on her feet. A Durham woman told the 1939 Women's Health Committee that she sent her children on errands because she had no coat to wear and so could not go out herself.

Even those whose circumstances were less extreme found that

clothing required considerable effort as well as ingenuity. Winifred Foley recalled that, in her youth, few people owned more than one change of clothing and that 'clothes that today [the 1970s] cannot be got rid of at a penny a bundle at the tail end of a jumble sale would have been thankfully washed and hung out with pride'. Rose Gamble's mother spent a lifetime going without. 'She had no vanities, but now and again a pretty pattern would catch her eye, perhaps on a scrap of cloth in Dodie's basket or on a roll of lino standing outside the ironmonger's. 'I'd like a frock of that,' she would say, showing just for a moment that she still had an occasional thought for herself.'

Fashion and poverty co-exist. Flora Thompson described how, towards the end of the nineteenth century, young women working away from home as domestic servants 'helped to set the standard of what was worn' by passing their mistresses' cast-offs on to their mothers. 'The hamlet's fashion lag was the salvation of its wardrobes, for a style became "all the go" there just as the outer world was discarding it, and good, little-worn specimens came that way by means of the parcels . . . This devotion to fashion gave a spice to life and helped to make bearable the underlying poverty. But the poverty was there.' For the poorest, a change of clothing could achieve an especial transformation. A member of the Fabian Women's Group recalled that 'the astonishing difference made by a new pink blouse, becomingly-done hair, and a well-made skirt, on one drab-looking woman who seemed to be about forty was too startling to forget. She suddenly looked thirty (her age was twenty-six), and she had a complexion and quite pretty hair – features never noticed before. These women who look to be in the dull middle of middle age are young; it comes as a shock when the mind grasps it.'

The access to new horizons wrought by the cinema, wireless

and women's magazines between the wars, plus the greater accessibility of affordable and fashionable clothing, led to an apparent merging of the social classes. For all the upward mobility of the period, there was still little understanding between them and some of those who remarked about factory girls now looking like duchesses could barely conceal their anxiety about young women not knowing their place. Others, like Lettice Cooper, applauded the change. Her state-of-England novel, *National Provincial,* set in 1930s Leeds, introduces Olive, who operates a newly installed button machine in a clothing factory and is one of those upwardly mobile young women. 'Olive's personal daintiness, her exquisitely ordered curls and polished nails, her fresh, fashionable clothes, were the result of much determination, and of a prolonged and valiant struggle.' Few would guess Olive came from a two-up two-down in which all water has to be boiled, and where her mother, with whom she shares a bed, constantly battles against the dirt from belching chimneys. Olive achieves the latest styles via a combination of home-dressmaking and off-the-peg clothes; her friend and fellow machinist, Violet, whose wages are her family's mainstay, has an even greater struggle. 'How Violet managed . . . to have the fur-collared coat and eye-veiled hat, the bag and gloves, powder and cream and permanent wave, and always to be abreast of changing fashion among her friends was one of the lesser miracles of modern civilisation.' Olive and Violet may be fictional characters but they typify the resourceful young women who made considerable efforts to dress fashionably and considered it a mark of personal pride to do so. Small miracles like theirs were performed every day of the week.

A 1930S BUTTON-MAKING MACHINE

He stood at the end of one of the long tables watching a girl who was working a machine that fastened buttons on the waistcoats. The waistcoats slid towards her out of a wooden funnel that disgorged them flat onto the table, the side awaiting the buttons marked with chalk crosses, and turned towards the machine. One sure movement of her hands flicked the waistcoat into place, a second dropped the buttons into a small tray at the side of the machine, which immediately absorbed them. As she pressed a treadle with her foot, the machine released the buttons each into its place on the chalk crosses. Needles shot down and stitched the buttons on to the cloth with firm, strong stitches. Another pressure of her foot raised the needles and released the cloth, a quick twist of her hand pulled the waistcoat past the machine into another flat wooden funnel that conveyed it to the next table, where another girl was waiting to operate on it with a machine for making button-holes. This button machine was new and one of the show pieces of the work-room. Stephen had brought his mother to see it, but she had observed placidly, 'They'll all come off at once, dear. I've never worn anything ready made without sewing on the buttons first.' Those five movements of hand and feet, endlessly and exactly repeated, distressed her as they distressed Stephen, and she asked, 'Don't you get very tired of doing it?' but the girl, who was pretty, with carefully curled hair, delicately plucked eyebrows, and a bright painted mouth, smiled and said that she liked it. How can she, Stephen thought, as he stood now watching her warm young flesh and blood moving with the precision of a machine.

Lettice Cooper, *National Provincial* (1938)

8 **THE BABY'S BUTTON:** 'PRAY LET PARTIUCLARE CARE BE TAKEN'EN OFF THIS CHILD'

The three pearl buttons on a dress in my possession are defined by their milky sheen. Less than half an inch wide, with four holes punched for thread, they seem indistinguishable from others of their type, but the dress itself has a special value and the fact that it survives is testament to that. It was made by my grandma and worn by my mum shortly after she was adopted in 1930.

I do not know if this was the dress my mum was wearing when my grandparents brought her home, but she was photographed in it soon afterwards. My grandma held her up for the camera and although the pose is not triumphant, the story is a triumph of a kind. My mother escaped institutional life, thank goodness, and the more I think about it, the more I realise how unlikely an escape hers was. She was a London baby and could easily have become a child in the care of the Foundling Hospital, or an infant in a Dr Barnardo's Home. Instead, she was handed to the National Children Adoption Association (NCAA), one of the two key interwar agencies that worked to unite couples seeking children with children in need of homes. How that lucky decision came about is lost to history.

Many years separate the establishment of Thomas Coram's Foundling Hospital in the eighteenth century and my mum's adoption but, regardless of the century, the stigma and difficulties faced by women who found themselves pregnant and unsupported was intense. The first eighteenth-century women who gave up their children did so under cover of darkness. The Foundling Hospital opened its doors at 8 p.m. on 25 March 1741, the late hour especially chosen to shield the women and their shame. The occasion was advertised in the press and, one by one, young mothers came forward. By midnight, when the doors were closed, thirty children had been admitted: eighteen boys and twelve girls.

The Foundling Hospital's full title, The Hospital for the Education and Maintenance of Exposed and Deserted Young Children, gives a clear statement of Coram's purpose. The call on the institution was such that a lottery system was introduced and the rules were soon adjusted so that only illegitimate children aged twelve months and under were admitted. Women already reflecting bitterly on the lottery of love may have looked askance at a regime requiring them to select a coloured ball from a bag but, for more than ten years, this was the procedure. A white ball granted admission, provided the child was healthy, a red placed the child on a reserve list, but a black ball spelled rejection for good.

For the first sixty years of the Hospital's existence, mothers giving up their children were advised to supply a token – a small object that would serve as an identifier should they petition for that child's return at a later date; mother-of-pearl buttons, coins, keys, medals, rings and coral bracelets were among the items left. Many mothers were illiterate and so were unable to provide other documentary evidence; however, even some of the women who could write chose also to supply a token. One young woman left a Coldstream Guards button *c*.1780. Denoting the Coldstream Regiment of Foot, this very likely originated with the foundling's father. If so, the man was an officer: the button is made of bone and backed with gilded metal, whereas rank-and-file buttons were pewter. He was not the only father in the Hospital's records to have 'gone for a soldier', and may have fought in the American Revolution. The woman he left behind probably wanted it known that her child's father was of officer class.

The children these tokens represent never saw them – their function was purely administrative – but though not intended as a parting gift, mothers sometimes used their token to convey their love for the child they were giving up, and made it themselves or personalised it in some way. The results can be seen in London's Foundling Museum; the passage of time has not made them any less heart-rending.

Each token suggests its own story. The majority were strips of fabric, the idea being that the mother would keep a corresponding piece which, when presented to the Hospital, would confirm the child as hers. If ever clothing revealed a larger narrative, this is it. Not surprisingly, hearts featured – one was cut from parchment and decorated with ribbon. Bits of blanket were personalised with extra stitches; squares of printed cotton and even beautifully embroidered silks were left to identify children. This extensive archive of scraps and heartache forms Britain's largest collection of everyday eighteenth-century textiles. The functional sit alongside the vividly patterned and the colourful, again giving the lie to the notion that poor women did not have pretty things. Pieces of fabric were cut from children's sleeves (in the eighteenth century, sleeves were a separate item in children's clothing); the sleeve itself often cut down from the mother's dress. Time and again, these women demonstrated their dexterity with a needle and thread; time and again, I am struck by the intimacy of their endeavour and the magnitude of what these fabrics represent. A Foundling Museum exhibition, 'Threads of Feeling', could not have been more aptly named.

The handmade tokens are the most affecting. Some show diminutive beading, their individual beads barely discernible even in today's lighting and, surely, almost impossible to see when stitched or threaded in candlelight, back then. The phrase 'labour of love' is clichéd but some of these tokens involved considerable labour and convey a palpable sense of loss. The red-cloth heart stitched with tiny beads and further embellishment practically shrieks with love; the flower (or star) decorated with sequins and flecked with lace is equally dismaying. Covered with linen once upon a time, its message remains strong, though much of the linen has long since perished, exposing strips of card beneath. The women who fashioned these tokens with such elaborate care surely knew that this was likely to be the last time they saw their child.

Some mothers confidently expressed their intention to return – 'Pray Let partiuclare Care be taken'en off this Child, As it will be call'd for Again.' Between 1748 and 1798 over 500 parents petitioned for their child's release. However, infant mortality was high and those who had to wait several years before their lives turned around sufficiently for them to apply all too often returned too late. Lucy Reeves who, by 1767, had married a Suffolk farmer, applied for the child she left at the Hospital in 1760, only to discover that the infant had died years earlier. John Browne, a baby from Great Yarmouth, was admitted on 5 January 1760 with a piece of fabric with buttons and buttonholes attached. The buttons were Dorset High Tops, a type of thread button used to fasten eighteenth-century dresses and worn on underwear into the nineteenth century, which suggests that this fabric was cut from his mother's dress. (High Tops, also known as Dorset Knobs, were made by covering a small disc of sheep's horn with rag, and then working over the whole with fine stitching.) John Browne died before the year was out, probably while still with his nurse, one of the many infants carried off by disease.

On admission to the Foundling Hospital, children's names were changed and the children given a number to wear on a disc around their neck. The use of discs was eventually dispensed with, but the change of name persisted, as was generally the case in the history of adoption. Newly admitted babies were sent to wet nurses, usually in outlying rural districts, with whom they stayed until the age of five. Once returned to the Hospital, the children endured a strict regime, rising at 5 a.m., and received a rudimentary education before being sent out into the world. As with the workhouse and industrial schools, the boys were generally apprenticed to the Navy or a trade, and the girls sent into domestic service. This regime was probably no harsher than those practised in other institutions in earlier centuries, but this story does not only belong to the distant past. Tom MacKenzie, one of the Hospital's last foundlings, admitted in 1939, was also subjected to this punitive regime. He too was fostered for the first five years of his life, and then taken away and boarded with the Foundling Hospital. There he wore a uniform to fit him for his future station in life. Harsh regimes like these obtained until the publication of the 1946 Curtis Report into the conditions of children in care.

It is impossible for me to read of Tom MacKenzie without thinking of my mother's lucky escape and her good fortune in being placed for adoption via the NCAA, with its glittering list of committee members and supporters drawn from the great and the good and the upstanding. Its Annual Report for 1927–8, which doubled as a promotional booklet, was sent to my grandparents prior to my mum's adoption and shows NCAA president HRH Princess Alice and founder and director Clara Andrew smiling with Queen Mary on her visit to its babies' hostel, Tower Cressy. The young girls photographed are dressed in white and the boys wear pale knitted jumpers; evidently they have benefited from bathing in the brand-new bathrooms of which the NCAA booklet boasts. The picture painted of the adoptees' brief stay – and their stay *was* brief – was very different from that of institutional life. 'It must be jolly to be a babe at Tower Cressy,' its promotional foreword gushed; a *Woman's Own* feature from 1936 shows a nursery-like frieze of hopeful adoptees wreathed in Mabel Lucie Attwell smiles. In a vastly quicker process than today's adoption procedures, would-be adopters were told to be patient: enquiries as to their suitability generally took a few weeks.

My mother was an early beneficiary of the Adoption of Children Act 1926, which came into law the following year and laid the foundation for adoption as we know it today. Anxieties about adoption meant there was talk in the press of 'hereditary taint'; as a counter to that the children photographed by the NCAA look as clean and hygienic and 'untainted' as anyone could wish: shiny modern bathrooms and pristine clothes separated the adoptees from their beginnings.

Heredity held no fears for my grandparents in any way. Adoption was threaded through my grandma's family history. My mother's was not the first adoption in the family: hers was the last of three. The adoptions stretch back into the nineteenth century and convey something of the eras in which each one took place. My great-grandfather was abandoned by emigrant parents in the 1860s and left in the care of a Chesterfield barber; my great-aunt Eva spent much of her childhood in an Industrial School (later called a children's home), before being plucked from a line-up in 1909 and brought home to join the family. My mother's was the only adoption orchestrated through the courts. When her adoption was finalised in 1931, the court officials said she was the first child legally adopted in Chesterfield, following the Adoption Act.

When this Act came into force, the mother whose child was legally adopted was saying goodbye for good. Before 1927 there was always the chance that a woman giving up her baby could reclaim the child later – like the eighteenth-century mother presenting her matching strip of fabric. One of the eighteenth-century success stories relates to a boy christened Charles but given the name Benjamin Twirl. He was reclaimed by his mother, Sarah Bender, on 10 June 1775. When giving up her child some eight years earlier, Sarah left a strip of patchwork, a selection of fabrics, oversewn with flowers and decorative stitches, and completed by a heart in red thread. One half of the patchwork was left with the Hospital. 'The heart was made whole' when the mother reclaimed her son.

Just as the eighteenth-century buttons, fabrics and home-made tokens have a larger meaning than those items might initially suggest, so the small dress my grandma made tells its own large story. If I look closely at the cream silk dress, I see the gathers at the neck and the sleeves and the double frill circling the hem. I note the delicate smocking below the bodice and the fine drawn threads, discreet additional features. Several elements combine in this complex but understated garment. Most frequently my eyes are drawn to the final telling details: the two white flowers that decorate the bodice – each petal a single stroke of embroidery silk. Annie stitched her hopes into every gather, running thread and seam of that small dress: her hopes for herself as a mother and her hopes for her child, and it was her decision to hold on to the dress down the years. It was kept without any fanfare, and

I came upon it almost by chance. At first I thought it was just a baby's dress, but its meaning became clear when I saw the photograph of my grandma with her new daughter. And while it is true that, like a great many mothers, my grandma bought pearl buttons, fabric and thread to make her child a dress, these are no ordinary buttons and this is no ordinary dress.

9 **EVA'S GLOVE BUTTON:** MODEL GOWNS AND INEXPENSIVE DRESS

My great-aunt's gauntlets, with their broad buttoned cuffs, suited her slim hands. Eva wore clothes well and enjoyed them; I've enjoyed wearing Eva's gloves since they came to me. These chocolate-coloured wool-lined gauntlets with buttons, buttonholes, gusset and cuffs edged in caramel-coloured leather were ideal for the dressy woman going out on a cold day.

In the 1920s, gauntlets were still associated with the sporting woman's wardrobe. *The Needlewoman* confirmed their dashing pedigree: 'At the moment the fashion seems to be for coloured sports gloves. A young woman who caused quite a sensation in Bond Street recently, was driving a smart coupé in black and green, and wore a black leather coat with elaborate gauntlets of green to match the upholstery.' Within a few years they were a popular choice for day wear and were worn by women like my great-aunt Eva when they dressed up to go shopping.

Eva's chocolate-brown gloves complemented her leather clutch purse or 'pochette' as it was also known. With an asymmetrical pattern in toning shades on its front flap, the clutch is absolutely of the moment; an internal mirror enabled the interwar woman (though not Eva) to apply lipstick and a dab of powder. Accentuated by the gauntlets' own pedigree, the bag's sleek trim line and 'pick up and go' style, gave the immediate impression of a woman with places to be.

Clutch purse and gauntlets were the mark of a woman shopping for pleasure, not necessities, and in Eva's case, this meant leaving her own shop counter to examine others of a more luxurious kind, usually in Chesterfield town centre. Like other provincial towns, Chesterfield had its own large stores, including Swallow's and John Turner's, sedate establishments whose air of affordable refinement was still apparent in the 1960s. Though smaller and less glossy than city department stores, they nonetheless drew shoppers from outlying districts. Earlier in the century, the town made a brave attempt to promote itself as an alternative venue to Sheffield, Derby or Nottingham and, with that in mind, held its first Shopping Festival in 1910 and a further 'Grand Shopping Week' in April 1914, promising myriad attractions. Swallow's, with its 'unique and artistic' windows, and Turner's, 'the fashion house where the ladies gather', vied with one another to carry off the prizes for the best displays.

The most elaborate gloves of that era were elbow-length evening gloves. The Army and Navy Stores catalogue lists numerous examples, some of them fastened with as many as twenty buttons apiece. Favoured by Edwardian ladies – and only 'ladies' wore them – these gloves followed the contours of the hand and forearm so tightly that assistance was required to put them on. Glove-stretchers were needed, a dusting of talcum powder and, 'if you had a maid or were being fitted in a shop you put your elbow on the table or counter and held up your hand while the glove was smoothed over it'. The difficulty of keeping white kid clean meant that gloves like these were kept in their own box. And, of course, pristine gloves confirmed that ladies never dirtied their hands.

Glove buttons fastened with the help of a hook even smaller than those used to button shoes; after washing, the glove's shape was restored with further help from the long, thin stretchers; a lady's maid, a glove box, a hook, a dusting of powder, plus stretchers – and all for a pair of gloves. No thought given to the women who strained their eyes stitching all those tiny buttonholes for between 2½d and 8½d per dozen pairs of gloves.

Gloves completed an outfit; not to wear them was, like the failure to wear a hat, to be undressed. 'Gloves must be in harmony with the costume, in texture as well as colour.' *How to Dress Well* advised the interwar woman. 'An incongruity between gloves and costume may ruin an otherwise perfect ensemble.' By the time my great-aunt Eva pulled on her buttoned gauntlets, Chesterfield had a population of just over 64,000, its own small shopping arcade and a Tudorbethan row of shops. Swallow's continued to make an appeal with 'Gloves with a Reputation' and 'Costumes of Distinction'; while the woman wearing a smart overcoat and clutching a pochette and gauntlets in a Turner's advertisement from 1934 might well have been my great-aunt herself.

Annie made some of Eva's clothes but Eva also bought ready-to-wear. Hours spent behind the corner-shop counter left little time for running up her own frocks. Though many still baulked at the quality of ready-to-wear clothing others, including *How to Dress to Well*, appreciated its reliability. 'One can always be certain how a ready-to-wear garment is going to appear. There is no gamble. And few women have not had clothes made at home which turned out to be utter failures.'

In 1920, 75 per cent of clothing and footwear was purchased from independent retailers, with department stores responsible for only 10 per cent of sales. By 1939, the independent share had dropped to 50 per cent, as chain stores increased in prominence and department stores gained in popularity. A Chesterfield directory for 1936 listed 5 fancy drapers, 1 tailoress, 28 drapers (including Swallow's and Turner's, which combined drapery with dressmaking and ready-to-wear), 7 costumiers; 5 ladies' outfitters, and a choice of 12 milliners to supply the hat to go with Eva's smart gloves.

My great-aunt Eva shopped at ladies' outfitters Miss Greaves, whose clothes were thought to be 'a cut above' well into the 1950s; Marjorie Willett, who trained at Chesterfield's Madame Lucille before branching out alone, was also worth visiting for something distinctive. Chesterfield Market was the place to buy cheap fabric and to rummage for buttons and make a lucky dip for rick-rack braid and strips of lace. Far more discreet were Eva's forays into Swallow's or Turner's for skirts and 'art' silk blouses, good stockings for best-dressed days, and the Californian Poppy scent and Cuticura talc she liked.

The development of the department store is also the story of the draper's shop. The majority evolved from drapers, family concerns which grew in size and popularity over the years and which, recognising the advantages of having fabrics, sewing silks, trimmings and their own dressmakers under one roof, were well on their way to establishing multiple departments. Browns of Chester was founded by Susannah Towsey whose family had been associated with hattery and hosiery from the early 1700s, and who ran a drapery and haberdashery with her sister Elizabeth before marrying druggist John Brown. William Whiteley purchased his first draper's shop in 1863; the young John Lewis was a silk buyer at Peter Robinson's before setting up on his own. Long before department stores existed, draper's shops stood out from their neighbours: they needed to be well lit in order for women to appraise the quality of the fabrics and eiderdowns piled high in their windows.

Women have sought department stores since improved transport
in the mid-nineteenth century enabled them to travel into the city.
For all the indulgence associated with them, they offered a safe
and comfortable space at a time when the city could be a dangerous
place for women out alone; they offered anonymity too, in contrast
to small local shops. A considerable part of the department store's
appeal, and a key principle behind its development, was the ability
to enter without obligation to buy: the freedom of the store, as
Harry Selfridge termed it. Their attraction was all the greater once
restaurants and cloakrooms were added.

The freedom of the store was a real plus, but department stores
require customers to spend money and they seek ever more
seductive ways to entice them, or, to quote Virginia Woolf's more
jaundiced view: make 'the effort to persuade the multitude that
here unending beauty, ever fresh, ever new, very cheap and within
the reach of everybody, bubbles up every day of the week'. A
1924 guide took a loftier tone, praising Peter Robinson's 'perfec-
tion of detail', its ground floor paved with unpolished blocks of
marble in the style of Milan Cathedral and its inlaid zodiac signs
near the lifts. The lifts themselves, those gateways to the store,
were lacquered in 'sealing-wax red, with black bands picked out
in gold', while the doors were 'bronze faced round with pale
green marble'. Marshall & Snelgrove was like 'the East of one's
dreams, where silks and cushions, gorgeous lamps and ornaments
of jade and amethyst are piled with an apparent carelessness that
is the subtlest of temptations'. Some might have expected the
Sheik to appear at any moment. According to the company's own
literature, the very name Marshall & Snelgrove signified 'quality,
something necessary to a woman's sense of well-being'. Its reputation among the well-heeled was long established; the store was
fondly satirised by *Punch* as early as the 1870s: 'Well, Master
Tom,' a nanny asks her young charge, 'the twins are going to be

christened tomorrow. What shall we call them?' 'If we want to please Mama,' the little boy replies, 'we'd better call them *Marshall* and *Snelgrove*!'

In Lettice Cooper's 1936 novel *The New House*, a Leeds department store offers reassurance as well as pleasure. 'The warm air, scented with cosmetics, lapped round [Evelyn] . . . Once you got inside those big doors, you were in a world which, provided that you had money to spend, existed . . . to give . . . pleasure, to wrap you in soft furs, dress you in rich or delicate colours. It saw to it that the small doings of your everyday life, smoking a cigarette or powdering your face, were surrounded with luxury and grace.' By now, the freedom of the store was wrapping women in a glamorous art-deco embrace. Following its own elaborate refurbishment, the interior of Selfridges was like stepping on to a film set. Its lift operators – that enticing lift again – dressed in shiny satin Oxford bags, brass-buttoned majorette jackets, striking hats and broad-cuffed gauntlets, looked ready to break into triple-time steps.

As a penniless (and occasionally light-fingered) teenager, Angela Rodaway went window shopping in the 1930s. 'Sometimes, after school . . . I would go round these shops in the way that I had once wandered round museums and art galleries, just gazing and getting a kind of spiritual stimulation from it. I needed food for dreams.' Dreams are, of course, what department stores were built on. 'The air was scented; it smelt a bit like bluebells but richer, deeper. "What *does* it smell of, exactly?"' Cassandra asks her sister Rose, when, in Dodie Smith's novel *I Capture the Castle* the sisters venture into a department store for the very first time. 'Heaven,' Rose replies.

Two-thirds of the women who responded to a 1939 Mass Observation survey said their clothes purchases began with window shopping. Jean Rhys described women peering through the windows of Oxford Street stores: 'If I could buy this, then of course I'd be quite different.' Then, as now, magazines also provided inspiration – and for retail staff as well as shoppers. Lewis's department stores in Liverpool and Manchester instructed their employees to 'read fashion magazines and study advertise-ments . . . You must cultivate a sense of good taste; in other words you must have the ability to gauge the materials, colour and styles most suitable for the customer.'

Cultivate a sense of good taste – a terrifying proposition. How to 'look right' could be nerve-racking, particularly during an era when it was hard to keep pace with changing fashions and waist-lines went down as skirt lengths shot up, only to reverse a few years later. Most women knew how easy it was to Get It Wrong and were grateful for advice, especially when what you wore announced whether you were 'our kind of people' or not. There were unspoken rules to be observed whatever your social class, but most especially if you were a working-class woman (or man, for that matter, although their rules were more straightforward) edging your way into the expanding middle classes.

It was perhaps with this in mind that, in 1936, *Woman's Weekly* produced a series of features advising women how to dress. Priced 2*d*, the magazine appealed to those who were mostly home-dressmakers, but nonetheless wanted to stay abreast of fashion. At this time, large numbers were making their own clothes and visiting department stores for fabrics; the fabric and paper-pattern department of London's newly refurbished D. H. Evans occupied half of its extensive ground floor. After reassuring its readers that the advertised patterns (6*d*, plus coupon) were available in large sizes, *Woman's Weekly* proposed three outfits:

Green patterned silk with brown and beige flowers. Sling scarf lined with plain green, lighter cuffs. Wear with brown waffle-weave wool coat; brown felt hat with green trim; brown suede with small buckle shoes; copper brown stockings; beige washing suede gloves and brown suede handbag and large jewelled clip.

Or black crêpe moracain, with tin roll collar and soft black satin belt and novelty pearl buckle; a fancy black velour coat; fine black felt hat, black patent leather shoes; moon mist grey stockings, pearl grey kid gloves; pearl necklace and stud earrings and black silk pochette.

Or soft blue and navy checked tweed; navy leather belt; tailored coat in matching tweed; navy blue felt beret; court style navy blue kid shoes; soft fawn stockings; navy blue kid gauntlets; navy blue cravat and navy kid handbag.

Hats, gloves, the exact shade of stockings, the correct jewellery; a later feature advised on the best buttons to select for a navy blue dress (white, square). Coordinated clothing was a must. Many women's magazines offered advice in columns called 'London Notes' or something similar, but *Woman's Weekly*'s detailed hand-holding suggests the especial anxiety of the women whose rise in the social scale was relatively recent and who understood all too well that clothing had its role to play in the 'universal game [of] class assessment and judgement'. Although unlikely to be able to afford all the accessories and create an outfit from scratch, readers could add to and adapt an existing one with greater confidence than formerly.

Whether the modern woman wanted fabric and paper patterns, a fancy black velour hat or chocolate-brown gauntlets like Eva's, department stores worked hard to capture her custom. Large stores offered gradations of quality and pricing across several departments. For example, Lewis's Liverpool Bon Marché which, following its own refurbishment in the early 1920s, promoted itself as the city's 'most modern, forward-looking department store', offered ready-made clothes and three separate dressmaking departments: a bespoke service, available in the Model Gown Salon, where a gown might cost anything from five to fifty guineas; an Inexpensive Dressmaking department, where a customer's choice of fabric and style would be made for her in-store, following a fitting; and the 'Cut and Fit' department where a customer's own pattern and fabric was cut out and tacked for her to sew at home.

This did not necessarily make life more straightforward. Once again, *Punch* had fun, via a sketch in which a woman heads for Inexpensive Gowns, only to discover that everything on sale there is too large. Redirected to Small Ladies, she finds its dresses too expensive. 'Modom wanted the Inexpensive Gowns on the first floor,' she is told. 'But they're all too *big*,' she protests. 'The department I want is the Inexpensive Small Ladies.' 'I'm sorry . . . but I'm afraid there's no such thing.' Some customers may have felt tempted to cut and run.

For those without deep pockets, the Model Gown Salon was unbreachable, but even wealthy women shopped across different departments. Many of the clothes belonging to Emily Tinne have survived. The wife of a Liverpool doctor, with a family fortune built on the sugar trade, Mrs Tinne ordered clothes bespoke, but she also bought ready-to-wear, albeit of a different calibre from that sought by women like my great-aunt. There were further, much harsher, gradations: Emily Tinne shopped in Bold Street, one of Liverpool's premier shopping streets, which is where the impoverished Helen Forrester, clothed in rags with no shoes on her feet, was appalled to catch sight of herself in a shop window. Depression-era Liverpool was a very different place for those with no money at all.

The social hierarchies behind the counter were every bit as telling as those on the other side. Ms T. J. Rendell, who joined the staff of Liberty as an apprentice milliner in 1926, was shocked by its 'rigid social hierarchy'. Liberty was regarded as a forward-thinking store, but its three dining rooms were designated by rank and those who came into direct contact with customers were higher up the social scale than someone like herself, behind the scenes. Their clothes also reflected their status:

> All the saleswomen working in the Tudor building . . . wore a uniform of soft brown wool, a plain design in the current mode, square neck and long sleeves, a low waist and mid-calf in length. They looked very elegant . . . When I was in my third year I made myself a somewhat similar dress in the same colour in Tyrian Silk, with a vee neck to wear at business. How snobbish we all were in those class-conscious days!

In 1922 a Mrs Mary Pennyman and the WI's Mrs Blackwell kept lists of their clothing expenditure. Mrs Pennyman of Tanton Hall, Stokesley, was a wealthy woman from a county family (Ormesby Hall, the Pennyman family home is now owned by the National Trust), who kept a record of her expenses. In 1921 her personal income was £300; it rose to £356 9s 0d the following year, and in 1923 was £301 15s 7d. Mrs Pennyman appears to have spent between one-third and one-sixth of her income on clothes – a similar proportion to that recommended by Gladys Burlton for shop-working bachelor girls, although the sums involved were vastly different. Mary Pennyman's expenses were not confined to new purchases, but included repairs and alterations, the dyeing of a coat and skirt, and the cost of cleaning a pair of gloves (8s). Novelist Naomi Mitchison recalled the quality of service available during this period: 'If a small alteration was needed, any of the big shops did it cheaply, quickly and willingly; expecting service, we got it.' Mary Pennyman, like Emily Tinne, also combined bespoke clothing with ready-to-wear; much of her wardrobe was made up privately by a dressmaker.

Mrs Pennyman's purchases for 1922 included: a hair wreath (4s), brogue shoes (£2 12s 6d), a covert coat (£4 4s), a coat and skirt (£7 17s 6d), 2 pairs of silk combinations (£1 13s 6d), a black-and-gold evening dress (£12), blue suede shoes (18s 9d), 3 pairs of evening shoes (£2 4s 5d), a kilted skirt (12s 9d), a serge coat frock (£7) and cape (£2 10s), a velour coat (£6 10s), ski boots (£2 10s), mackintosh breeches (£4 14s 6d) and a silver dress (£3 3s).

By contrast, the WI's competition winner Mrs Blackwell, the wife of a working man, produced a far more basic list. 'Boots, clothes and sundries' represented one-eighth of the overall expenditure for herself and her husband on a weekly housekeeping budget of £2 5s. The annual outlay for these items came to £14 12s 6d. (That year Mary Pennyman spent £12 – by far her most expensive purchase – on one black-and-gold evening dress.) Mrs Blackwell's prosaic list included: a coat (£1 1s 6d), a hat (5s 6d), 2 skirts (15s 11d and 6s 9d), 2 blouses (9s 6d) and 2 overalls (8s 6d), as well as woollen vests, woollen stockings and fleecy knickers.

As Mrs Blackwell detailed her expenditure for a competition, it is fair to assume that she provided a blueprint for the kind of items her budget needed to cover, whereas Mrs Pennyman itemised actual spending (although Mary Pennyman clearly had other funds, presumably courtesy of her husband: some of her most expensive purchases, including the black-and-gold dress, are not in her cheque book). Nonetheless, the items listed give an idea of their different purchasing and of their very different lives. Evening dresses do not figure in Mrs Blackwell's list (nor does a covert coat or ski boots). Both women bought gloves, however. Mrs Blackwell spent 1s 6½d on a pair; Mrs Pennyman (who bought six pairs in 1920) purchased white kid evening gloves like those worn by Edwardian ladies and which, in 1922, retailed at 6s 6d.*

My great-aunt Eva had other dressy gloves: black leather gloves (for funerals) and some chamois leather gloves with decorative stitching. Both pairs also came to me, although a chammy disappeared along the way. The lone glove has its own pedigree, the odd glove, without a match, giving rise to the phrase 'the odd women' coined by George Gissing (whose novel of that name depicted the difficulties faced by single women at the turn of the century, including those working in draper's shops). In Tudor times, the single glove symbolised lost love, while Tudor courtiers wore gloves whose fingers extended beyond the wearer's fingertips, 'adding a fashionable elegance to the hands, while also demonstrating that the wearer was exempt from practical tasks', just like those white kid gloves.

I have a second pair of gauntlets, leather gloves in rose madder with broad sharp cuffs and pinprick decoration; three rows of stitching mark their taut backs. Found on a Chesterfield market stall in the early 1970s, they were, I think, the very first vintage items I paid for, my appetite whetted by my finds at Annie and Eva's. Then, as now, I was drawn to their colour and crisp outline. I would like to think that, like the 1920s driver who chose green gauntlets, these were once worn by a confident young woman who bought them to match the rose madder upholstery of her coupé and startle the shoppers on a provincial high street.

---

* Mrs Pennyman's story has a sobering coda: in 1924, she died in childbirth at the age of thirty-four.

10 **THE INTERWAR FASHION BUTTON:** TENNIS AND AFTERNOON TEA

My grandma's two-tone green button with square 'eyes' and modulated shape speaks of the 1930s. I only have to look at buttons like these to picture women going about their lives – walking down provincial high streets to change their library books or take tea in Kardomah Cafés. The front-fastening blouses of the period placed an emphasis on decorative buttons, many of them in the art-deco style, which were often labelled 'fashion' or 'novelty' when sold as a carded set. The composite materials from which they were formed and their moulded shapes and patterns demonstrate the degree to which art-deco design percolated down from the grandest of skyscrapers, cinemas and restaurants to even the simplest of interwar buttons. Buttons like these reflected expanding opportunities for leisure, and the clothes to go with it.

Tennis was increasingly the thing. In a memoir fittingly entitled *Anyone for Tennis?* Eileen Whiteing, who grew up in an outer London suburb she described as 'unbelievably enclosed and exclusive', recalled its importance as social glue and the difficulty of obtaining membership to her local sports club which was something of a 'closed shop'. Emma Smith, another child of the period, has described the agonies suffered through her father belonging to the *wrong* tennis club. It was even harder for single women. *Home Chat*'s 'Mrs Jim' advised Shy Suzanne of Hampstead, 'I think you should take up golf, as you can always play alone until you are sufficiently proficient to play with other people.'

The looser clothing of the period was ideal for sport. Stripes were permissible on the golf course long before they hit the high street. In 1927 it was reported that the 'vogue for colour is spreading so rapidly that even the sacred precincts of the tennis courts and golf courses are not immune.' The 'gaily coloured' bandeaus worn by tennis players Helen Wills and Suzanne Lenglen made the newspapers along with their winning scores. The *Illustrated London News* anticipated a colourful Wimbledon that year with 'eye shades in every colour imaginable'. From now on, players could dazzle their opponents with their fashion sense as well as their sporting prowess.

Anything loosely fitting and vaguely bright was deemed suitable for sport. In traditionalists' eyes, the two were linked and equally suspect. 'Men who might, in the absence of the war, have been content to grow roses and don sombre attire on Sundays, now speed along the highways in a "sports" car, or array themselves in "plus fours" of diverse colours. Their wives, instead of knitting or sewing, may put on richly coloured coats and depart to the tennis courts.' Modernity terrified some, though one pleasurable aspect of the advent of more casual dress was that it was now possible to look *sportif* without being remotely sporty.

Swimming was at least more democratic. New beach clothes revealed far more flesh than formerly and offered the brave opportunities for glamour and the chance to strut with a parasol. Beachwear gave rise to the pyjama craze, a way of introducing the Venice Lido – 'La Plage du Soleil et des Pyjamas!' – to the British beach (and London's West End: commenting on the 'vintage period of sunshine' experienced during the 1932 summer heatwave, the *Illustrated London News* reported the appearance of bright yellow pyjamas in Tottenham Court Road and beach trousers in Oxford Street). For all the talk of swimming, a fashion-page description of a one-piece bathing suit for those who 'really can swim' suggests that many were still just posing. Posing was probably the wisest option when the majority of costumes were home-knitted and, as well as becoming uncomfortably heavy when wet, sagged revealingly when the bather emerged from the water. Bathing costumes still had the power to shock an older generation unaccustomed to so much flesh. When, in 1925, the chorus of *No, No, Nanette* wore bathing costumes for one scene, Queen Mary looked away from the stage.

Calisthenics and other bends and stretches were a less revealing way to stay fit. Office workers were not exempt: 'If your job is sedentary . . . watch your hips,' women were advised in 'The Rolling Road to Beauty', a feature on massage rollers. Dance classes gained in popularity for children as well as adults: many mothers, my grandma included, wanted their own Shirley Temple: my mum attended classes for several years. One of her ballet teachers, all arched eyebrows and peek-a-boo lips, could have stepped straight out of a Busby Berkeley musical. My mother also loved to run and was awarded a typical thirties prize, a Bakelite jewellery box, for winning a race. An uncle gave her a gramophone record, 'I'm Happy When I'm Hiking', a popular song of the time, although she tells me she was more intrigued by the record's translucent blue colour than its message.

Hiking had come into its own (and was marvelled at by some: Elizabeth Bowen, compiling an anthology, observed to a friend,

'Quite a large number of short stories are told, do you notice, by hikers'). More seriously, public right of way was granted and pathways opened following the 1932 mass trespass on Derbyshire's Kinder Scout. Walking tours became an acceptable way for young women to holiday with friends. Jenifer Wayne and a fellow Somerville student combined walking with a reading holiday shortly before the Second World War. Some of the more playful buttons of the period reflected a fondness for sport and games, including an Olympic button, a button resembling a checked yellow-and-black racing flag, and a rectangular domino.

Board games and card games required the least exertion. My great-aunt's copy of *Home Management* lists the rules for nearly a dozen. Those higher up the social scale (or determined to climb there) could take up bridge. Along with the newest sport dresses and 'Fashion Parades on the Beach', *The Needlewoman* promised its readers 'The All-Conquering Bridge Coat', an evening jacket for those after-dinner games, which, with its elegant long fringing, may have given women the confidence to play a particularly difficult rubber. Really dedicated players could embroider a set of cushions with diamonds, hearts, spades and clubs. Like tennis and golf, card games played their role in affirming social circles and cementing neighbourly relations – or not. M. V. Hughes, who disliked card games almost as much as she disliked sewing and social pretensions, deftly resisted the overtures of the neighbour who knocked on her front door shortly after she moved to a new district.

'We hope you will like to join the "Cuffley Ladies" – our little social circle here.' Scenting working parties – card parties – musical evenings – my brain had to work quickly . . . I heard myself saying, 'I'm so sorry, but I can't join your circle. I can't sew, or do anything useful, or play cards, or be sociable in any way; and I'm not a lady.' It was this last remark that brought her to her feet.

M. V. Hughes loved reading, however. A friendship with another new neighbour was instantly secured by mutual love of books. ('Books!' a neighbour 'exclaimed in rapture', on stepping into her house.) Molly was more than happy to dispense with housework, or anything else, and read. The interwar years saw a boom in reading as a leisure activity, especially among women; this was the first period in which universal literacy prevailed. Public libraries saw the benefits. In 1911 libraries issued 54,256 volumes; by 1924 the number had risen to 85,688, and in 1939 reached 247,335.

Circulating libraries were also popular; there were several to choose from, provided you could pay their fees. Boots Library had supplied women with books since the turn of the century; in 1926 it cost 42*s* a year to take out their books 'on demand; 17*s* 6*d* to choose from all works in circulation and 10*s* 6*d* for the ordinary service'. By the mid-1930s, Boots was the largest circulating library of its kind with over 400 branches and half a million subscribers. Boots was cheaper than the smaller, exclusive London libraries such as Mudie's and the London Library, of which Virginia Woolf was a member, but more expensive than W. H. Smith. Exciting developments were taking place in publishing: in 1935 Allen Lane published the first Penguin paperback, priced 6*d*.

These were extremely fertile years for novelists who used their work to address key issues in women's lives, especially the ongoing quest for independence and identity, a desire shared by more than just bachelor girls. Vita Sackville-West's elderly, widowed Lady Slane bemoans the fact that she has been a daughter, wife and mother, but has never been herself. E. M. Delafield's *Diary of a Provincial Lady* was light-hearted, yet still skewered contemporary concerns. The Provincial Lady herself is depicted as a great reader; the *Diary* teems with references to books and authors its readers are expected to recognise. The interwar woman could delight in her shared knowledge and blush – in recognition? – at the Provincial Lady's admission that it was so much easier to express an opinion about *Orlando* before she had actually read it.

Women's magazines proliferated. *Woman, Modern Woman* and *Woman's Own* were among the new weeklies to appear. By the early thirties, *Good Housekeeping* was selling around 100,000 copies a month. Winifred Holtby baulked at the falsely romantic messages delivered by magazines at the lower end of the market, despairing of the young women who 'swing daily to their offices in suburban trains and trams and buses, carrying in their suitcases a powder-puff and a love-story or *Home Chat*'. Holtby knew of what she wrote: readers of *Woman's Life* could sample the four-penny delights of 'Her Passionate Lesson', 'Stolen Fruit' and 'The Flame of Love'.

When not reading, the interwar woman could listen to the wireless; by 1939, 75 per cent of all British families owned a wireless set. An advertisement for Ardern's Crochet Cotton from the early 1920s, illustrated with a wireless and listening trumpet, managed to make even crocheting sound up-to-the-minute: 'while you listen in.' Many of the embroidered tray cloths and cushion covers of that era were created with the wireless murmuring in the background. So many home-sweet-homes, cottage gardens and crinoline ladies were embroidered then, and have been found in antique centres since, thanks to an expanding and house-proud lower middle class. Women moving into married domesticity and with fewer children than their mothers, had more time on their hands. No wool-work fire screens and tapestries for them: they wanted colour and plenty of it (except when crocheting those ubiquitous doilies, fawn-coloured as well as white).

In Elizabeth Bowen's 1938 novel *The Death of the Heart*, Mrs Heccomb surrounds herself with the symbols of interwar leisure. She has a 'glossy' wireless cabinet, 'a scarlet portable gramophone, a tray with a painting outfit, a half-painted lamp shade [being painted to supplement her widow's pension], a mountain of magazines'. However, her full glass-fronted bookcase, has 'a remarkably locked look' and her gate-legged table, 'was set for tea, but the cake plates were still empty – Mrs Heccomb was tipping cakes out of paper bags'. Oh dear: no home-made cakes.

Afternoon tea became so popular that Royal Doulton produced a china afternoon-tea figurine. Eileen Whiteing and her mother luxuriated at Kennard's tea room in Croydon with its palm trees and ladies' orchestra (a china ladies' orchestra was also available). Schoolteacher's daughter Jenifer Wayne enjoyed occasional treats at a Lyon's Corner House, while Virginia Woolf rounded off her shopping with tea at an ABC cafe. Other women sampled cafes like Pamona's Parlour, with its 'orange curtains, purple-and-orange check cloths [and] Art Pottery'; the period's liking for afternoon tea provided ample opportunities to flaunt exuberantly patterned crockery. The china manufacturer Shelley put the young tea-drinking woman at the heart of an advertising campaign. In her jazzily patterned shift dress, dangling earrings, white fur stole, multiple coloured 'slave bangles' and cloche hat embellished with feathers, the Shelley Girl was trying out every fashion at once. She appeared in 1926 when modernity was starting to hit the provinces and no one was quite sure what to do with it (or how to dress for it, either).

One Saturday afternoon in the early seventies, wearing my great-aunt's buttoned gauntlets and clutching her art-deco bag, I took myself to a Chesterfield hotel to meet a friend for afternoon tea. Dressed for the 1930s, I wanted to recreate the mood. Today's passion for mismatched vintage tea cups and home-made cakes would make such a mission straightforward; then, we were faced with thick white earthenware and a few dry biscuits in an otherwise empty, gloomy interior. It was hard to channel the 1930s in provincial towns – unless accidentally, in premises yet to be refurbished: one of my favourite venues as a young child was Woodhead's cafe. There, the 1930s were still in full swing with wood panelling and fittings in chrome and pistachio green.

Jenifer Wayne's grandmother insisted on dressing for tea when staying with the family at Christmas. She 'would wash up the lunch things, rub her hands on a piece of lemon she always kept by the sink, go upstairs for her rest and come down at 4 o'clock in her printed silk dress and black velvet bridge jacket; then we would have . . . thin white bread and butter'. Those eating bread and butter needed a decorative cloth. No tea table was complete without a cloth with embroidered roses and tulips clustered in each corner. 'Most women like to make these at home,' *Home Management* advised, making the hearts sink of those who, like M. V. Hughes, had other ideas as to how to spend their time.

11 **THE EDGE-TO-EDGE CLASP:** KISSPROOF LIPSTICK AND GINGER ROGERS FROCKS

Nothing in the button box proclaims art deco as loudly as the edge-to-edge clasp with its smoky oyster discs circled in Bakelite. Spanning some five inches, the two discs have a decorative function, any real work done by utilitarian hooks and eyes concealed beneath their broad flat span. Clasps like this ornamented smart afternoon- or eveningwear – a jacket, coat, dress or belt. There is no need for jewellery; the clasp is the thing, drawing attention to the cut and line of a garment, and affordable in a way that a jewel of this size is not. The edge-to-edge clasp speaks of leisure and modernity and, above all, glamour – a glamour many women discovered via the cinema.

The interwar years were full of contradictions and a minor personal one is the fact that such a dramatic clasp was among my grandma's buttons. However, one of Annie's 1930s creations was an art-deco-patterned edge-to-edge jacket with rippled seams, so why not a showy clasp? It sits in the button box, as it has for many years, a shining example of a period in which there were many occasions – excuses – to dress up.

In 1914 there were 3,500 cinemas in the UK; by 1939 their number had risen to 4,800 and all but the poorest were finding sixpence for their regular fix. At that time, the majority of cinema-goers were working-class women under forty. My grandma was one of them. A photo-booth snapped her in a tight cloche hat, my mum a surprised toddler on her lap, afternoon co-conspirators. While Annie sank into the Lyceum's gold seats and imagined herself as a sultry Theda Bara, my mum ran up and down the aisles. Soon she too was sitting on her own bristly seat, as trans-fixed as Annie.

My mum, Cora, went to the pictures every week of her childhood, mostly with Annie or Eva, occasionally with her grandma Betsy; later, in a gang with friends. In no time at all, she had a Shirley Temple cut-out doll and paper clothes in which to dress her, and a book of cowboy tunes with a lassoing cowboy on its front cover. She carried a Minnie Mouse bag and a Mickey Mouse mirror in which she could check the tilt of her Donald Duck hat, and surprised piano teacher Miss Alice Brocklehurst, whose baby grand had never known anything but classical tones, with the sheet music for *Snow White and the Seven Dwarfs*. Later came a Zorro cape and a gingham 'Dorothy' dress, courtesy of Annie's faithful Singer. Influences came thick and fast, 1930s kiddies just as susceptible to them as adults. My mum has always said she grew up in the cinema. A true child of her era, she took her lessons there, graduating from Shirley Temple via Deanna Durbin and Judy Garland to Rosalind Russell. Soon she was reading *Photo Play* magazine and writing to Hollywood, Burbank, California for signed photographs of the stars.

In Winifred Watson's 1938 novel *Miss Pettigrew Lives for a Day*, the cinema is Miss Pettigrew's one extravagance in an otherwise meagre life. It is also where she picks up American slang and learns all manner of things a 'spinster', and most especially a curate's daughter, would not be expected to know. Life imitating art, the cinema was where many girls – the majority of them far more sheltered then than now – learned how to become young women. This was not just a matter of how to speak and behave, but how to dress.

A Clara Bow bob, Betty Grable curls, a Garbo coat, a dress like those worn by Ginger Rogers – the cinema stamped a whole new look on the period. Most women's magazines were only too willing to tell their star-struck readers what Gladys Cooper wore, so that they could aspire to a similar look. Professional dressmakers who learned to copy by eye could adapt the styles; others, professionals and home-dressmakers alike, looked to paper patterns for inspiration, or to *Film Land* which purported to reproduce actual film-star fashions.

Dressing for dinner was expected among the well-heeled, but parties and dances of all kinds required formal clothes. Eileen Whiteing recalled 'the joy of saving up for, and choosing really pretty evening dresses in lace or net, with silver slippers and fresh flowers for a corsage'; Derbyshire schoolteacher May Smith was equally happy to spend her wages on an evening gown. Some of the creations that graced provincial dance floors and civic functions were surprisingly elaborate. The 'Inexpensive Dance Frocks' *Good Housekeeping* advertised for mail order included every imaginable style: scalloped hems, semicircular skirts with heavy lace edging, tinsel-striped satin and silk net, skirts dressed with handkerchief petals. Similar clothes could be bought in department stores, styled by professional dressmakers or made at home by anyone dextrous with a sewing machine. New crease-resistant and washable fabrics simplified matters. 'Celanese [goes] from ballroom to wash tub' advertisers reassured fashion-conscious women who needed serviceable glamour. Others who 'cut out for chic' were reminded that Ferguson Fashion Fabrics were 'noted for their draping qualities'.

Daywear could be equally sophisticated: stripes in all directions, fancy buckles, buttons from elbow to wrist, and from neck to below the waistline, each fastened with its own tiny loop. It took skill to make multiple loops and cover some thirty buttons before stitching them in a perfect line. Some of the clothes worn by Emily Tinne are enough to make a vintage fashionista's mouth water and reflect that era's fondness for elaborate styles. A dress ornamented with a large scarlet Bakelite buckle with a lizard decoration captures the liking for all things oriental. Exoticism was modern; in the language of art deco, anything could be given a modern take.

The queen of artful, extravagant design was Elsa Schiaparelli. Schiaparelli's ideas were not for mass-consumption, but in her vocabulary a button or buckle could be anything she pleased. Brass curtain rings, lips, gold escargots, harlequins, insects, pyramids, lovebirds, plastic mermaids, ship's-prow figures, tiny umbrellas, glass paperweights, gold baubles, silver tambourines . . . These were not mere fastenings, but audacious proclamations of surrealist style. No one designed buttons like she did. In 1934 Schiaparelli appeared on the cover of *Time* magazine. The caption read: 'Mme Elsa Schiaparelli . . . glorifies the gadget, persecutes the button.'

Schiaparelli's designs had couture price tags. Nonetheless, this was the era in which buttons known as 'realistics' were introduced. Annie's willingness to add decorative flourishes meant that Cora could request buttons that looked like animals or stars. Thanks to the development of plastics and advances in technology, intricate shapes could be created or objects set within moulds and plastic poured on top to achieve a 3D effect. The new compositions, such as Bakelite, Perspex, Plexiglas and casein, the latter a by-product of milk, allowed for great flexibility. Eye-catching buttons in an archive collection range from stark geometric patterns which would distinguish any smart dark dress, to chunky blocks of Perspex with striated colours locked within them, and architectural forms whose tiers of opaque green and chrome-coloured plastic echo shapes seen in mansion flats, American diners and garage forecourts. Whether playful or sophisticated, all demonstrated the possibilities of the new.

The interwar woman seeking glamour had much more to consider than buttons. Styles for evening gowns were almost as fickle as those for daywear: backless or not, short or long, the tone changing in the mid-1920s and then again at the close of the decade, giving rise to a slinky, feminine look that followed the curves of the body and frequently saw yards of silk or satin pooling on the floor. *The Times* described the new long evening dresses from Chanel, 'the long caterpillar bodices with skirts flowing wide to the ankles'. Few home-dressmakers wanted to tackle those, and although some yearned for a Madeleine Vionnet-inspired gown, it took skill to achieve the bias cut. The introduction of the zip fastener was a godsend, and further democratised fashion. Women could now wear elaborate gowns without needing help to dress, an invention that assisted the working woman invited to a social 'do' just as much as the leisured one struggling to manage without a maid.

Glamour could be achieved on the never-never. By the 1930s, my grandma was working as a part-time agent for the Provident Clothing Company, issuing credit cheques to women who bought clothes on hire purchase. Most needed workaday frocks, but every now and then a best dress was needed and saved for, week by week. Bristol-born Joyce Storey, a school-leaver working as a child's-nurse-cum-skivvy, saw a coat in a shop window, with a fur collar 'that would make me look like a film star. The more I looked at it, the more convinced I became that I must have it.' Each Thursday, her 'half day', Joyce paid 5*s* towards the £2 10*s* coat. At a higher end of the scale, Corot on Old Bond Street offered the well-heeled but cash-strapped customer a sumptuous choice. In the 1920s the 'Isolde' panne velvet evening gown with a peplum line and flowing skirt could elevate a wardrobe for a monthly payment of 19*s* 6*d*, while by the 1930s, the 'Luxury Lady' coat in woollen weave, with a shoulder yoke of seal coney, could be bought outright for 8 guineas, or 24*s* monthly.

For many young women, an evening dress symbolised the transition from girl to woman and was the first opportunity to assert their own identity. For Jenifer Wayne, the treasured dress was 'solid purple taffeta', with complicated styling:

> ruching; gathering; yards of bias-cut skirt; stiffened epaulettes tapering to a point. My mother and I bought it at Chieseman's in Lewisham and it cost nearly £3. My first 'bought' evening dress, for my last school dance . . . there was I, nearly nineteen, standing in front of Chieseman's cheval mirror, stunned with amazement and gratification. I could never have told my mother how much I appreciated her letting me have that dress.

Jenifer bought her first pair of evening shoes – 'stubby-toed courts,· encrusted with variegated glitter' ('Go with anything,' the shop assistant said) – to wear with it, for which she paid an extravagant 12*s* 11*d*. Historian Sally Alexander has noted how many women recall the price they paid for the garments which signified a rite of passage. Jenifer Wayne kept the purple dress for more than forty years, 'a hoarded rustle of the thirties in which [she] "Grew Up"'; it even provided the title for her autobiography.

'Our lives were narrower, our minds more naïve', Wayne said of those years. With young women 'coming to fashion conscious-ness' much later then than now and wearing what their mothers decreed until they reached maturity (and with far less choice to begin with), their first grown-up dress had an even greater signifi-cance than it does today. In *Invitation to the Waltz*, seventeen-year-old Olivia expresses a view many of Rosamond Lehmann's readers would recognise. 'Olivia considered serviceable dark-brown or navy-blue winters, holland and tussore summers; cream viyella blouses, white piqué tennis skirts; all plain, neat, subdued, unbe-coming . . . Now that I'm grown up and can choose my own clothes, I'll wear bright colours always.'

Olivia selects a piece of red silk to be made into a dress for her first ball. School dances, first balls – 'This then is a ball. This is life, what we have been waiting for all these years,' wrote Nancy Mitford – marked that longed-for moment of transition, but then as now, the difficulty with an important dress is the weight of anticipation carried with it. Women wrapped their dreams as well as their yards of fabric in the brown paper parcels they delivered to their dressmaker's door. Somewhere between daydream and reality disappointment lies, as Olivia discovers. Before setting about the red silk with her scissors, village seamstress Miss Robinson seeks inspiration from *Fashions for All*, but, alas, the finished gown dips at the back, the armholes catch 'and there was a queer place in the waist where, owing to a mistake in the cutting, Miss Robinson had had, in her own words, to contrive it'.

Before ready-to-wear garments predominated, every district had its Miss Robinson, little dressmakers to be treasured or avoided. Far below the dizzy heights of the couturier came the self-employed woman working from home or, in the case of larger concerns, rented premises, with varying degrees of enter-prise and success. May Bell branched out alone after working as a trainee tailoress in Hanley. She started work at fourteen in 1921, earning 6s 6d a week, and was not earning much more when she left five years later. Like many juniors, before and since, she spent much of her time sewing buttonholes. Thereafter, working from home during the Depression years, she made clothes for 'the wives of men who were still in work, or the wives of professional men'. She did not charge much, 'perhaps about a pound for making a coat'. In those days, 'women only had one or two dresses made a year, one for summer and one for winter'. May sewed skirts and blouses too, and wedding dresses and elegant evening gowns with tiered skirts like those seen on the films.

Rachel Brewis started her own dressmaking business in Norwich in 1932 after her godfather paid for a three-month course at the Katinka School of Dressmaking. Her prices ranged from '15s for a simple skirt or blouse, to £2 for an evening dress or at the very most £3 for a wedding dress'. She sometimes felt 'quite faint with fear before a fitting that I might have spoilt a customer's material, but if I had they were too kind to tell me so'.

Esther Rothstein worked on a different scale. A two-year trade scholarship awarded at the age of fourteen led to coveted work with a London court dressmaker. Four years later, with capital from the aunt and uncle she lived with, Esther started her own business and was soon employing four 'girls'. Later, she became a well-known Worthing dressmaker. 'Dressmaking at this time was much more of an art,' Esther told an interviewer.

The styles and materials . . . necessitated so much more work . . . There were handkerchief skirts, squares and squares of material had to be sent to the hem stitchers for picot edging . . . There was also a style that had rows and rows of fringe from the neck right down to the hem. Georgette was very fashionable – this meant having to make a lining . . . There were full straight skirts too, these had rows and rows of gathering all done by hand; they also took hours, even though we used a method called fly running – nowadays done with machine stitch.

Life was far from glamorous for the women who strained their eyes to cut and stitch exquisite fabrics. As a fourteen-year-old apprentice, Gladyis Stonier worked for six weeks at 1*s* a week before her wages rose to 3*s* ½*d* an hour. At the age of twenty-two she became a fitter:

My wages then was two pounds and I worked all hours God made for that two pound . . . they had our life. I mean you were absolutely glued to it, you didn't dare take your eyes off it to look up, if anyone was talking in the work room . . . and you happened to stop work – Oh, my goodness me, 'You can work another hour for that'.

Gladyis was luckier than some; she wanted to design, and later succeeded, designing for private customers at 15*s* a time, and for large fashion houses, including Derry & Toms and Marshall & Snelgrove, before being taken on by a family-owned department store.

The most poignant description of the little dressmaker belongs again to Miss Robinson. She may be a fictional character but in the landscape of the 1930s, when many single women eked out a living some of them were ill-equipped to achieve, her plight sounds all too real. Poor Miss Robinson, living precariously at the edge of other people's dreams, hampered in her own attempts at independence, stuck with a querulous mother for the rest of her life. She 'looked at [Olivia] with hungry curiosity: seeing perhaps lights, flowers, silks and satins; hearing music and the vibrating tones of gentlemen in evening-dress . . . She made frocks for other girls to dance in.'

Regardless of what a good dressmaker could achieve, the right dress alone was not enough: glamour required a trim figure and a good complexion. Eileen Whiteing recalled the extent to which physical beauty was 'greatly admired and cultivated . . . A good skin, large eyes, well-shaped nails, slender ankles, to say nothing of a good figure – all these things added up to, I suppose, one's potential value in the marriage market.' A contemporary advertisement for Palmolive soap left women in no doubt: 'Men ask, is she pretty? Not, is she clever?' Weight was also an issue – those sheath-like dresses of the 1920s demanded sheath-like figures and flattened breasts; the long-line numbers of the thirties were no less demanding. This was the era in which slimming began to be discussed.

By 1935, *Good Housekeeping* was reporting that women of all social classes were making a conscious effort with their appearance. 'The films have had much to do with it.' One young woman wrote to *Woman* asking how she should wear her hair (with 'three fetching curls on the top and curls all round' came the reply). Perms were ubiquitous – home perms as well as trips to the hairdresser; my grandma had some evil-looking metal crimpers for the job, my mum had her first perm aged seven. Make-up became more acceptable. Once considered the mark of a woman who was 'no better than she should be' – in 1918 Vera Brittain sacked a maid for wearing face powder – make-up gradually acquired respectability. Interwar products were bright and unsubtle, which was probably why make-up took so long to lose its theatrical tag. Vanishing cream and a light dusting of face powder were considered acceptable in many households, though not all. Jenifer Wayne's mother thought 'perms and powder' were, like 'parlours and serviettes', not quite respectable and something for the working or lower-middle classes.

Boots launched its 'No. 7' range in 1935; that year *Good Housekeeping* asked, 'What Price Beauty?', and imagined six different women and their probable outlay on hair, skin and nail care, and bathing preparations (make-up accounted for only a small proportion of the whole). The town-dweller spent almost twice as much as her 'country cousin', who was at least allowed two pairs of gardening gloves. Each of the women used lipstick, although eighteen-year-old provincial typist 'Miss Brown', who was reckoned to earn 25s a week, was still applying one purchased two years earlier. The boldest of the six (and by far the wealthiest, with an imagined income of £5,000) was 'Mrs Gold', a 'well-preserved' London actress, aged forty-two. Mrs Gold owned fourteen lipsticks, though some were presumably for stage use. Lipstick's increasing popularity was helped by the cinema – all those peek-a-boo lips – though it still had the power to shock, a fact Winifred Watson had fun with. 'Powder, thundered [Miss Pettigrew's] father the curate, the road to damnation. Lipstick, whispered her mother, the first step on the downward path . . .'

The Bank of England did not tolerate its staff wearing any form of make-up, and even employers who allowed a dab of powder drew the line at painted nails. 'Although bright nails are the thing,' *Miss Modern* advised its readers, 'they are out of place in business hours, and however modern the "Chief" and the office furniture no businessman likes his girls flashing carmine over typewriters.' Miss Brown's three bottles of nail polish must have been reserved for her days off. Those still too young for make-up of any kind measured out their sophistication in shakes of talcum powder and Hearts of Roses bath salts.

A stylish dress, a slick of Kissproof lipstick, a splash of scent for the wrists and hair (as recommended by the *Daily Mirror*), all were components of interwar glamour. But even the right dress and make-up were not enough; confidence and panache were needed. *How to Dress Well* described how to achieve it: 'If you say to yourself, "I am about to greet one whom I respect and admire," you will find that you are unconsciously making yourself erect and tall. You assume a victorious attitude. You feel yourself "sun-crowned above the fog".'

In a picture postcard of the period, one of the type found crammed into a box in antique shops nowadays, an unknown young woman poses in an evening gown. The chic slide buckle securing the belt at her waist is shaped like a chunky moon; the composite material from which it was made probably shone just as brightly. As with Emily Tinne's lizard buckle and my smoky oyster clasp, the slide moon draws the eye, according both dress and wearer instant glamour. Another 1930s woman chose a heavy amber-coloured clasp. When clutching its partner edge-to-edge – cheek to cheek – two radiant circles were formed, overlaid by a small matt black one. Today, one half survives, transformed into a brooch. This solo clip spans an impressive three inches; the pair would have made a magnificent six, and shouted glamour in abundance. Pleasure too – the pleasure of the woman wearing it.

INSTRUCTIONS FROM MISS TOWSEY, DRAPER, 1782, FOR A TRIP FROM CHESTER TO LONDON, TAKING SIX DAYS EACH WAY

If Wednesday be a fine day go up as soon as you well can to be out early. In the first place call at Steward Spavold and Smiths, where settle our accounts and look at modes of all sorts, at the white silk, the blue and green. Do not buy any. Ask if they have any black . . . coat, as had last at 62s. Then go to Harris and Penny, pay their bill, and just look at what kind of fancy gloves they have to sell. Tell them that the gloves they called maid were most of them small girls, that they were too dear, that as their account was a small one it had indeed been almost forgot, that I had advised Weatherall people we should draw upon them in favour of Harris and Co., but in hurry of business we had quite forgot it. Next place you may call at Moores, or not, as you will have a good deal to do and the morning will be pretty far advanced. You may then go to Bread Street. Just call in at Adams, and if they have any pretty fancy ribbons pick out a few. Get the bill made out and take it with you to Drury's which is just by there. Perhaps they may not have sent out the goods last ordered. Get to look at the order whether they have or not, and you will be able to judge what is wanted of those kind of things. And be sure to get some white soufflee for tippets as we have some bespoke for next week. If they have none done, as I do not suppose they have, they may perhaps let you have a yard or two of some that may be done for other customers, which we shall be obliged if they will let us have. A small quantity must be had at any rate to send on Wednesday.

You may call at Tibets and see if there is anything particularly pretty in the ribbon way there. As Barton and Simpson live in the same street call and balance their account, then go to Price and Cook, who lives in the same street, balance their account, look over their gloves, ask the prices of all the different sorts. If there is anything particularly nice you may look them out and order them to Drury's as the parcel from there will not be a large one.

Browns and Chester: Portrait of a Shop 1780–1946,
Mass Observation, H. D. Willcock, ed. (1974)

12 **THE TWINKLING BUTTON:** STITCH IN THE CHIC

Haberdashery is the place where buttons of every size and shape reside: carded, colour-coded and sometimes boxed in small squat drawers, each one labelled with its own button – glass, mother-of-pearl, vegetable ivory (made from the corozo nut and polished until it gleams), gilt, enamelled and silk-covered, plus composition buttons of all kinds. Here they exist in profusion.

The British button industry was for many years based in Birmingham. Established in the 1660s, and assisted by protective legislation to prohibit the importation of buttons, the trade came into its own in the eighteenth century when clothing had ceased to be defined by rank and became an expression of wealth and fashion. Buttons formed part of the 'toy' trade, the name given to the silver clocks, brass candlesticks, snuffboxes and other small metal objects with which an expanding class of merchants and industrialists decorated their homes but, whether gilt, silver or cut-steel, the buttons that scintillated by candlelight decorated male not female clothing. A woman wanted the newly imported silk and a walnut tea caddy; her husband had his eye on elaborate buttons for his waistcoat and topcoat, and shiny buckles for his breeches and shoes.

Birmingham made the fortunes of numerous button manufacturers. By the 1770s, there were more people making buttons than anything else; a 1773 directory lists 104 firms. Buttons depicting delicate Watteau-like landscapes, or made from exquisitely patterned mother-of-pearl were produced in a city described by Southey in the early nineteenth century as a place of 'noise beyond description . . . The filth is sickening . . . active and moving, a living principle of mischief, which fills the whole atmosphere and penetrates everywhere.'

In 1852 *Household Words* described button manufacture: the punching, drilling, stamping machines, the polishing wheels and 'all the bright and compact and never-tiring apparatus'. With industrial advances, gilt, silvered, electro-plated, silk, Florentine, mother-of-pearl, steel, wood, bone and horn buttons could all be produced. Dies for stamping patterns were created via a complex process; the drawing of tiny portraits, animals or crests involved intricacy and skill. This was men's work. Women were engaged at tasks such as covering and carding buttons; it was said that, in years gone by, the covering of buttons was 'one of the most important lessons given to the infant needlewoman'. As the century advanced, buttons captured the coming world as well as current trends and pleasures like ballooning, sport and photography; buttons depicting insects reflected the growing fascination with botany and science.

By the late nineteenth century, elaborate picture buttons were fastening women's clothes. In 1895 *Home Notes* advocated the purchase of 'beautiful buttons with miniature paintings' to ornament the satin blouse each fashionable woman should wear. 'One of the great charms about these buttons is their expense,' its columnist advised. 'I say "charms" and I mean it too, for this will be the means of preventing their becoming common.' It would not do to have the same buttons as everyone else.

Buttons are but a small part of the haberdasher's theme. Ardern's Crochet Cotton; Clark's Embroidery Thread; tuppenny packets of Flora Macdonald needles; Stratnoid Knitting Pins; floral paper baskets opening to reveal rows of needles and pins; knitting wools; feathers, ribbons, beads and braids; 'Wizard' bodkins for whizzing ribbon through machine-embroidered night-gowns, plus a selection of darning aids – for woollens, stockings and gloves – comprise some of the many items needed for decorative and functional sewing, plus making of various kinds.

A prosaic list cannot begin to convey haberdashery's pleasures. Novelist Lettice Cooper describes a child's fascination with a box 'full of bits, scraps of lace and coloured satin, lengths of narrow shaded ribbon with picot edges, fragments of embroidery, threaded with gold, some studded with bright things . . . called beetles' wings. To be allowed to dip in that box was like being offered the treasures of Aladdin's cave.' Adults, myself among them, have been similarly wooed. In *The Ethics of Shopping* (1895) Lady Jeune confessed that, 'We are not able to stand against the overwhelming temptations which besiege us . . . We go to purchase something we want; but when we get to our shop there are so many more things that we never thought of till they presented their obtrusive fascinations on every side. We look for a ribbon, a flower, a chiffon of some sort or other, and we find ourselves in a Paradise of ribbons, flowers, and chiffon, without which our life becomes impossible and our gown unwearable.' Fashionable ladies were not the only ones craving pretty things. The folk song 'Oh Dear, What Can the Matter Be?' conveys a young girl's longing for blue ribbons to tie up her bonny brown hair; even those desperate women handing their babies to London's Foundling Hospital found ways to prettify their clothes.

A paradise of ribbons, flowers and chiffon, haberdashery may be found on a counter or department within a draper's shop or have a whole shop to itself. In earlier centuries, every village and hamlet had its travelling salesman or market stall selling buttons, fabric and trimmings, or found ways to purchase what was needed. Edith James recalled visiting her country grandmother by carrier's wagon in the early 1900s:

> We left Wellingborough at four o'clock and it took until eight to cover the twelve miles. On the outward journey in the morning the carrier's daughter used to collect, from the villages through which they passed, all sorts of commissions to buy this and that, and in the evening these items were all delivered. It might be a couple of bloaters, or a reel of cotton or a card of buttons, or some 'shop' cake – anything, in fact.

'Anything, in fact' might be a wayward definition of haberdashery. Even a 'highly respectable draper' told Henry Mayhew that 'he never could thoroughly understand where hosiery, haberdashery, or drapery, began or ended'. Traditionally, Haberdashery was the department in which shop assistants learned the ropes. Its extensive stock and fiddly transactions, not to mention innumerable sub-divisions of the most prosaic items, provided the ideal training ground. In the days when customers expected personal service, Haberdashery required patience too: all those rolls of organza, silk and satin and yards of unspooled ribbon had to be put away again. The length of time women spent looking far exceeded the amount of money they finally parted with. And there were beady-eyed customers to deal with; Margaret Penn's grandmother among them, who, to ensure that 'woollen' fabrics were actually wool, put a match to one corner because wool does not burst into flame.

A similarly vexing customer may have led one haberdashery assistant to flex her superior knowledge. In 1940 Derbyshire schoolteacher May Smith

> Decided to pop off in search of a hat and clover trimming for my spotted frock . . . but had a fruitless mission. The only trimming produced by Stockbridges was a hectic clover, not at all the right shade, but when I said so the girl said she thought it was a Perfect Match and added threateningly that I Wouldn't Get a Better. She gave me a lecture on Trimming, its Uses and its Selection, proclaiming profoundly that Trimming is Only a Decoration and shouldn't be The Exact Colour.

London-born Lu Gamble, tired of skivvying as a cleaner, longed to dress in black and stand behind a haberdashery counter, but was rejected because her hands were ingrained with dirt. 'A business girl should take as much care of her hands as an actress,' *Miss Modern* advised interwar young women hoping to get on. John Lewis had no such problems with the graduate trainees it appointed in the 1920s. For a brief spell, before she found her vocation, pilot Amy Johnson was one of them. The scheme promised graduates and 'Ladies of Gentle Birth and Breeding' a minimum salary of £3 a week and training, with the hope, no doubt, that their refined tones would attract new custom. Delighting in the 'delicate shining materials' beforehand, Amy Johnson quickly discovered that the idea of selling chiffons, silks and ribbons was very different from the real thing.

The ha'pennies and farthings shop assistants were obliged to tot up in those by-gone, pre-decimalised days had a particular meaning for Haberdashery. Before the First World War, this department customarily gave women 'a paper of pins' in lieu of their farthing in change. While appearing to spare store and shopper alike from pocketing coins of little value, retailers made a profit on pins 'sold' this way, and most shoppers felt unable to request the actual farthing. Some small draper's shops gave out farthing novelettes instead, enabling their customers to feast on poorly printed images of high society along with their reel of cotton or carded thrupenny buttons. Morley's department store was more high-minded: it gave out 'Wonderful Books' and 'Citizen Books' instead. The 'paper of pins' was such a quaint custom that Mollie Panter-Downes referred to it when ramping up her portrait of Second World War Britain for readers of the *New Yorker*.

Pins were bought in quantity, of course, as well as 'given away', and were the bane of the apprentice dressmaker's life. Professional seamstresses cast quantities of them to the floor when sewing; it was the junior's job to pick them up. When not scrabbling for pins, apprentice seamstresses, be they employed by couturier, department store or a little 'Madam' (or 'Modom') shop, could be found in Haberdashery each morning, matching sewing silks to fabric pieces: which shade of Silko – juniper berry or petunia – to correspond with a piece of shantung silk? Matching silks taught young women to judge by eye, a skill they would need later, when required to copy and cut out garments without using paper patterns.

The sewing machine, whether used by a professional or home-dressmaker, was crucial to the democratisation of fashion. By the 1880s, treadle machines were fast becoming part of the furniture and Butterick was producing around forty to sixty patterns a month, priced between 3*d* and 2*s*. 'Most Exquisite Embroidery & Art Needlework as well as Ordinary Plain Sewing can be done on Singer's new Sewing Machine', the manufacturer advised women in 1895. By the 1930s, a different approach was needed: 'No longer need you "make do" with last year's wardrobe. The Singer man shows how a length of fabric can be transformed into a "straight from Paris" frock at a fraction of the cost of a ready-made garment.' By the 1960s, Mary Quant patterns for Butterick were selling in their thousands.

Butterick, *Mabs Weekly*, *Weldon*'s, *Fashions for All* – names like these transformed home sewing. *Vogue's Guide to Practical Dressmaking* (1s) advertised patterns 'made for just those women in every community who wish to dress in the metropolitan manner'. Women's magazines offered paper patterns along with love stories and advice. *Woman's Life*, aimed at a lower-middle-class readership, promoted a weekly free pattern as a banner headline, in addition to advertising sixpenny patterns within the magazine. 'Do you make your own frocks or are you afraid to attempt them?' an advertisement in *Modern Home* enquired. Even young women dragooned into sewing perfect hems at school did not necessarily have the skills to turn out a 'smart new frock', and those making household economies might be making their own clothes for the first time. Although the looser styles of the 1920s simplified home-sewing, women who wanted to be up-to-the-minute still had to tackle complex designs; dresses could have tiered skirts, tie-cuffs, and scarf necklines. A pattern accompanying the button-and-buckle set (in tortoise-shell or amber) that came free with a 1928 issue of *Woman's Life* required readers to master a pronged belt, gored skirt and half a dozen buttonholes.

The Woman's Institute of Domestic Arts and Science prom-ised to solve all difficulties via a correspondence course. Advertisements placed in *The Needlewoman*, *Good Housekeeping* and *Home Chat* made an appeal across the social classes: 'I made all these clothes myself – quite easily' is the headline above the illustration of a woman with arms brimful of different garments. 'And they cost me less than half the usual price.' A woman looking chic in a patterned evening cloak with a shawl collar gazes out in silent sophistication in a more upmarket publication. Correspondents were promised 'all the little tricks and arts of the highly skilled dressmaker – the subtle touches that mean so much – the perfect fit that gives style . . . Write today for our free booklet: "Dressmaking & Millinery Made Easy."'

Abetted by women's magazines and fashion manuals, haberdashery departments made a virtue of necessity. *Vogue* cheered its readers in January 1931: 'At this time of year, when the rich woman is buying new items to refresh her winter wardrobe, the girl with nothing a year is dyeing, turning, or altering hers, and having just as good a time at it.' *How to Dress Well* was similarly reassuring: 'attractive designs and artistic touches are simply the result of experiments in remodelling . . . . A little touch of handwork, such as embroidery, beading, or braiding, is almost always acceptable and is an attractive means of camouflaging a seam or the insert of an extra piece.' The Miss Robinsons of the dressmaking world took heart.

Home-dressmakers, like shoppers, drew inspiration from multiple sources. In writer Alison Uttley's youth, 'the village dressmaker was the glass of fashion'. She copied styles from *Weldon's Journal* but she also took 'ideas from attendance at church where she saw the latest modes in the Castle pew'. Women have always taken ideas from the gentry; from at least the seventeenth century commentators remarked on young women imitating and aping 'their betters'. Sewing machines and ready-to-wear clothing, plus the development of cheaper, washable fabrics, made imitation that much simpler, which accounts for the numerous observations about factory workers dressing like duchesses – although, from the 1930s, they were more likely to dress like film stars.

For all the advertisements and encouragement, sewing was the last thing some women wanted to do, and whether they liked sewing or not, few could delight in mending, a chore for which there was no fashionable gloss. M. V. Hughes discovered an excellent solution: 'I would bring [my pile of mending] out when a friend came . . . "I can't sew alone," would be my excuse, "because I keep on thinking of all the other things I would rather be doing." Then my friend (whether truthfully or in a Christian spirit I did not seek to know) would say, "I love sewing; let me do it *all* while we talk".' M. V. Hughes also had her own approach to knitting, explaining away her many dropped stitches as 'a new kind of open-work, much in vogue at the moment in London'. Knitting requires a different kind of concentration and, for the skilled knitter, is soothing; it is a respectable activity too, its respectability underlined in an incidental moment in *The Weather in the Streets* when, after dinner, the matriarch and her married daughter, Kate, sit and knit while Olivia contemplates an illicit love affair. As Alison Adburgham pointed out in the *Guardian* some thirty years later, 'The Other Woman Never Knits'.

While some women sewed reluctantly, from necessity, others sewed for pleasure. Some of the dressmaker's 'little tricks and arts' came from embroidery. *Home Chat* advised its readers that 'Mab Says Stitch in the Chic: Get busy and smarten up your frocks with modish embroidery.' Embroidery also had its own magazines. Priced 2*d* a month (postage 1*d* extra), *Fancy Needlework Illustrated* was down to earth in its approach, containing patterns for crochet jumpers and the ubiquitous crochet corners for tablecloths; *The Needlewoman* cost twice as much and appealed to a different market. This 'magazine of exclusive fashions' included the pattern for a compact brush and comb bag with elaborate tassels. *The*

Needlewoman also featured a social diary. A column in January 1929 announced Diana Mitford's engagement to Bryan Guinness and, managing to make a set of silver buttons look cheapskate, advised a little car as the perfect twenty-first birthday gift.

The needlewoman is not a seamstress. Whereas plain sewing demonstrated thrift and domesticity, embroidery was seen to add refinement to femininity, suggesting the decorum and gentility only fancy work could convey. An early instruction book, *Treasures of Needlework* (1855), advised that needlework 'brings daily blessings to every home . . . without its ever watchful care home would be a scene of discomfort indeed'. Even in 1926 the *Guardian* advised that a room did not 'feel very liveable without some evidences of needlework'. However, like the young subject of Colette's short story 'The Sempstress', who terrifies her mother by *thinking* as she sews, its reporter observed that the nineteenth-century woman 'must have enjoyed the liberation of thought that comes from an occupation that is partly mechanical'.

Most women choosing embroidery silks are choosing skeins of leisure; the home-dressmaker seeks serviceable thread, but even women sewing from necessity enjoy a little flourish now and then. My great-grandma's house was full of crochet edging, drawn-thread-work runners and lace doilies; the word 'pyjamas' scrolls across my great-aunt Eva's pyjama case in thick icing-sugar pink. Many women stitched colour into their lives; by 1930 Mercer crochet silk advertised buttercup, orange, coral, sky blue, marine blue, jade green, spring green and light amethyst among its brand-new shades. Interwar women 'stitching in the chic' were asserting their individuality, albeit in small ways. At a time when, for all the talk of freedom, domesticity was much to the fore, small ways of personalising clothes and asserting individuality were important. Embroidery decorated homes as well as clothing. Those without a garden could make one to hang on the wall by stitching blazing hollyhocks, vibrant nasturtiums and every other cottage-garden flower – and a crinoline lady to water them. Embroidery stitches are veritable gardens in themselves: fly stitch, leaf stitch, stem stitch, spider . . . daisy . . .

Haberdashery was a female domain and, as such, was a place where women could buy dress preservers for those occasions when they 'glowed' a little too much; and also discreetly purchase sanitary napkins and pins, and sanitary towels. Tampax was trade-marked in 1932, but the introduction of a new product did not guarantee its immediate widespread use; historian Elizabeth Roberts explains that none of her respondents remembered even disposable sanitary towels until after the Second World War. In the 1940s, Naomi Mitchison watched her future daughter-in-law joshingly push a packet of Kotex at her son, and compared that easy gesture with the horrified silence that surrounded menstru-ation during her own youth – a horror between women, let alone in front of men. Women of my grandma's generation were too ashamed and embarrassed even to speak to their daughters.

In 1930 Kotex tied in itself in knots promoting sanitary towels to drapers without once referring to the term; Kotex may have been coy because some drapers' assistants were male (bolts of cloth mean heavy lifting). A full-page advertisement in the *Draper's Record*, illustrated with young women drivers, and headed 'Kotex says it's not so much the car you ride in as the road you ride on . . .', expended a considerable number of words talking around the subject. Finally, Kotex cut to the chase:

> 'Make it easy for them . . . Many women dislike asking for this product. Why not appreciate this and help them avoid embarrass-ment . . . Simply wrap a few packets, place them on the display so that any of your customers can simply step up, take a packet and complete the sale for you.'

Hurrah. The manufacturer of Pheltose Sanitary Belts was bolder. Disdaining 'Victorian discomforts', it illustrated its modern approach with a young woman clutching a pochette and striding ahead with her dog. In years to come, her equivalent would be leaping about in tennis whites.

For more than 150 years, Haberdashery was where you placed an order for Cash's name tapes, those essential labels for gym kit and school blazers, provided by J. & J. Cash of Coventry. There was something tidy and pleasing about names spelled out in coloured thread on narrow ribbon. Many more tapes were ordered than were needed; all over the country, a lifetime's name tapes exist in buff-coloured packets pushed to the backs of drawers. In 2014 J. & J. Cash went into administration (though a reduced operation continued). Thanks to indelible pens and the growing reluctance of mothers to spend their evenings stitching names into school uniforms, tapes like theirs fell out of favour.

Ordinarily name tapes had a mundane function, but aspiring novelist and playwright Enid Bagnold found an unexpected use for hers. Shortly before the First World War, she was invited to join a lunch for actor Sarah Bernhardt:

> I was wild with excitement. But how should I be dressed? I had what I knew was a smart coat and skirt, black, pin-striped, like a businessman's, and so daringly short that it showed my ankles. White silk stockings and patent shoes with a big buckle. But what about a hat?
>
> On the day of the luncheon, in Bond Street near Cartier's, I saw a white hat in a window, with a big gull's feather. I went in. It cost three or four guineas. I had five shillings on me and a pound in the bank.
>
> I pointed out the urgency, the immediacy, the total necessity – and the steady seventy-five pounds [a considerable sum for an

allowance] which, though not there at the moment . . . I pointed out my father's name in the telephone book.

'But how am I to know that you're his daughter?' I still wore my school vest. By wriggling and dragging, the sales lady could see the Cash's name-tape sewn at the back of my neck. I went out with the hat.

13 **THE BLUE SLIDE BUCKLE:** A PAINTBOX OF SUMMER COLOUR

The blue slide buckle sings of summer and the patterned frocks of earlier decades. The shift dresses of the mid-1920s had low, false belts but the more defined shapes of the late 1920s and '30s were frequently belted at the waist in matching fabrics. The blue oval slide was one of three in my grandma's button box; the others are square and circular. To step into a vintage summer dress today is a colourful exercise in nostalgia, but for women like Annie and Eva, these were everyday wear (and, during wartime, could be cheaper, cotton frocks requiring seven coupons to wool's eleven).

'How lovely to get into cotton or silk and fine linen' after eight months wearing wool, Naomi Mitchison said of those years. We forget how heavy winter clothing was before the wide introduction of man-made fibres, and how necessary before central heating. The ease of slipping on a light summer dress and the instant creation of a look instantly lifts the spirit. 'I noticed the semi-transparent beauty of a parasol in the sun,' Virginia Woolf told her diary in May 1920, 'how the air has this tenderness now that coloured dresses seem to glow in it.'

Some floral patterns of the period were created by women who were among the first generation employed in large-scale industrial textile design. Increasing access to art schools and widening opportunities enabled them to gain a foothold in what was still a predominantly male preserve. As in other industries, opportunities were scarce: to become a designer required dedication as well as talent. The Silver Studio, established in London in the 1880s, served many of England's key textile manufacturers with designs that retailed at fashionable stores such as Selfridges and Liberty. At its peak, the Studio had more than ten designers at any one time; in all, seventeen women were employed. Winifred Mold, its first woman designer, started as a learner in 1912 after taking evening classes at the Paddington Technical Institute for 10s 6d a term. Part-time scholar or no, she felt sufficiently confident about her chosen sphere to define herself as an Art Student on the 1911 census.

Unlike the male designers engaged by the Studio, the women worked from home and communicated with their employer by letter, an entirely manageable practice in the years of three or four posts a day. Working from home gave them a flexibility their male colleagues lacked, and would have suited those with children; married woman numbered among the Silver Studio staff. It also enabled women to carry out other domestic responsibilities: in later years, Winifred Mold was caring for sick parents.

A six-day working week was the norm. A timecard for the designer Madeleine Lawrence, an employee during the 1930s, shows that she earned just under £2 for a forty-eight-hour week, even less than some retail workers. According to a 1931 staff census within the John Lewis Partnership conducted for the *Draper's Record*, the majority of its female employees received between £2 2s and £2 11s, and most of these were shop assistants. The role of designer enabled women to exercise creative flair, but brought neither riches nor autonomy. Like many designers in other fields, they worked to a specific brief and had to satisfy commercial trends. Letters between 'Miss Lawrence' and Rex Silver, who succeeded his father, the company's founder, give some insight into how prosaic creative work could be and how hard designers worked for their pay. In 1928 he asked her to

> try for me as quickly as you can a few dainty ideas in pencil suitable for Dress Silks in the character of cutting attached. They should be allovers that look equally well any way up and should be daintily drawn in outline and should be composed of quaint little flowers and pods and berries etc all based on nature . . . Just send me 6 pencil ideas all as different as possible with the above qualities.

The results Madeleine Lawrence and others like her achieved were far from prosaic. The colours and scents of summer rise from watercolours in the Silver Studio archive: edge-to-edge dahlias, one petal touching the next, delicate pale pink dicentra, bright nasturtiums, irises and primroses; sprigs of daisies; stylised blooms both large and small, and aching blue forget-me-nots. There are beguiling, wistful intimations of spring and summer, and of bee-buzzing heat and sunshine, hedgerows, herbaceous borders and butterfly-flitting gardens. The style emphases of the 1930s were so abundantly floral that not only did dress patterns imitate flowers, gardens could be described in terms of dresses: 'The flowers in cottage gardens, lilac and pink like cotton dresses, shone veined as if lit from within', Virginia Woolf wrote in *The Years*.

The introduction of roller-printing allowed many more colours to feature within one design and enabled manufacturers to produce rich, dense palettes as well as delicate shades and to create multiple colourways far more easily than formerly. All-over patterns were favoured because of their versatility: complex repeats were more difficult to match when cutting out and led to wastage. A Mrs McPherson, who produced a small number of designs for the Silver Studio during the 1920s, made effective use of the liking for flowers set against black backgrounds, the black ground making a nod towards modernism and the Moderne look. Painterly designs were all the more vivid when foregrounded in this way.

In an era with a liking for all things jazzy, striped silks, especially those produced by the Macclesfield factories, were also popular. Up to the Second World War, Cryséde silks had a certain cachet. Produced by Alec Walker, who was much influenced by Raoul Dufy, these wood-blocked textiles translated Cornish life and landscape into acclaimed motifs. Patterns like 'Cornish Farm', 'Zennor' and 'Lobster Supper' were among those featured on the dresses and long wispy scarves initially designed by Walker's wife Kathleen (Kay). Both fabrics and dresses retailed through mail-order and Cryséde's own shops, the first of which opened in Newlyn in 1921 and by 1938 had reached as far as Harrogate, Manchester, Cheltenham, Birmingham and Edinburgh.

A 1926 London Underground poster lured home-dressmakers to the summer sales with an image of women picking over colourful fabrics. A Selfridges advertisement in the *Daily Express* gives some idea of the range available: silk crêpe, 3*s* 11*d*; all-silk crêpe georgette 5*s* 11*d*; all-wool stockinette 7*s* 11*d*; crêpe-de-Chine, 8*s* 11*d* and 9*s* 11*d*. Those visiting Liberty in 1927 could browse its squat fabric books and leaf through samples of Chinese Tyrian silk at 9*s* 11*d* or choose linen or cotton for a quarter of the price. Flowers bloomed in Whiteleys' sample pages, along with jazzily patterned prints, and salmon pink and white 'crêpe duleen' suitable for tennis parties and garden fetes.

Pearl buttons were pleasing additions to summer clothes, as were those made of glass or its imitator Lucite which was lighter and did not chip but allowed the pattern to show through without distracting the eye. Often incised or decoratively shaped (like the glass bow in my grandma's button box), glacial-looking buttons were a popular choice. The 1930s cruise-liner look called for more definition and a stronger statement: a *Pictorial Review* pattern circa 1937, priced 1*s* 6*d*, shows a white belted dress punctuated by navy blue buttons, with triangular pockets at breasts and hips.

John Lewis gave the names 'Lyme Regis', 'Lynton' and 'Ilfracombe' to some fashionable summer styles. Holiday resorts grew rapidly during the 1930s, with middle-class destinations like Torquay promoting their charms in newspapers and magazines. Blackpool spent £3 million on its parks, promenades and Winter Gardens; in 1937 it was estimated that 15 million Britons took an annual break, roughly one-third of the population. (However, it was not until the following year's Holidays with Pay Act that the right to a paid holiday was enshrined in law.) Members of the WI might wish to take a double room with Miss Thorogood at Westcliff-on-Sea (bed and breakfast from 22*s* 6*d* each person; full board from 35*s*). For those with smaller funds, day trips were an attractive option. For many years, my grandma's holidays were day trips.

Whatever their destination, women wanted to show off their summer finery. Promenade photographers were only too willing to oblige them for posterity. Photographs record the polka dots and florals chosen by my grandma and great-aunt. One photograph shows Eva striding forth in co-respondent shoes. Similar white shoes 'for cruising and holidays', with black, sea-blue or nut-brown trimmings cost the interwar woman 16*s* 9*d*.

By the 1950s, a slide buckle might fasten a cummerbund rather than a narrow belt. Patterns were changing too: the post-war years saw bigger, bolder florals and organic-shaped abstract prints. Instead of all-over designs, herbaceous borders circled and rose from the hemlines of fuller skirts. Scenic illustrations and sketchy line drawings were everywhere: pagodas and Eiffel Towers stood statuesque, little French poodles trotted across colourful cottons, reflecting the broadening taste for foreign travel – or the fantasy of it at least. My mum wore a Spanish-themed skirt with bull-fighters and flamenco dancers. (The British holiday resort was still going strong, however. A beach scene, complete with sticks of rock, was part of the Festival of Britain.) In the late 1960s, 1930s florals made their comeback in shops like Granny Takes a Trip and Antiquarius on London's King's Road. A few years later, it was time for me to rummage for them in provincial jumble sales and on market stalls.

I still have some of those vintage dresses: intense red poppies on silk; sky-blue, white and magenta patterned crêpe, sharp blue cotton stripes. A favourite print set mauve, blue and clover-pink anemones beside bronze-splashed yellow daisies. Frocks like these promise eternal sunshine, although it must have rained sometimes back then.

BUTTONS AND HOW TO MAKE THEM

Woven Buttons:

Cover a mould ['unpainted wooden beads are excellent'] with an uneven number of threads, and with a same or a finer cotton, weave in and out, over and under the bars, using a blunt needle. Pack the rows tightly, and continue weaving until the button is covered. This is one of the easiest forms of decoration.

A Linen Covered Ring Button:

Tightly stuff the centre of the [metal] ring with cotton wool; over it, strain a piece of fine linen and buttonhole it over the ring. Work a few French knots, or make a little chain stitch decoration, in the centre. Cover the back with a piece of linen slip-stitched on, and make a buttonhole or overcast loop for the attachment.

Embroidery (December 1937)

14 **THE SILVER-AND-BLUE BUTTON:** GOOD LITTLE SUITS IN WARTIME

Today, silver-and-blue buttons grace the jacket of a vintage suit, but the buttons were originally Annie's. Their silver has a pleasing sheen in keeping with the message of the day: during the Second World War, even buttons could be uplifting. I don't know the history of my pale blue suit, but it could probably tell its own wartime stories. Tailored suits were popular then, not only because of their versatility and the fact that a 'good little suit' will last, but with so many women wearing uniform, civilian clothing acquired a quasi-military style and a tailored suit always looks the part, instilling confidence, no matter what its wearer is feeling.

Suits were for best in my family. My grandma favoured a jacket with a complementary woollen skirt for everyday wear. My great-aunt Eva looked good in suits and, at the start of 1940, bought a trim black one with braid outlining its jacket and triangular pockets. When the jacket finally died some forty years later, after its second life with me (proof that those good little suits really were made to last), I snipped off the handsome octagonal buttons which sit in the button box to this day.

Buttons were still easy to obtain in 1940, and when clothes rationing was introduced the following year (seventeen months after food), buttons and other items classed as hard haberdashery were exempt from coupons. Over time, buttons, like so much else, rationed or not, were harder to come by; a wartime photograph shows a whole depot of workers snipping buttons from old clothes. With many raw materials in short supply, the manufacture of buttons for civilian clothing was a low priority and some of the compositions previously favoured found new uses – Lucite, for example, was needed for aircraft windscreens. Wooden buttons were produced in greater quantity, although even these were not abundant. Shortages bred inventiveness: wood could be hand-crafted and home-painted; buttons were made from cork, papier mâché and cellophane paper. Those who had held on to a 1937 edition of *Embroidery* magazine could follow instructions to make their own thread buttons, while at least one example survives of what appears to be a wartime 'habitat' button in which a cluster of grains and lentils has been encased within plastic and sealed with a wooden rim.

Whether being inventive with grains and lentils, or in some other way, 'making do' quickly became a keynote of civilian life. Not spending money was a patriotic matter: 'Once the family budget concerned just you and your family,' a National Savings advertisement advised, 'but now [it] has to help buy guns, tanks, and planes to defend a bigger family – the Family of Britain . . . Spend as little as you can. Save as much as you can. Be a stern and wise Chancellor of the family Exchequer.' By contrast, as its company literature reported some years later, Marshall & Snelgrove managed to turn shopping into a demonstration of British grit:

No woman who shopped at the Oxford Street 'Marshalls' will forget the calm (what our American friends would call the poise) of sales staff and customers alike when the spotters on the roof, during air raid alerts, signalled that bombers were near at hand. There was no undue haste, no hustling as, by rule, everyone went down to the underground shelters under the shop, coming up again to continue shopping as the all-clear was sounded.

Novelist Naomi Mitchison probably came nearer the truth when, in May 1941, she observed, 'I believe everyone except the really stupid is frightened of air raids. Pretending successfully not to be is a different thing.'

Pretending was easier with the right clothing. In the early months of the war, anything white was favoured. Selfridges advertised luminous buttons; white gloves, white gas-mask cases, arm bands, handbags and white fur stoles were among the items recommended by the *Observer* for fashionable blackout dress. Jan Struther's *Mrs Miniver* described how much more cheerful London looked with women wearing touches of white instead of their usual dark, autumnal clothes. Wartime posed new dilemmas, as diarist Joan Strange recorded: 'Mother remarked . . . as she set out for church: "Now, which shall I take this morning, my gas mask or my umbrella?"'

Zips came into their own, as did trousers. For 10*d* and a magazine coupon, readers of *Woman and Home* could buy a paper pattern for the 'ideal shelter suit', which they could make with buttons or a 'zipp' fastener. In the spirit of economy, the pattern could then be adapted for a pyjama suit, pyjamas gaining in popularity with night-time air raids. *Good Housekeeping* advertised the new 'slacks suit' for 'war work or shelter wear'. Mass Observation diarist Nella Last was surprised to receive a siren suit in the post as a birthday gift: 'It's the maddest, most

amusing thing a sedate matron of fifty-one ever possessed!'
More conservatively, *Housewife* magazine asked, 'Should Women
Wear Trousers?' and concluded not. Women themselves thought
differently. By 1943, Nella Last saw trousers as a statement of
new-found confidence: 'I know why a lot of women have gone
into pants – it's a sign that they are asserting themselves in
some way.'

My grandma did not resort to making her own buttons, nor
a siren suit, alas, but in 1940 she took up sewing professionally.
That year, following a long illness, my grandfather died, and
Annie needed to find new work to support herself and ten-year-old
Cora. She was still working for the Provident Clothing Company,
a job she loved, but, even with her widow's pension, this work
alone was not enough. Becoming a 'little dressmaker' meant that
Annie could combine two jobs. She was already making clothes
for herself and my mother and, thanks to a tailoring course she
had taken some years earlier, was able to offer a professional
service, aided by her silent assistant, Nellie, a pigeon-chested
tailor's dummy.

'NOW! . . . more than ever you need a SINGER sewing
machine,' a wartime advertisement insisted. Along with the rolling
pin, that essential kitchen tool, sewing machines were described
as weapons of war and became part of the civilian woman's
arsenal. 'Make one of your old coats into a panelled pinafore
dress for your schoolgirl daughter,' *Woman and Home* advised,
which was all very well, but even women who confidently ran up
summer frocks thought twice about converting coats into dresses.
This was where Annie came into her own.

My grandma could have made Eva's trim black suit, and lined
it too, had she the time, but tailoring required hours of close,
concentrated work, whereas most of Annie's tasks consisted of
letting out and taking in, and of conjuring two garments out of

one. Winter coats became skirts and jackets – and pinafore dresses; dresses were converted into skirts and blouses; panels in complementary patterns were added to last year's summer frocks for those women who could no longer squeeze into them. Multiple ingenious ways were found to refresh garments that had already done good service – a new belt, different buttons, silk edging or a silk flower to revive a tired dress. Thanks to her years of home sewing, Annie had a full rag-bag, and buttons and trimmings to call on, as well as a store of ideas. People commented on the clothes she made: something about them was just that bit different.

Something that bit different was welcomed once rationing was introduced. In April 1940, a Limitation of Supplies Order imposed restrictions on cotton, rayon and linen goods. The extension of rationing to clothes, fabric and footwear in June 1941 put ingenuity to the test. 'Rationing has been introduced not to deprive you of your real needs,' the Board of Trade explained, 'but to make more certain that you get your share of the country's goods.' Not everyone saw it that way. Inevitably, the wealthy fared better than those with fewer, poorer-quality clothes and many women who had resisted the temptation of a new winter coat the previous year came to regret it. Coats, the most coupon-heavy item of expenditure, used fourteen of the sixty-six coupons with which adults were initially supplied to meet their yearly needs (the total fell in subsequent years). A jacket took eleven coupons, as did a woollen dress; a blouse needed five; a skirt seven; stockings and gloves two. Hats, caps, boiler suits and bib overalls were among the exempt items, as were sanitary towels, thank goodness. Those who needed reminding of their allocation could purchase a Jacqmar silk scarf depicting an underslip, dress, shoes, gloves, etc. with the number of coupons for each written beneath; other Jacqmar scarves instructed women to 'Dig for Victory', and so on.

From now on, dressing well required a certain amount of

dodging and contriving. In 1941 a neighbour complimented Nella Last on her outfit: 'we started to assess my rig-out. Broad-brimmed summer hat, four years old; sleeveless linen frock (three times remodelled), five years; white linen mesh fish-net gloves, three summers; woven braid sandals – lost in the mists of time – certainly seven years old; and navy flannel "swagger" coat belonging to a two-year-old suit.' Her clothes would see even longer service before the war was out.

For women like Nella Last and Annie, mending and remod-elling clothes was already a way of life. Over the next few years women countrywide turned counterpanes into dressing gowns, made bras from silk blouses and parachute silk and wedding dresses from curtain material, while the range of garments made from blackout cloth exceeded all imaginings. One of the many suggestions for reviving tired clothes came from *Home and Country* which advocated using half a pint of gin to renovate 'treasured silks'. Under the circumstances, most women would have sooner taken a swig.

Wartime restrictions applied as stringently to trimmings as to bath water (no more than five inches). Braids and ribbons of three inches or less were, like buttons, classed as hard haber-dashery and so exempt from coupons, as were mending silk, wool and sewing thread – if they could be found in the shops. The Board of Trade's own survey discovered that three in ten 'Mrs Sew and Sews' could not find any needles, and that one in four was unable to locate the darning wool for the woollens that 'must last longer'. A floral blouse I found on a market stall was a perfect example of wartime expediency. Its seams were as narrow as possible, its elasticated waist saved on fabric. Clear Lucite buttons allowed the pattern to predominate (and had been chosen for this reason). The whole garment illustrated the care that went into some home-made clothes. This papery silk blouse had an almost invisible butterfly-shaped breast pocket, and hooks and eyes as well as buttons and a gathered waist. It was loved by someone else before it came to me.

Leaflets informed women 'how to patch an overall', 'how to darn holes and tears', 'how to use old garments for children', and so on. There were 'Useful Jobs That Girls Can Do' and 'Jobs Boys Can Do Themselves', including sewing on their own buttons. Knitting was part of the initiative and frequently involved the unravelling of old jumpers to re-use the wool for new ones. A thrupenny Bestway pattern enabled women to give 'a bright new look to their "getting shabby suit"' with a Harlequin-style 'two-coupon' jumper – if they could find the two-ply. Knitting could soothe frayed nerves and help to occupy the long hours spent in air-raid shelters. Knitting and sewing parties brought together women of different social classes 'for the duration', only for them to separate again thereafter. In Mollie Panter-Downes' novel, *One Fine Day*, Laura reflects on 'some classic pattern which went on recurring for ever in different fancy dresses, the group of women sitting sewing round the lady of the house while their men were at the wars . . . Men must fight and women must sew – of course in this war women had fought too.'

The Utility Clothing Scheme, which came into force in September 1942, looked set to stultify fashion completely. Strict regulations determined the number of buttons on jackets, coats, dresses and blouses, the length of hemlines and the depth of actual hems, as well as the width of sleeves, belts and collars. The number of pleats and tucks were restricted and feathers, lace, velvet trimmings and appliqué no longer allowed. The very name Utility made hearts sink, although the president of the Board of Trade described the restrictions as 'one obvious occasion for rejoicing. There has been a most unreasonable use of colour in normal times . . . and it has been fanned into fiercer unreason in these abnormal times by the practice of making dresses, and especially coats and cloaks out of hearth rugs, dogs' blankets, and other coupon-free materials.'

The coming years were far less bland than predicted. Luminaries such as Hardy Amies and Norman Hartnell were famously invited to submit a coat, suit, afternoon dress and a cotton overall dress for civilian wear and the results met with general approval. The public was grateful for affordable clothing that reflected practicalities; most women agreed that Utility wear could be stylish. I remember finding in a vintage shop an elegant wrap-around dress in green and cream patterned crêpe, Diane von Furstenberg-style (no buttons in sight) stamped with the Utility mark, and would have enjoyed wearing the Utility suits and dresses stocked by the Hodson sisters in their Willenhall house-shop. By July 1943 70 per cent of the clothes being manufactured bore the Utility label. From now on, all clothes were subject to the new restrictions, including those made by a dressmaker with the customer's own fabric. My grandma had to literally cut her cloth to suit the times.

Derbyshire schoolteacher and diarist May Smith was twenty-six when war was declared. As teaching was a reserved occupation, she was not 'one of Ernie's Girlies' (Ernest Bevin was Minister of Labour), but taught throughout the war while living at home with her parents. Like many women, May was unprepared for clothes rationing – 'Oh dear! Why have I put off for so long buying essentials?' – but, thereafter, beautified an old blue frock with embroidery, embroidered camiknickers to make them less Utility, and transformed a blouse into a bra. She invested in sensible crêpe-soled shoes, bemoaned the need to wear lisle stockings ('oh monstrous!'), and sometimes went without stockings altogether. Glamour was attempted via a new evening dress – 'a startling affair in black, with a red corsage and gold spots' – and, less successfully, with a series of tortured perms and a face pack. Each month was a struggle to stay solvent: 'I'll be glad when pay-day comes. I have 2/6 to live on until then.'

Like many wartime diarists, May Smith combined the matter-of-fact with the momentous, describing the growing scarcity of everything, air raids and blasted shop windows, along with films viewed, parsimonious Kardomah Café lunches ('measly lunch of sardines on toast and coffee') and frequent tussles with her local dressmaker Mrs W. On 16 May 1940 she notes that she has washed her hair in a Stayblond shampoo, 'in order to introduce a flaxen Sheen', before quoting Minister of Information Duff Cooper: 'The greatest battle in the history of the world is now in progress.' A few months later, May and a friend arrive in Leicester for a shopping expedition at the very spot that was bombed earlier that morning, and with no more than an exclamation mark to record that fact, head straightaway for lunch, which they eat in style in the Grill Room of the Grand. Wartime or no, she was a young woman getting on with her life.

May Smith's class (of forty-seven pupils) found air raids exciting and enjoyed the sing-songs she led in the school shelter. May, by contrast described the 'Awful feeling when we're inside'. The essays she set in 1940–41 give a flavour of early wartime schooling: 'The House that was not Blacked Out', 'What to Do in an Air Raid', 'Helping Our Country', and 'Adventures of a Spitfire'. My mum wrote similar wartime stories. She was nine years old at the outbreak of war and fifteen when it ended, a span of time in which she exchanged her Mickey Mouse gas mask for a plain one, passed through primary to secondary school and started to contemplate work. 'Owing to the outbreak of hostilities', her primary school closed for the first four weeks of the war, but its pupils were soon back at their desks, with the Australian and Canadian anthems new additions to their musical repertoire. The following summer, the annual appearance of the fair on the town's

old racecourse was designated a 'Holiday at Home' and Cora
was painting airmen, khaki soldiers and women wearing military-
style suits, stylish hats and gauntlets in her home-made notebooks;
a glitter ball radiates light across a watercoloured dance floor as
bright today as when it was first painted. She sampled Whittington
Moor's British Restaurant (excellent puddings) and, for the first
time, heard American voices undiluted by the cinema. Careless
talk cost lives and so Cora invented a secret code which she and
her friends could use at break, when they met in the girls' toilets
(where else?). During air raids, her form mistress, like May Smith,
led her class in song: 'All men must be free/ March for Liberty
with me . . .' Singing was not all pomp and circumstance, however;
in the week that *Casablanca* was shown at the Lyceum a new
song was quickly learned and practised in the playground: 'You
must remember this . . .'

In 1941, a Mass Observation survey, 'What Does Britain Mean
To You?', asked Britons to define themselves. Despite the fact
that the majority were town and city dwellers, they saw themselves
as an overwhelmingly rural nation. The following year, war artist
Laura Knight produced an intensely poignant and patriotic
painting, 'Betty and William Jacklin'. Betty in her jumper and
spotted frock and young blond William in his knitted woolly and
red buttoned shoes are an idealised mother and child. Behind
them, a hedgerow and trees separate one furrowed field from the
next. A painting with multiple messages, it is the stuff of England
as conjured many times over during the Second World War.

THE WOMEN'S LAND ARMY: UNIFORM

On joining the W.L.A. every girl is supplied with the following: 2 green jerseys, 2 pairs of breeches, 2 overall coats, 2 pairs of dungarees, 6 pairs of stockings, 3 shirts, 1 pair of ankle boots, 1 pair of shoes, 1 pair of gumboots or boots with leggings, 1 hat, 1 overcoat with shoulder titles, 1 oilskin or mackintosh, 2 towels, an oilskin sou'-wester, a green armlet, and a metal badge. After every six months of satisfactory service she receives a half-diamond to be sewn on the armlet; she has a special armlet after two years' service, and a scarlet armlet to replace the two-year one after four years' service.

Every twelve months she is entitled to some uniform replacement. All uniform is of course given free of charge, though she has to surrender a certain number of coupons.

Vita Sackville-West, *The Women's Land Army* (1944)

15 **THE LAND ARMY BUTTON:** UNIFORMS NOT UNIFORMITY

Shirley Joseph emerged from her Women's Land Army interview 'already mentally clothed [in a pair of] coveted khaki breeches'. She was not the first young woman to have her head turned by those honey-coloured corduroys – nor was she the last. I found a pair of Land Army breeches on Camden Market when I was in my early twenties. I loved their deep pockets and the ease with which they fastened, with three buttons on each side of the waist. They were extremely comfortable to wear but, having seen Evelyn Dunbar's paintings of Land Army workers, I have to conclude, with Shirley Joseph, that 'khaki breeches . . . do not make for glamour, whichever way you look at them, least of all from behind.'

Breeches like these were a key element of the uniform with which the 80,000 members of the WLA were issued on registration. And, thanks to government recruiting posters, they are the image of the Land Army worker – or Land Girl, as they were known – that always comes to mind: the young woman gathering in the harvest on a golden afternoon. The majority were not country women: one derived her idea of rural life 'from an office calendar depicting scenes which existed only in the imagination of the artist'. This and the 'picturesque uniform' made her decide to join up; another Land Girl, aged sixteen, only knew horses from cowboy films. There were many rude awakenings. Romantic visions of cowslip-dotted country lanes were soon scotched by the reality of hard, heavy labour and the conditions in which the WLA worked: rain driving into their faces, the sun beating on their backs, up to their ankles in water, or fingers numbed with frost. 'Nobody sees her; nobody but the men whose ordinary life it has always been, and who, she knows, will be only too glad of a chance to catch her out,' Vita Sackville-West wrote in the official publication *The Women's Land Army* (1944).

Women started registering for war work as soon as war was declared. They could choose between the WLA, the Women's Services – the ATS (Auxiliary Territorial Service), the WAAF (Women's Auxiliary Air Force), the WRNS (Women's Royal Naval Service) – or civil defence, industry, and a wealth of other war work. For many young women, putting on uniform marked their transition into adulthood and independence. In November 1939, May Smith noted 'the appearance of uniform in almost every public place . . . Almost every other girl and woman is swaggering about the streets in her khaki stockings and costume, and soldiers are nipping about here and there, with or without stripes.' However, it was the introduction of conscription for women, for the first time in British history, in December 1941, that altered the wartime landscape for good; this was the most significant change the war brought to women's lives.

'[Y]our finest clothes are those that you wear as soldiers,' Virginia Woolf wrote in 1938, noting the regimental ribbons, braid and dress-uniform folderols worn by high-ranking military.

She did not have uniformed women in mind. In Vita Sackville-West's view, 'You cannot look fashionable in uniform; you can usually look only trim, neat and correct.' The look of the uniform determined which Service many young women chose, however. With no way of knowing what Service life really entailed, a surprising number, as Virginia Nicholson has noted, judged by appearances. For many 'it was enough to know, and let other people know, that they were doing a job which entitled them to wear a uniform'. In her fortnightly 'Letter from London', Mollie Panter-Downes informed readers of the *New Yorker* that, with conscription, young women could 'no longer decide that they look better in navy blue than in khaki and act accordingly'.

The navy blue 'Wrens' uniform was generally reckoned to come top in both colour and style. ('Efficient, neat, yet soignée too', according to an advertisement for Miner's Liquid Foundation.) Their refashioned hat met with such approval – Christian Lamb maintained she 'only joined for the hat' – that it was copied in different colours for civilian wear. Barbara Pym thought the hat 'lovely, every bit as fetching as I'd hoped, but my suit rather large though it's easier to alter that way. I have also a macintosh and greatcoat – 3 pairs of "hose" (black), gloves, tie, 4 shirts and 9 stiff collars, and two pairs of shoes which are surprisingly comfortable.'

The ATS uniform was redesigned to make it fashionable, but Lucia Lawson was not alone in thinking she looked 'AWFUL' in khaki, 'but alas, it is not because the clothes don't fit because they fit beautifully.' Hilary Wayne was struck by the 'dinginess of the clustered khaki uniforms under electric light. The colour is designedly dull and inconspicuous by day: by night it is dead.' An unbecoming jacket did not help. Air Force blue was generally liked as a colour, but the WAAF broad belt accentuated the hips and, even worse, one young woman was horrified at the prospect 'of the underwear she [would] have to endure – vests with short sleeves, and woolly pantees!'

Hilary Wayne described how lavishly the ATS were kitted out.

To people feeling the coupon pinch and wondering where the next pair of stockings was coming from, it was miraculous to be handed four pairs. The kitbag which was given out first was, indeed, soon overflowing with underwear of excellent quality, khaki shirts, ties, sweater and gloves. Then cap, tunic, skirt and greatcoat were tried on and critically inspected by an officer before they became one's own. Then to the 'Haberdashery' counter for studs, shoe-laces, tooth-brush, hair-brush, comb, button-cleaning equipment, shoe-brush, field dressing and housewife. Then two pairs of shoes. And the only thing to disburse at the end of this orgy of acquisition was a signature as receipt.

Cleaning equipment was essential. Belts, buckles, buttons had to shine. Lucia Lawson wrote to 'Darling Mummy', requesting 'Some cleaning rags *important* & a duster.' Three days later, her desperation became clear. 'I've never known anything like the cleaning that goes on buttons, shoes & goodness knows what else . . . I'm afraid there isn't nearly as much time for writing letters as I thought, owing to this awful spit & polish.' Arriving at her Army quarters in 1942, she described being marched into lunch and marched out again: '(in future, the abbreviation of marched is M because it seems to be the only [way] we move about) . . . then M to medical inspection . . . we then M to collect luggage, got same & M to our hut,' and so on.

Sylvia Townsend Warner, who had put on overalls to relieve munitions workers during the First World War, now lectured to over a hundred ATS on behalf of the Workers' Education

Association. 'The sight of so many depressed tunics was soul-searing . . . the poor things were living in such horrid chilly hencoops, and it was melancholy to hear them leaping to their feet as their officers walked in, the two hundred odd uncomfortable Heavy Oxfords thundering as one – all the disadvantages of being soldiers and none of the fun.'

Uniformed life took some getting used to. Lucia Lawson told her mother that 'lunch at Claridge's in uniform was a little hard, I tried telling myself how much superior I was to all the be-foxed, be-minked, be-scented & altogether pretty be-stinking & I think it worked.' Lunch at Claridge's was not exactly the norm; there were fewer be-minked women dining in British restaurants or Lyon's Corner Houses (although quite a number were be-foxed and be-scented) and, in no time at all, uniformed women were everywhere.

Barbara Pym 'felt funny being in uniform – more like fancy dress than anything'. Hilary Wayne thought that

> There is no doubt that 'dressing up' helps soldiers, as it helps actors, to play their parts. I think we not only looked different, we felt different. For one thing, I personally felt less self-conscious . . . the very numbers and the fact that day and night we were all dressed exactly alike gave me the comfortable feeling that, whatever happened, I could not be conspicuous.

While Hilary felt comforted, she also saw how easily the power that uniform conferred could be abused. Novelist Betty Miller was also fascinated by 'the astonishing effect on quite ordinary civilians of army life. No sooner had they donned uniforms than these men (and women too), who in everyday life were respectable, God-fearing citizens became – under the influence of a *very* peculiar CO – quite unrecognisable.' 'War is a strange thing,' Shirley Joseph noted.

The grander the uniform the more important your job must be. Values, ideals, and morals get mixed as if in a cocktail shaker. The result, for a time, is stimulating. In the shaking-up process girls who before the war were doing menial work – or what they regarded as menial work – found that they were welcomed into houses with as much enthusiasm as a conquering hero, just because they happened to wear a uniform. It was all very unsettling. The uniforms would have to come off one day.

Despite the democratisation uniform imposed, and the fact that women were required to mix with those they would not otherwise have known, social class remained an issue. Hilary Wayne described how the division of the ATS into S (Specialised) and G (General) gave 'the impression that the categories labelled G, which included cooks, orderlies, messengers and so on, would absorb the socially lower entrants'. Marghanita Laski's family invited their Land Girls to choose a book to read and 'placed' them according to their choices. The receipt of uniform was itself a demarcation: for some it meant their first pair of shoes that were not hand-me-downs. Vita Sackville-West criticised the Land Girls' tendency to mix their uniform with their own clothes, but who would not wear the warm overcoat with which they had been issued? Behind some criticisms lay the assumption that members of the WLA had a wide selection of clothing to choose from, and plenty of opportunities to wash and dry the clothes they had. It was an old argument dressed up differently. The WLA issued guidelines, as opposed to strict rules; some felt this could make for ill discipline – and ill discipline let the side down. Vita Sackville-West bemoaned 'a flowery frock showing under their khaki overcoat, or a magenta jumper combined with dungarees. And as for the things some of them do with their hats and their hair!'

'Uniform, yes, but not Uniformity,' an advertisement for Boots Cosmetics declared, and many women did do their bit to assert their individuality. Joan Wyndham, who hailed from bohemian Chelsea, felt 'There is not much you can do to make a WAAF's uniform look sexy (apart from pulling your belt in till you can hardly breathe), but jumping up and down on your cap to loosen up the brim does help to give it a rakish air.' On completion of her officer training, her uniform acquired a thin blue band, 'not to mention £2 14s 10d a week – though I understand that most of this goes on what's known as "living up to your uniform". Can't wait to live it up – let's hope I get posted near London.'

Later Joan told her diary, 'I have been given a superb new job – Messing Officer. This means I'm in charge of the booze cupboard, and can order make-up for my friends . . . I am now one of the most popular girls in the Mess.' Make-up was now widely accepted, indeed was an expected part of uniformed life. Elizabeth Arden was quick to support uniformed women, inviting them to use her London salon as a place to meet friends, take a shower or telephone. She also offered cosmetic advice: 'burnt sugar is the colour Miss Arden boosts to go with khaki', Mollie Panter-Downes noted; Tangee lipstick was also popular. Laura Knight's 1941 paintings of Corporal Elspeth Henderson and Sergeant Helen Turner, both of whom received the Military Medal for bravery, presents them both in scarlet lipstick; Corporal Henderson has matching nail polish too. Make-up was not just a matter of individual pleasure: young women driving ambulances in France were advised to wear lipstick to cheer the wounded. The most telling account of the role lipstick played in wartime is provided by Linda Grant, who, in *The Thoughtful Dresser*, describes the restorative power that gifts of lipstick had on newly liberated concentration-camp survivors.

Attractive uniforms, scarlet lips – enough, but not too much make-up. As ever, women struggled with mixed messages. Abram Games's recruitment poster for the ATS was famously withdrawn because the 'blonde bombshell' had excessive sex appeal. Wartime phraseology – 'Up with the lark, to bed with a Wren' etc. – made it all too clear how women were perceived.

It was not merely servicewomen who were denigrated: Sheffield bus conductor Zelma Katin complained that a woman in a uniform was thought 'easy'. New roles, the same old judgements.

By 1943 women aged between eighteen and fifty were being directed into war work. By then, at least 80 per cent of married women and 90 per cent of single women were contributing in some way, whether in full-time, part-time or voluntary work. The services accounted for less than 10 per cent of these millions of working women. To Jenifer Wayne, 'any form of militarism seemed . . . fatuous and obscene, and an utter waste of anything I had learned at Oxford'. Instead, in the autumn of 1939, she joined what was then a somewhat makeshift ambulance service. She recalled 'the faint smell of petrol; the blacked-out windows; the radio playing "Run, Rabbit, Run"; Spam sandwiches and siren suits . . . We were a kind of Dad's Army set-up, but with both sexes.'

Zelma Katin enjoyed wearing her blue uniform with its nickel buttons. As her bus ran to and from the centre of Steel City, she took in the breathtaking vistas across the rubble heaps, while watching early-morning factory hands give way to shop assistants and clerical workers, shoppers and, eventually, ladies of leisure.

Was this woman in navy blue myself? There must be two 'I's': the original 'I' is a married suburban woman who once studied botany in a university college, speaks with a southern intonation, confines herself to her house, and belongs to the petty bourgeoisie. She must have indulged in a burst of dichotomy and procreated another 'I' – an aggressive woman in uniform who sharply orders people about, has swear words and lewd jokes thrown at her, works amid rush and noise, fumbles and stumbles about in the blackout, and has filthy hands and a grimy neck.

Zelma relished her new freedom and her new personality. Like servicewomen, she too observed, 'It's extraordinary what a profound part in your and my psychology a uniform plays.'

Zelma Katin's passengers may have included some of the young women taught welding by Valentine Pearson. Valentine joined her father's Sheffield firm and undertook university evening courses in metallurgy when her work as a graphic advertisement designer 'dried up' as war approached. She was proud of her reputation as 'the young woman teacher with long, red nails' and, in quiet moments, reconstituted old lipsticks by holding their ends over a welding torch.

The women Valentine trained repaired castings for tank parts and ship valves or welded parts for bridges and tank vents. Those engaged in electric arc welding required strength as well as great concentration, an ability to withstand heat, and steady hands. Like the young women who worked with munitions during the First World War, some of them transferred their peacetime skills to wartime. Agnes Helme, a nanny used to decorating cakes, was an excellent welder, while Enid Hiley, a former seamstress, was assisted by her skills in invisible mending. Also like their forebears, the women met resistance from men on the shop floor; they also suffered work-related injuries. Whereas male welders wore masks that fitted on to their heads, the women had hand-held masks which did not disturb their hair. A common problem was arc eye, caused by accidentally looking at the 'flashes' of the flame, and those working in intense heat for eight hours a day all experienced heavy periods; two had problems following childbirth.

Novelist and memoir-writer Emma Smith took on another unconventional role. She was delighted to exchange a dull clerical posting for work on a narrowboat transporting cargo on the Grand Union Canal. Emma relished the freedom and the chance to wear scruffy clothes – dungarees in summer and her brother Harvey's old flannel cricket trousers, in winter – with a brass-buckled leather belt slung low around her hips and an iron windlass, for winding up lock-gate paddles, tucked into it. Some years in, however, Emma's fervour palled and she yearned for 'pretty frocks, and shoes with high heels, and silk stockings and lacy underclothes'. She wanted to go dancing like her WAAF sister Pam and give up the life of a boater. By contrast, Kaye Webb (later editor of Puffin) maintained her pre-war occupation and rose through literary journalism. She described herself as 'a war profiteer' and felt guilty for having such an interesting job 'while [her] girlfriends were yawning their heads off on night duty in the RAF Operation Rooms, or getting chilblains on Ack Ack sites.'

For Nella Last in Barrow-in-Furness, the war was transforming. Though too old for conscription, she blossomed as a member of the WVS (Women's Voluntary Service). 'I'm in the rhythm now, instead of always fighting against things.' Like Nella Last, my great-aunt was too old to be conscripted. Eva joined her local ARP (Air Raid Precautions), where, at the end of a day at the corner shop, she learned first aid and was issued with a notebook and whistle, and a rattle to swing in order to notify her neighbours in the event of a gas attack.

Some of the corner shop's customers were the young women now working in neighbouring factories. Factory workers found ways to personalise their own 'uniform' – baggy trousers and overalls, and those ubiquitous head scarves twisted into turbans, Ruby Loftus-style. In September 1941 London diarist Vere Hodgson described a munitions procession designed to attract women to the factories. 'All firms sent contingents in marvellously coloured overalls – on lorries containing parts of Spitfires etc with the words: We Made These . . . One lorry had elderly women. We are all between 60 and 80 . . . we are still working – why aren't you? How happy they all looked.' *Housewife* magazine advocated patterned smock overalls and matching turbans. Wearing your hair up was a safety precaution, not just a matter of style. *Vogue*'s Audrey Withers was one of several magazine editors invited by the Ministry of Information to encourage women to 'Be in the Fashion – Cover your Head'. Neat hair was also a priority for servicewomen, albeit for different reasons. Many of them chose 'the regulation roll; hair clamped into an almost circular sausage, well clear of the collar, but with enough smooth crown on which to park a tin hat'.

Wherever you looked, a uniformed woman was working. Trousers or no, as Nella Last observed, women were asserting themselves in new ways, although not without attracting criticism. Uniformed women came top of a *Daily Mail* list of gripes; factory workers were also chastised for their appearance. *Housewife* defended them in June 1941: 'The woman who can look as bright as a flower during twelve hours of night work . . . deserves credit, not criticism.'

Criticism of women and their appearance seeped everywhere. Doreen Fairclough was called up in 1944, and directed to work as a BBC engineer, a job that had formerly excluded women. The response was generally positive, if patronising, as a BBC manual reported: 'We have every reason to be satisfied with the performance of these girls to date . . . provided we keep them strictly to operational work.' But although women were used to being patronised, some found themselves unwelcome in any context.

> An Engineer In Charge sought to limit their activities as much as possible, because their clothes got caught up in the components. In the next breath, he was complaining about women wearing trousers on his station. He had forbidden them to do so, except on the night shift, in contravention of the official line that there was no objection to trousers, provided that they were of a reasonably quiet colour.

All these anxieties about the high visibility of women – too present, too exuberant, too vocal, especially factory workers, singing on buses and trams and going into public houses with money in their pockets at the end of their shifts – was a criticism levelled at uniformed women too. Far better that they should sit quietly and knit. Jaeger offered patterns for a waistcoat, matching scarf and gloves, 'Essentials for the Forces', and all for 6*d*. Those seeking *Vogue* patterns could knit a pair of fishnet stockings – sexier than the dreaded lisle stockings women were forced to wear once silk became impossible to find. *Woman's Weekly* included a pattern for a short-sleeved jumper for 'When You're Off Duty'. When Joan Wyndham, whose wartime diary is spliced with whisky, pernod, benzedrine, black-and-gold Balkan Sobranie cigarettes, love affairs and hangovers aplenty, decides to 'give up men and lead a quiet life', she knits a scarf from Air Force wool, 'the consistency of tarry rope'.

My mum acquired her own militaristic uniform. For a couple of years during the war, thanks to the English and Arts mistresses, Miss P. and Miss M. (until Miss P. married and gave up work), Fridays after school were devoted to the Girl Guides. As leader of the Daffodil Patrol, she had two vertical stripes on the front pocket of her Guide dress, a strong leather belt, and a lanyard to go with her daffodil badge. Like other young women up and down the country, Cora learned to march in time and read signals. Hers were benign skills – lighting fires, tracking, making beds and earning badges in the process. The Guides met in the art room and, in summer, laid tracks in the school gardens, making signs with stones on the ground. When Lady Baden-Powell visited Chesterfield, the floral patrols joined the town's other Guides in marching round the football pitch and offering a three-fingered salute. On less ceremonial days there were campfire sing-songs (minus the campfire), 'Riding Down from Bangor on an Eastern Train', and similar rousing numbers. There was also a camping trip to Richmond, Yorkshire, for a real taste of life under canvas: my mum demurred.

VE Day brought celebrations all round and the sale of red, white and blue commemorative buttons. Frances Partridge described children wearing red, white and blue ribbons in their hair; Naomi Mitchison saw similarly beribboned children waving flags on the train from Scotland to London, and again in London itself. 'Most people were wearing bright coloured clothes, lots of them red, white and blue in some form.' Mollie Panter-Downes reported exploding squibs, exuberant conga lines, linked arms and singing and 'girls in their thin, bright dresses . . . In their freshly curled hair were cornflowers and poppies, and they wore red-white-and-blue ribbons around their narrow waists. Some of them even tied ribbons around their bare ankles.'

My mum and grandma were holidaying in Llandudno with a school friend and her mother in August 1945, the first week's holiday they had ever had. When news of America's victory over Japan was announced there was dancing on the end of the pier and my mum twirled around in the arms of an American soldier. But the revelation of the Nazi concentration camps and news of

Hiroshima and Nagasaki meant that all celebration was tinged with shock and no one was certain what would happen next. A young ATS officer Naomi Mitchison met in 1944 could not imagine what it would be like 'to be grown-up but not in the Army' and, in 1945, Lucia Lawson, by now a Company Sergeant Major in Paris, working in the public relations office of the Allied Expeditionary Force, contemplated the end of the war.

Already I am scared – what's going to happen afterwards, what is it like when there isn't a war . . . What will I do when I don't have to get up in the morning, don't have to dress the way I'm told, all these questions to which I can find no answer, and questions which people like me are asking all over the world?

Emma Smith's sister Pam commemorated peace with

a symbolic gesture . . . chopping off the plaits which were normally twined around her head like a sort of halo, and allowing her blonde hair to swing loose in a shoulder-length pageboy bob . . . Overnight she reverted, effortlessly, to the character of an eighteen-year-old student, as though the war, that long dark passage of suffering and loss, had not after all been the destroyer of carefree youth, but merely, instead, an interruption to what could be resumed at the exact point where it had so arbitrarily been broken in upon.

Sylvia Townsend Warner took a different view: 'the temple of Janus has two doors, and the door for war and door for peace are equally marked in plain lettering, No Way Back.'

16 **THE VELVET FLOWERS:** HATS

'If you are going to wear a hat at all, be decisive and go the whole hat,' Alison Adburgham decreed. Many women have followed that maxim. Chocolate-box confections, cream puffs, galleons, outsize doilies – hats have been many things, including occasions for mirth and music-hall merriment. There are everyday hats, hats that cheer, hats for Sunday best, even hats to steal a march on friends. In Lettice Cooper's novel *The New House* (1936) Evelyn is advised by her mother, who has learned a thing or two about keeping up appearances on limited means, that she should 'have a new winter hat at the very beginning of the autumn, and a new summer hat very early in the spring'. That way, friends noticed your new hat while they were still wearing their old ones.

Hats like soup plates were all the rage when my grandma was a young woman. Not only were their circumferences large, their decoration knew no bounds: flowers, fruit, shells – sometimes all at once – plus plumage so extravagant it threatened British birds. The Edwardian taste for things feathered led to the creation in 1904 of the Royal Society for the Protection of Birds to curb millinery excess. A hat Annie wore during this period was relatively restrained, being limited to flowers, but was a whopper nonetheless. At a wedding she attended, the female guests stood some distance apart from one another to accommodate their different headgear. Turner's department store promised modish styles that were neither 'extreme nor conspicuous', but definitions of conspicuous change: its advertisement featured hats whose ostrich plumes stood at least eighteen inches proud of the crown.

The velvet flowers that lay on top of my grandma's buttons when they came to me belong to the 1920s. By this time common sense reigned and hats were now more discreet. The cloche hat was in vogue and women like Annie, who could not afford to buy a new hat each year, let alone each season, decorated their own, applying new trimmings as fashion or fancy dictated. Women's magazines offered advice on how to trim one hat six different ways; the tills of haberdashery departments rang with purchases of ribbon, braid, and flowers. Eileen Whiteing recalled that hand-made artificial flowers shaped in silk or velvet were 'quite exquisite' back then. The button-box flowers, with their papery green leaf and solid stamens (now, sadly, cracked) were once bright and blooming, and are not unlike the appliqué trim decorating the Victoria & Albert Museum's pink straw hat made by Kilpin Ltd, circa 1925. Millie Levine recalls with fondness, more than eighty years later, her first grown-up hat, a cloche circled with marigolds.

Whatever their style and function, hats were an essential part of a woman's wardrobe well into the twentieth century. Hats conferred respectability; to go without was to be improperly dressed. (In the eighteenth century, a top London hotel refused admittance to any woman without a hat.) *How to Dress Well* was of the opinion that, of all items of clothing, hats performed a 'diplomatic mission' by bringing an outfit together.

In the era of my grandma's velvet flowers, cloche hats could

be purchased off-the-peg in the wide variety of colours that signified modernity. *Good Housekeeping*'s Shopping Service offered
straw hats in copper beech, poppy, cyclamen, hyacinth and jade.
Green was so popular that *The Green Hat* even gave its name to
a fashionable novel. An Irish linen cloche hat cost the interwar
woman 14*s* 11*d*, but little felts or straws were nearer 6*s*, and a
bobbed or shingled hairstyle to go beneath them 1*s* 6*d*. My great-
aunt Eva bought a decidedly chic cloche hat, closer to a skull
cap in shape, which gripped her head like a helmet and whose
brim swept back on each side of her face; a photograph shows a
well-heeled young woman wearing something similar. Mistress
Fashion ruled the day and evidently hats could be as democra-
tising as dresses. Those with means shopped at little milliners
like Brighton's La Maison Blanche which advertised 'exquisite
millinery and evening head dresses'. Chesterfield had Madame
Lucille and Maison Meta, whose very names were a draw; in
1936, the town had twelve milliners as well as millinery departments providing a personal service within larger stores. Women
fortunate enough to wear bespoke hats advertise their milliner,
which is why, when Nancy Astor took her seat in Parliament,
she received free hats by the dozen.

   T. J. Rendell joined the staff of Liberty as an apprentice milliner
in 1926. In this role she was paid the statutory rate of 1½*d* an
hour, a token fee while training, for a forty-four-hour week. With
the exception of the Workroom Head and First Hand, even fully
trained milliners were only paid 7½*d* an hour, which amounted
to approximately 30*s*. This 'was insufficient to live on, since a
bed-sitting room with food generally cost about that amount . . .
[and] meant that only girls with comfortable homes or working
husbands could do this kind of thing. We had a maid once who
said that she would have liked to have done millinery, but owing
to lack of money was obliged to go into service.'

Millinery had long been regarded as a respectable profession for young women with artistic flair. Ms Rendell progressed from making linings for simple felts and straws to cutting out the famous silk scarves with which many of Liberty's hats were trimmed, before progressing to the milliner's skill of shaping hats on blocks. She decorated raffia hats with posies and individual flowers, creating the pattern as she went, and during the summer of 1928, when all things painterly were in vogue, actually painted hats. Millinery was a seasonal trade, and so during slack periods Ms Rendell made up hats for the next season and, occasionally, stitched soft toys. Margaret Broughton, a young milliner working in a provincial establishment, had the more sobering task of stitching shrouds in quiet moments.

There were few quiet moments for Marjorie Gardiner who sold hats during the 1920s, when retail workers were reliant on commission and *not* to sell was a cardinal sin. She enjoyed her first job in a small exclusive shop with an artistically dressed window containing the obligatory single gown, hat and vase of flowers, but her next establishment, although equally smart, and with two showrooms, a Head Milliner and four girls, was a much harsher regime. Dressed in black from head to toe, including black satin shoes, Marjorie and the other sales staff stood throughout the day – often until 9 p.m. on Saturday evenings – with the shop door open, regardless of the weather, their faces fixed in smiles – like the young worker in Katherine Mansfield's short story 'The Tiredness of Rosabel', who must tolerate the customer who tries on every single hat before saying she will 'call in tomorrow and decide definitely'. A steely-eyed madame observed Marjorie's every move; incurring her displeasure meant instant dismissal with no reference.

It takes confidence to wear a hat well. 'The oddest little shapes alighted like birds on [Evelyn's] trim pale gold hair', but not everyone has the fictional Evelyn's knack of finding a hat to suit her. Christian Dior advised readers of *Woman's Illustrated* not to copy his models, but to try a hat several ways until they found the most becoming angle for them. Most women simply followed fashion. The lengths some went to be in the swim was captured by a cartoon in which a woman wears her feathered hat at a rakish, tipsy angle: 'Darling! It's perfect,' a friend tells her. 'You look absolutely blotto.'

Magazines advised how the right ribbon flourish could add a note of individuality but, more often than not, uniformity triumphed. Invited to speak at the Women's Institute, the Provincial Lady is 'introduced to felt hat and fur coat, felt hat and blue jumper, felt hat and tweeds, and so on'; some twenty-five years later, a Barbara Pym heroine observes that

> there was a particular kind of hat worn by ladies attending Parochial Church Council meetings – a large beret of neutral-coloured felt pulled well down to one side. Both Mrs Crampton and Mrs Mayhew wore hats of this type, as did Miss Doggett, though hers was of a superior material . . . Indeed, there seemed to be little for the ladies to do but observe each other's hats, for their voices were seldom heard.

Best hats were a different matter. Whether following or disdaining fashion, women took pride in these. Picture postcards record all manner of headgear. At a time when hats were ubiquitous, some postcards may have simply recorded special occasions at which hats were worn, but others undoubtedly recorded special hats.

Though some hats were unique, hats were seldom singular: women wore a hat *and* gloves. How to find the right hat and gloves to complement an outfit was a mission in itself. May Smith conveyed her pride in succeeding. 'Garbed myself in my new autumn attire – blackberry coat, black hat with petunia ribbon, petunia scarf, black gloves, shoes and handbag – and, thus attired, swaggered forth feeling like Solomon in all his glory.' On this occasion, as on many others, May's new clothes received their first airing in church. Until 1942, when, with wartime shortages worsening, the Archbishop of Canterbury decreed that women's heads need no longer be covered in church, no respectable woman attended hatless.

Post-war relaxation saw a revival of frivolity. Alison Adburgham recorded 'A wonderful year for hats' in 1956. 'One rose, or roses galore . . . soufflés of whipped-up tulle, charlottes of frothed organza . . . toadstools of black net . . . hair-dryers . . . big white drums . . . beehives . . . mob-caps'. And that was only five months in. Nonetheless, the war had loosened the hat's grip; women no longer felt compelled to observe the rules in quite the same way. What really finished off the hat as an insistent symbol was the 1960s, which finished off so many other symbols of conformity. Jean Shrimpton's appearance at the Melbourne Races in 1965 wearing neither hat nor gloves was considered newsworthy and sounded the hat's death knell. Soon, young women wore hats only when they chose – the crochet caps of the 1960s (which were not a million miles away from the cloche), broad, floppy brimmed hats or Faye Dunaway berets. More recently the special-occasion fascinator has held sway. Wearing what you like is a long way from wearing what you must.

Elsa Schiaparelli's surrealist shoe hats raised eyebrows in 1937; today, we look in awe at some of Philip Treacy's millinery creations: hats have always inspired the adventurous. During the 1930s, the Newcastle branch of Fenwick's department store proudly announced The Glass Hat, 'transparent . . . glinting . . . with a picture brim to see your eyes and curls! But wearably pliable, and stitched with a band of soft blue velvet.' It is hard to think who might be tempted by this creation, except, perhaps, the occupant intended for Oliver Hill's all-glass room, seen at an exhibition of modern design in 1933, with its glass bed and glass table, standing on a glass floor. And if any woman *was* brave enough to step out wearing the Glass Hat, then – hats off to her.

17 **THE COAT BUTTON:** POST-WAR AND THE NEW LOOK

'I think we all feel that after the war we shall just throw away the whole bloody lot of things and never darn or mend or make do again,' Naomi Mitchison told her diary, but with clothing rationed until 14 March 1949, improvisation of one kind or another still came high on the list. Newly demobbed Joan Wyndham dyed her WAAF uniform 'a smart forest green' and enlivened it with a tight leather belt; Katharine Whitehorn and fellow students at Newnham College, Cambridge, also dyed their clothes 'when we could not bear them any longer' and relied on the college sewing machine, the inexperienced among them crossing their fingers that the thread would not break.

My mum delighted in a neighbour's gift of a very nearly new wine-coloured coat in bouclé wool. Coats are your greeting to the outside world and she was thrilled with this one and its six buttons in descending sizes, five of which I have in my button box today. A welcome parcel also arrived from her new American penfriend which, in a private echo of the wartime clothing scheme, Bundles for Britain, contained a stylish dress and two wool skirts and jumpers. The majority of Cora's clothes were still home-made, including, in a late flowering of Annie's tailoring skills, a fully lined sand-coloured belted coat which drew compliments from those who saw it. Cora wore the coat with a pair of high-heeled lace-ups similar to those in a 1946 advertisement for Church's shoes: 'Just arriving', its shout line announces '. . . but still, of course, in limited numbers.' This was the message frequently dangled before would-be shoppers. 'Smart frock seen in Piccadilly – copied at home in "Spava" fabric: scarce but obtainable.' Utility clothing was still being produced, although in smaller numbers; manufacturing restrictions still applied to buttons, as to so much else. Rationing of one kind or another staggered on until 1954, with some of the worst scarcities, including a textile shortage, actually experienced after the war.

Wartime stringencies were still in place, but the mood had changed. Nella Last wanted to 'explain to Tom Harrison [the founder of Mass Observation] just how laughter has fled'. Even as a young woman discovering adult life and with plenty to distract her, my mum observed that too: the sense of camaraderie that had bound people together had passed. As if to exemplify this, *Modern Woman* advised on 'Food for the Fed-Up'. Something was needed to lift the spirits. Visiting Paris three months after the war ended, *Vogue* editor Audrey Withers saw

a remarkable vindication of the belief . . . that not only our needs but our whole outlook is determined by the way we dress. In England we were wearing big overcoats with hoods, and flat-heeled shoes . . . We wanted to be ready for anything asked of us. Paris was in a totally different situation. Occupied by the Germans, its people wanted to cock a snook at them . . . They were wearing shoes with platform soles inches high, and towering hats.

With its gusts of fabric and insistence on Plenty, Christian Dior's 1947 New Look certainly cocked a snook. Reporting from Paris that autumn, *Vogue*'s fashion editor explained, 'The skirt may be full-petal-shaped or spreading with unpressed pleats. It may be straight. But either way it descends to anything from fourteen to eight inches from the floor.' The New Look's appearance in Britain six months later immediately aroused controversy. The style hit the headlines as well as the fashion pages, with questions asked in the House of Commons by a number of Labour MPs. MP Mabel Ridealgh, ex-Regional Coordinator of Britain's 'Make Do and Mend' campaign, was outraged by the prospect of women succumbing to what she saw as an extravagant and wasteful fad at a time when manufacturers were struggling to find materials, and asked Harold Wilson, then President of the Board of Trade, to prevent the production of large quantities of longer coats and dresses; Wilson wisely refused to become embroiled in debates about how women should dress. MP Jean Mann wanted to know why a New Look skirt, which may require up to twenty yards of cloth, 'can be had for four coupons while a gentleman has to sacrifice 26 . . . for a suit which contains only 3¼ yards'. Bessie Braddock MP described the style as 'the ridiculous whim of idle people'. 'Women today are taking a larger part in the happenings of the world,' Ridealgh wrote in *Reynolds News*: 'The New Look is too reminiscent of a caged bird's attitude.' It was the late 1920s all over again, with arguments about descending hemlines. Were women to be returned to an extreme femininity?

Correspondence in *The Times* straddled the different opinions. Women were instinctively seeking 'variety and change', or else 'bullied, cajoled and subtly inveighed' into altering their wardrobes; the New Look was either 'deplorably ugly' or pleasingly feminine, depending on your point of view. Femininity was key after all those military-style suits. No more ramrod backs; the New Look had sloping shoulders as well as a considerably fuller, longer skirt and a cinched waist. It was not just a question of style, however. Audrey Withers recalled how the New Look required a change of posture. 'Suddenly I found myself having to pick my skirt up in two hands to go up the steps of a bus and I realised that I hadn't seen that gesture since I'd seen my mother before the First World War.'

In an echo of the eighteenth-century court mantua whose even more exaggerated shape required women to turn sideways to enter rooms, photojournalist Grace Robertson saw a woman struggling to board a London bus. 'A crowd had gathered. Her skirt was so wide, she couldn't negotiate the door. At first, I laughed with everyone else. But then I suddenly thought: are they putting us into these clothes so we can't get on buses, and take their jobs?', a pertinent fear in the post-war climate of economic uncertainty.

The look *was* new, however, and women wanted it. Conversely, many saw the style as an expression of freedom from restraint. Art-school student and later RCA tutor Joanne Brogden made 'the biggest skirt in the whole world, apart from a genuine Dior, out of blackout material'. Retail assistant Jo, who worked in a smart hat shop that was part of Claridge's hotel, was delighted to be 'among the first in London to wear it' when a friend's mother copied the style for her; Jenifer Wayne, by now a trainee BBC radio producer, recalled the excitement and romance of her first New Look suit. 'For one post-war summer, at least, I felt I was "with it".'

Selfridge's advertised high-heeled shoes 'to enhance the new look'; Marshall & Snelgrove reported that it was selling nothing but the new style. Its sales assistants wanted to wear it too. In the autumn of 1948, Margaret M. Trump 'bought a good pattern and a length of navy-blue Moygashel linen, and made [herself] a passably fashionable dress, with a rolled collar over a simple "V"-neck, a gently flared new-length skirt, and those ubiquitous, so-useful three-quarter sleeves', before setting off for London and a job in that department store. A fellow junior member of staff who 'saved up and bought herself everyone's heart's desire – a grey flannel New Look suit – nipped-in waist, perky basque standing out over the almost ankle-length skirt', was the envy of all her peers: 'she looked perfect in it.'

'The "New Look": Chesterfield Women "Just Not Interested"' was a 1948 headline in the *Derbyshire Times*. Unlike Paris and London, its stores had no plans for extensive New Year sales to clear existing stock to make way for the new style. 'One enterprising shop' introduced two coats in the New Look, but although several customers expressed approval, they 'lacked the coupons and the courage to wear them!' Fashion will out, however. Rosalie Bailey caused a 'minor sensation' when she appeared in Chesterfield town centre in May that year dressed in a 'startling vivid scarlet "New Look" two-piece'. People stared, and one seventeen-year-old was so overwhelmed that he failed to see an oncoming bus (a mistake that earned him a broken leg and a plaster cast as well as some column inches). The following morning, Rosalie enhanced her New Look suit with a smart veiled hat, and armed with a Red Cross collection box, set off into town again.

She pounded the pavements . . . in the morning, held up the crowds going to the football match in the afternoon, and, still not satisfied . . . did a round of the Recreation Ground during the match. Tommy Lawton [a football celebrity] . . . suffered a debit of 3/- when this young lady stuck a flag on the lapel of his hacking jacket.

The £16 2s she achieved was said to be a record for an individual collector. 'Note for the Ladies', the *Derbyshire Times* journalist appended his article: 'Miss Bailey told a representative . . . that this new length (hem 14 ins. from the ground) was all the rage in the West End of London, where the costume was made.' 'Chesterfield is too drab,' Miss Bailey said. 'Someone has to bring things up-to-date and it might as well be me.' My mum's first New Look garment was a lime-green coat with large Perspex buttons, bought from Voce, a stylish town-centre costumier. Striding under the colonnades of the town's Tudorbethan shops, Chesterfield's young women introduced the new world to a mock version of the old one, swishing past pedestrians in their sweeping coats and skirts.

By the end of 1948 it was estimated that as many as 10 million women either had or desired the New Look. Desire was the thing of course. No more shabby suits or matted woollens, but something elegant and chic and, as historian Sheila Rowbotham has noted, the sheer joy of having what you wanted after years of doing your bit and going without. If so, the New Look also highlighted what some women could not have. Lorna Sage recalled a 'memorable fuss' when, aged five, she cut out – or cut up – 'the ladies from the Oxendale's catalogue in their New Look long skirts and picture hats'. Unwittingly, she had mutilated 'the very stuff of . . . dreams'. The pictures were the closest her mother would come to the desired new style. Historian Carolyn Steedman recalls her own mother

> tearing up the ration book over my sister's pram, outside the library in the High Street when meat came off points in the summer of 1951 . . . and then looking across the street at a woman wearing a full-skirted dress, and then down at the forties straight-skirted navy blue suit she was still wearing, and longing, irritatedly, for

the New Look; and then at us, the two living barriers to twenty
yards of cloth.

Later, they visited her mother's home town, Burnley. There was
'no New Look . . . in Burnley either. The post-war years were
full of women longing for a full skirt and unable to make it.'

WOMAN'S CLOTHING BUDGET

This is how one thirty-eight-year-old mother of three children managed to keep her spending down to the minimum in 1949.

	Per Year £	s	d
Dress at £2 2s 0d every 3 years		14	0
Coat and skirt (second hand)		12	6
Odd skirt (second hand)		2	6
Overcoat at £6 6s 0d once every 3 years	2	2	0
Raincoat (second hand)		12	6
Jumper		3	6
Hat at 17s 6d once in 3 years		5	10
Shoes at £1 10s 0d once in 2 years		15	0
Stockings, 12 pairs a year at 3s	1	16	0
Under slip		7	6
Vest, 2 a year at 5s 6d		11	0
Knickers, 4 pairs a year at 6s 6d	1	6	0
Corset	1	1	0
Nightdress, one in 2 years at £1 10s 0d		15	0
Apron, 3 a year at 4s		12	0
Wool for gloves		2	0
Handkerchiefs, 2 a year at 1s		2	0
Shoes repaired every 3 months at 10s 6d	2	2	0
Total	**14**	**2**	**4**

The Pound in Your Pocket 1870–1970, P. Wilsher (1970)

18 **THE SMALL, DRAB BUTTON:** OFFICE LIFE IN THE 1950S

Small, drab buttons have always been essential to women workers. Whether black, brown, grey or navy, shank or sew-through, these are not the pearls of the button box in any sense. Undistinguished buttons like these exist in quantity: my button box holds a small drab button for almost every working day of the month. Similar, yet different, like weekdays themselves – they fasten functional garments and, as surely as Monday morning comes around each week, are part of working life.

In 1945 Cora took a year-long secretarial course at her mother's expense. At the local technical college she learned to type to music and, after 'We'll make a bonfire of our troubles and watch them blaze away' was taught, in accordance with Pitman's Shorthand Notebook, how to apostrophise '6 doz. Men's Caps: 4 doz Boys' Vests: and 3 doz Girls' Tam o' Shanters.' On her first day in the secretarial department of a large industrial firm, Cora typed a letter to her grandad, outlining her various tasks – taking dictation, Gestetnering, distributing post, and so on. 'It's a bobby's job,' she told him, adopting the family phrase associated with any work that was none too taxing (so-called because the bobby on the corner-shop beat saw little to disturb his perambulations).

Miss Maskrey, the department supervisor, read poetry and encouraged sing-songs and knitting to occupy quiet moments. Those who, back in the 1900s, thought women should be at home in their pinnies and not unspooling wool across typewriter keys, would have had their worst fears confirmed. In 1950 Cora graduated to something more demanding, with better pay (£6 and more a week), as assistant to the Managing Director's secretary: a desirable post with longer hours, more responsibility (and no time for knitting pullovers).

The MD's secretary wore suits, as did Miss Roberts, secretary to the Company Secretary; Miss Maskrey favoured a smart conservative dress. Cora wore skirts and blouses, the majority made by Annie. Rationing was still in force, but my grandma continued to produce her trademark flourishes: blouses buttoned off-centre or tied at the throat. My mum added detachable ribbon bows, shortcuts for enlivening a plain blouse or dress – plaid bow Monday, scarlet Tuesday . . .

The other office junior with whom she initially ran errands and out-smarted whomever got in their way (as young women in an overwhelmingly male firm they needed to be deft at back-chat) was her close friend, who later became my godmother. She too went on to something more rigorous than distributing Friday cakes and, when I was a child, was the only woman close to me who was an office worker. My godmother came to tea each Tuesday in the navy blue skirt, white blouse and navy court shoes that comprised her office 'uniform'. These clothes were a window on to a mysterious adult world; even her Perspex pencil box and leather office bag fascinated me, as did the way she wore her hair in a neat French pleat which was nothing like her off-duty look.

This female corner of office life conveyed something altogether different from that suggested by my father's weekday suits and was far more intriguing because, one day, it might be mine.

My grandma's work for the Provident Clothing Company was of a different order; my great-aunt Eva's shop-work too; neither job held the faintest intimation of glamour. I gave no thought to my mum returning to paid work, but I knew I would work one day. I remember standing before the window of a (small, drab) dress shop as a very young child and deciding what I would wear when my turn came. By then, man-made fibres had transformed life for the office worker. She could hang her skirts and pastel-coloured blouses, as well as her stockings, over the bath to drip-dry. 'Terylene – The Wonder Fabric of the Future . . . has outstanding advantages', Marks & Spencer's in-house magazine announced in 1955: 'it resists stretching as well as creasing, it is quick drying and most important, it is shrink proof, moth proof and rot proof. What qualifications for a smart and practical skirt!' Home-dressmakers were equally blessed. *Woman's Illustrated* recommended the 'Jiffy Dress' in candy-striped 'Super Tremendo' non-iron cotton. 'You can make it in a jiffy, wash it in a jiffy . . . And you *never* need to iron it!' And all for 5s 11d a yard.

The world of work had changed since my grandma joined it. Personal service (a figure including waitresses as well as domestic servants) still ranked top of the list, but did so with lower numbers (23 per cent of women in 1951 compared with 39 per cent in 1911); and the number of women entering clerical work had risen considerably: 20 per cent, compared with 2 per cent back then. The picture of post-war work was a chequered one. Some of the women who disappeared from the workforce in 1945 were soon needed again as part of the post-war reconstruction. Joan Holloway who applied for posts as a nursery nurse in 1945/6 'received a sackful of mail offering interviews'. Within a few years, diverse shortages in areas such as textiles, clothing, midwifery, nursing, domestic service, transport and secretarial work led to recruitment drives. Not everyone was as fortunate as Joan Holloway: Gail Lewis's Aunt Verna, who came to Britain from Jamaica around 1956 to train as a nurse, 'endured and survived incredible racism . . . as she made her contribution to the super-exploited pool of overseas nurses who helped Britain supply "the best public health service in the world"'.

The number of married women in the workforce was rising and would continue to do so. Whereas only 14 per cent worked in 1911, by 1951 they numbered 40 per cent. Despite this, the abiding image of the woman worker was that she was young and single – like Lucy, who, thanks to her breakfast of Kellogg's Corn Flakes, is so full of energy that her fingers fly across the keys of a newfangled adding machine: 'Lucy's a bright girl, that's easy to see.' (So many messages in one advertisement.)

Professional women were making gains. By 1951 there were 6,487 women doctors, 150 barristers and 397 women engineers, and graduates such as journalists Katharine Whitehorn and Joan Bakewell, and children's publisher Kaye Webb, were embarking on exciting careers. Nonetheless, when Kay Smallsure wrote *How to Run Your Home Without Help* (1949), she assumed that the majority of career women giving their homes a 'brisk once over' before they left in the morning only had themselves to please (and that those who were married would find life difficult unless husbands did 50 per cent of the housework). Most women still had jobs, not careers, and the default assumption remained that women were best suited to caring roles. 'There is nothing healthier for a full body and mind than a day's work in a job that creates happiness for yourself and others,' *Woman's Illustrated* advised its readers in 1957. Inevitably, the world of work meant different things to different women. My mum loved her job but gave up work to start a family: there was never any question of her doing anything else. By contrast, Carolyn Steedman, whose own mother worked all her adult life 'had no awareness of the supposed stereotypical mother of that era – lipsticked and aproned, waiting at the door'.

Bobby's jobs or not, creating happiness or otherwise, much women's work was repetitive. Sandra Levine's job was different, however, and must have seemed the height of sophistication when, in 1956, she was interviewed by *Woman* for a series depicting 'Young Success'. Sandra was the receptionist for the London-based Finders Limited, 'the agency that undertakes to find anything anyone can reasonably want'. Educated at North London Collegiate (the school that, back in the 1880s, required M. V. Hughes to stitch a buttonhole before admitting her to its ranks), she worked as an optician's receptionist (for £4 10s) and a lab technician (£3 10s) before a secretarial course led to a job 'finding the unlikely and doing the all-but impossible'. Sandra found a stuffed crocodile for a psychiatrist's waiting room, two 'cute cast-iron casseroles' for a Texan's wife, and having located a giant tortoise in Ecuador, arranged for its transportation to Michigan. 'My head is crammed with the oddest facts,' she told her interviewer, 'such as where to buy red-headed parrots and out-of-print Agatha Christie novels . . .' Finders Limited was Google *avant la lettre* – and with knobs on: not only did Sandra Levine locate the hard to find, she delivered it. 'I learned more about life in six weeks here than I could have learned in six years at the laboratory,' she said. 'I've learned to dress smartly, talk easily to strangers, cope with odd situations and handle six phones at once' – efficiency personified on a salary of £8 a week, plus luncheon vouchers.

The other women in the series offered more standard fare,

although the variety of jobs some tackled and the speed with which they moved from one to the next confirmed how easy it was to obtain work. Not all interviewees gave their salaries but, among those who did, a £15-a-week executive as 'agent for an American business firm' ranked highest; then came the journalist responsible for the 'Miss Manchester' column on the *Manchester Evening News* (£14 4s). A ballroom dancer and a show jumper provided a perhaps predictable period allure, as did the nanny to the children of actor Jack Hawkins (£5 a week all found). The new world of television was represented by an ATV production assistant, a 'backroom girl', earning £9 a week, while 'Pamela' who 'parachuted into romance' by marrying the flight lieutenant who assisted her parachute instructor, probably fulfilled many a 1950s dream.

Sandra Levine had a head start in the matter of office clothes: her father, Isadore (Sid), was a tailor. Tailoring was in Sid's blood. He started work in his father's firm at the age of three, unpicking tacking threads and progressed, via buttonholes, to designing, measuring and tailoring, before graduating to his own business. (Still tailoring in his nineties, Sid never touched a sewing machine.) During the war, his factory supplied army uniforms, but when the need for these dried up switched to women's clothing, assisted by his wife Millie who joined the firm to do the paperwork. Two hundred and fifty thousand coupons were needed to make the transition and Millie knew how to get them. She recalls how, wearing a black silk shirt and a black coat with a black fur collar, both designs courtesy of Sid (but no hat, as hats were still hard to come by), she set off to persuade ministry officials. Throughout her meeting, Millie smiled and flattered and crossed her legs in her black silk stockings, explaining that there was a good job waiting if only they had the coupons to buy the necessary yards of cloth. Millie's flirting did the trick: they were issued with 350,000. Post-war shortages, including of textiles, meant there were still obstacles to overcome; bouclé wool was popular as it did not easily reveal flaws, and although the number of buttons that could be placed on coats was still restricted to six, Sid found ways to get round that. Millie and daughter Sandra were always the first to wear his new designs, effectively showcasing the business.

Earning money in the late forties and early fifties enabled my mum to buy new clothes, especially coats with their broad hug-me shapes of all-enveloping wool and often outsize buttons. Like many working women, she liked a new style each year: after the lime-green coat with Perspex buttons came a powder-blue swagger coat; and then a heavy black coat with a velvet collar and a dog-tooth check that could be belted or left to drape. How I wish I had those coats, let alone their buttons, but I do have a green button from the shawl-collared coat my mum wore in the late 1950s when she was expecting me and to which I gave new life as a young working woman some twenty years later.

The making and sale of clothes was changing. Department stores, with their ready appeal to women workers, were on the rise (as were the number of women employed in them). A retail assistant recalled selling a range of knitwear with the dolman sleeves that were all the rage: 'I remember one line at 35s 6d, made in black, navy and maroon, which sold at an alarming rate and must, I feel, have graced every office in town.' In store and out, however, the old divisions and demarcations of social class were still thriving. One *Woman* interviewee, a twenty-one-year-old Under-Buyer for the Model Suit department of an Oxford Street store, had risen through the ranks in every sense, having started out as a trainee, and in Inexpensive Dress. Margaret M. Trump, who arrived at Marshall & Snelgrove in her New Look suit, was extremely disappointed to find herself allocated to Inexpensive

Gowns and not to Model Gowns as expected. Staff took their
cachet from the clothes they sold and her Buyer, 'understandably
anxious to rise above the "Inexpensive" stigma', used 'every ruse
within her power to pull the trade of [the] department up-market'.
Other aspects of department-store life also harked back to earlier
times: like her nineteenth-century forebears, Margaret lodged in
a hostel (the Debenham Ladies' Club, at £1 10s of her weekly
starting salary of £2 5s) and, in a further and disconcerting
throwback, was told on arrival at the store that as a Margaret
already worked there, she would be known as Mary.

Model Gowns apart, the variety, improved quality and ease of
ready-made clothing was altering the landscape for good. When
Skylon rose from London's blitzed South Bank as part of the
Festival of Britain in 1951, *Vogue* included a feature on 'The Rise
of the Ready-to-Wear' in a special 'Britannica' issue and told its
readers: 'The most fastidious and fashion-conscious woman can
dress immediately for any occasion in ready-to-wear clothes.'
Vogue's own editor Audrey Withers favoured ready-to-wear
clothing; foreign fashion buyers sought British off-the-peg clothes.

Worthing dressmaker Esther Rothstein, whose staff had stitched
beaded frocks in the 1920s, figure-hugging bias cuts in the 1930s,
and conjured suits from linen sheets during the abstemious war
years, tackled the competition head on. In 1951 she opened her
own clothes shop.

> [T]here was much improvement in this field by then. Indeed I was
> rather taken aback on one occasion when one of my clients, on
> seeing the dress I had just finished for her, remarked 'my goodness,
> it is just like a ready made!' . . . I still had my very experienced
> staff who began doing alterations to the 'ready mades' in addition
> to dressmaking which by this time was gradually dying out.

Little dressmaking establishments may have been in decline, but the home-dressmaker was still a force. A 1950s advertisement shows a Singer Sewing Centre with a space-age appearance asserting its own place in the future.

Chesterfield had one or two of its own little shops similar to Esther Rothstein's, including Miss Grieves and Marjorie Willett who were still in business and who, from time to time, supplied my mum with interesting clothes. Although she enjoyed that era's hug-me coats, she preferred its slender suits and dresses. In 1953 she bought a double-breasted blue-grey suit with a hip-length waisted jacket for a wedding, and a short-sleeved blue dress with an extravagantly fluted peplum. Would that she had hung on to these. Both came from Miss Grieves who was given to wearing smart suits herself. Annie was still making some of Cora's clothes, although by now, her creations were reserved for eveningwear in a decade which afforded plenty of opportunities for dinner dances.

Whether elegantly draped or stiffly petticoated, both 1950s looks were accompanied by costume jewellery and full make-up – 'When you're really going to town your make-up must be Max-Factor Pan-Cake'. Models adopted 'kiss a butterfly' pouts, broad-brushed caterpillar eyebrows and pussycat eyes. Static creatures all and, above all, ladylike, a look widely copied by young women striving to appear grown-up and dress like their mothers. Joan Wyndham favoured Max Factor Pan-Cake number 2, Coty powder and a dash of Yardley's Cherry lipstick.

The highly stylised and exaggerated femininity of the period meant that permanent waves kept hair in its place, collars were stiff, blouses trim and neatly pressed, and that trousers – no longer sensible wartime wear – were unacceptable in many circumstances; a young employee joining Barclays Bank in 1952 was instructed: 'no "bare" legs, no sandals and definitely no trousers'.

Pierced ears were frowned upon – until the Queen had her own ears pierced. Lorna Sage described the 'rich variety of sumptuary laws concerning fashion and decency': what was and was not permissible for nice young ladies to wear; older women too. Jenifer Wayne recalled the effort – and the bravado – required to maintain this pristine look. Radio actor Mary O'Farrell, a woman in her fifties, was in those days, described as 'well preserved'.

> Her originally natural red hair was kept tinted; she always came to the studio in a hat, earrings, make-up, conservatively elegant suit, coat or dress with a spray costume-brooch on the lapel; fine silk stockings and Good shoes . . . I came to know what went on behind it: with what gallantry it was produced.

Mary lived in a mews flat near Broadcasting House, but the flat was down at heel and she shared the tiny airless space with a fragile elder sister she probably supported, and a great many cats and their 'half-licked saucers'. Mary's graceful appearance was exceedingly hard-won. On air, she was 'radiant. I find it very touching that she could have walked out of that terrible flat, day after day, looking as if she had just stepped up from Bond Street.'

19 **THE 'PERFECT' BUTTON:** THE ETIQUETTE OF DRESS

When Cora was fourteen or fifteen she came upon a slim book, *Etiquette for Ladies,* which she read from cover to cover because she wanted to know how 'ladies' should behave. She wrote her name on the fly leaf and the date, 1944, but the book itself was of a considerably earlier vintage and charted a life unlikely to be hers – Afternoon Parties, Evening Receptions, Little Dinners, Presentation at Court . . .

The book's first chapter dealt with that all-important subject, Dress. 'The appearance is a continual letter of recommendation,' Cora was told, which is where the 'perfect' button comes in. The 'perfect' button is no such thing. This button is synthetic and nothing like mother-of-pearls with their individual markings, chips and flakes. This pearlised globe has no character but is known to women and girls who, in the mid-twentieth century, wore the machine-made white summer cardigans with ribbon facings which spoke of femininity and conformity.

The women of my great-aunt's generation could take lessons from a music-hall song. Though performed with a saucy smile and

a swish of frou-frou petticoats, it nonetheless put its point across:
'I'm not too forward, not too bold, I'm not too young, I'm not
too old, I'm not too hot, and I'm not too cold, I'm just the kind
you'd like to hold . . .' and so on; Eva sang the song herself. By
the 1930s, she was looking to her copy of *Home Management* which,
in addition to advising on home cookery, decoration, engaging
servants et al., contained a chapter on etiquette for women (with
a short sub-section on everyday etiquette for men). Beginning
with introductions, and progressing through the complicated gradations of acquaintanceship and friendship – 'If . . . introduced to
you at a dance or dinner-party, you are not bound to recognise
him the next time you meet if you would rather not continue the
acquaintance' – it detailed the appropriate way to leave visiting
cards; though in Eva's experience, visiting meant Sunday-afternoon
get-togethers in the room behind the shop, where a knock on the
back door immediately preceded its opening. When making conversation, Eva was advised to avoid mention of the weather, if possible,
something even E. M. Delafield's Provincial Lady is unable to
accomplish: 'we talk about the weather, Gandhi and French poodles.
(Why? There are none in the room, and can trace no association
of ideas whatsoever.)'

How to dress, how to converse; all of these were lessons in
how to get on, and also, ultimately, lessons in how to find a mate,
requiring young women to learn how to behave and to absorb a
prescribed femininity. As a young teenager in the 1950s, biog-
rapher Fiona MacCarthy 'read avidly if anxiously' a manual called
The Years of Grace compiled by novelist Noel Streatfeild which,
as well as advising 'how to behave at parties, how to train as a
secretary, how to make yourself attractive to the opposite sex',
provided advice on sport, including the all-important instruction
that, while 'Every girl ought to love sport . . . if she wants to be
nice and adorable and completely feminine, she will let men win

ALWAYS.' *Etiquette for Ladies, The Etiquette of Today, The Years of Grace,* the titles changed but the essential lessons did not. They introduced the myriad ways in which girls and young women are judged, and being judged, judged themselves.

Some of the greatest errors could be made without uttering a single word or lifting a tennis racquet. In Rose Macaulay's novel *Crewe Train* (1926), Denham, a reluctant convert to urbane niceties, discovers that

> life was like walking on a tight-rope. The things you mustn't do, mustn't wear. You must, for instance, spend a great deal of money on silk stockings, when, for much less you could have got artificial silk or lisle thread. Why? . . . Why did not anything do?
>
> The same with gloves, with shoes, with frocks, with garments underneath frocks. In all these things people had set up a standard, and if you did not conform to it you were not right . . . You wore thick stockings and brogues in the country, thin stockings and high-heeled shoes in the town. You wore a hat if you gave a lunch party, a sleeveless dress in the evening. You had, somehow or other, to conform to a ritual, to be like the people you knew.

No wonder readers of *Woman's Weekly* appreciated some guidance on how to dress (though Denham would not have stooped to such a downmarket publication).

Wearing the wrong thing can afflict us all. Perhaps the most famous description of the Wrong Dress belongs to Virginia Woolf's short story 'The New Dress'. Poor Mabel does not even make it out of the cloakroom before having 'her first serious suspicion that something was wrong', a suspicion that grows as soon as she enters the party: 'for oh these men, oh these women, all were thinking – "What's Mabel wearing? What a fright she looks! What a hideous new dress!" . . . She felt like a dressmaker's dummy

standing there, for young people to stick pins into.' Virginia Woolf
knew of what she wrote. She loved clothes but had a complicated
relationship with them, feeling intimidated by shop assistants and
cringing at taunts from Vita Sackville-West and Clive Bell. Woolf's
diary describes her 'love of clothes . . . only it is not love; & what
it is I must discover'; also, her 'clothes complex' and her 'idiotic
anguish . . . that wave of agony; about 2 in the morning', over a
dress for a dinner party. But the diary also conveys her 'great joy'
in having the money to 'give way to the temptation of 30/- dress'.
Woolf was thrilled when Madge Garland, then fashion editor of
Vogue, commissioned a dress and jacket for her, made by couturier
Nicole Groult, Paul Poiret's sister. With Madge Garland dressing
her, Woolf said, she would have more time to write.

As Virginia Woolf knew all too well, observations from friends
can be among the most lethal, though they are not necessarily
spoken out loud. Julia Strachey pinioned novelist Edith Olivier
in her diary by describing her arrival to dinner in a 'suburban'
evening dress (the worst sin in bohemian circles). Even Mildred
in Barbara Pym's *Excellent Women* gives vent to her feelings while
out shopping with a friend:

> 'I'm not sure that it's your colour,' I said doubtfully . . .
>   'Now you're talking like a fashion magazine,' said Dora, strug-
> gling with the zip-fastener. 'I've always had a brown wool dress
> for every day.'
>   Yes, and look at you, I thought, with one of those sudden flashes
> of unkindness that attack us all sometimes.

Humiliation could overwhelm women before they even left the
shop. A *Punch* cartoon in which a woman begs a friend, 'Oh,
please don't let her make me buy that,' relies on an all too familiar
recognition of the intimidating power of shop assistants, something

to which Virginia Woolf was also susceptible, 'being persuaded into a blue striped coat by an astute & human woman at Lewises'. Even a woman's own dressmaker was not necessarily on side. May Smith finds Mrs W. 'in Narky and Independent Vein'; worse still is the fictional, bullying Mrs Form created by Storm Jameson:

> Mrs Form's position in the town was one of absolute authority. She told her clients what they must wear and refused to make them anything else. A lady who brought her a length of crimson satin to make into a dress was told to use it for curtains. Another, who fancied herself still young, left Mrs Form's . . . in tears, with a roll of yellow muslin under her arm.

Ageing is always a delicate subject, viz. Isabella and Evalie who, in Elizabeth Taylor's novel *The Sleeping Beauty*, face middle age together. 'They counted up calories, bought new corsets and tried new face-creams; cut paragraphs out of magazines for one another and went together to the Turkish baths. They remained the same – two rather larkish school-girls . . . "We haven't changed enough," Isabella once said. "We don't any longer match our looks."' Sitting side-by-side in the steam-room, Evalie reflects, 'We look discarded, sitting here . . . As if we were waiting for a train which never comes.' 'I'm sure I've done everything I could think of,' Isabella says, 'those beauty articles . . . I could write them myself in my sleep . . . What I detest is the way our breasts go out sideways when we get older. They look as if they're tired of one another's company.' On matters such as these, etiquette manuals were ill-equipped to advise, even if, like *How to Dress Well*, they included instruction on dress for a 'Woman of 40' quickly followed by the 'Twilight Years'.

Size is an equally delicate topic. Aroon, Molly Keane's self-deceiving protagonist in *Good Behaviour*, a substantial woman in all ways, discovers that her two evening dresses have 'shrunken miserably in cleaning'. Seeking a remedy from the village dress-maker, she presents Mrs Harty with both the pink chiffon and the gold lace. Mrs Harty, a stuffed satin heart full of pins swinging between her breasts, faces a monumental challenge. Both are required to drape Aroon's bulk. 'Well, Miss Aroon,' Mrs Harty searches for the correct response: 'wouldn't you make a massive statue?'

By the 1950s, those long white kid gloves favoured by Edwardian ladies had mutated into full-length cotton ones for eveningwear and cuff-length white gloves for daytime. 'It was tough, in the fifties. Girls wore white gloves,' Angela Carter wrote, summing up the impossible conformity of that decade and her relief when the sixties arrived. Lorna Sage described receiving lessons in vulnerable femininity via instructions on how to wear the palest of pale 'discreet mouse make-up', in a lesson organised by her grammar-school headmistress who knew that, brains notwithstanding, young women had to look the part. Hence the immense relief generated by Katharine Whitehorn's 1963 article 'Sluts' which exposed the pretence of perfect femininity and was 'dedicated to all those who have ever changed their stockings in a taxi, brushed their hair with someone else's nailbrush or safety-pinned a hem' (though the idealised mothers of Ladybird Books still wore white gloves to go shopping).

Then as now, most lessons began at home. 'You're not going out in that!' is a long-standing refrain, as mothers tell their daughters what they can and cannot wear. 'Inappropriate' shoes were smuggled into schoolbags and sensible ones discarded at the garden gate, and waistbands turned over and over, the greater rebellions possible once youth hit the high streets in the rock 'n' roll years and the Swinging Sixties, and on through punk, new romantics, Goths . . .

Exploring the delights of vintage clothes in early-1980s London, I sometimes visited the American warehouse, Flip. There I found a snowy-white twinset, a short-sleeved jumper matched with a crew-necked cardigan, just like those crew-necked cardigans I wore in childhood. This one had the same synthetic pearl buttons and ribbon facings, but was over-stitched with silver thread and studded with pearl flowers, ready for its original owner to slip on her ballet pumps, shrug off conformity and rock around the clock.

20 **THE DOLL'S-HOUSE DOORKNOB:** HOMEMAKING LARGE AND SMALL

As soon as you see a doll's house, you want to open its doors and look inside. The doll's house doorknob is part of that enchantment. It is one of the stray objects that found a home in my grandma's button box. The doll's house I played with as a child still has the wooden doorknob I remember; the ceramic version is an earlier vintage but is just as round and pleasingly button-like, which is why it landed in the box in the first place.

The doll's house was my mother's before it came to me, though she was not its original owner. The house was built by a local draper, Andrew Neild, for his daughter in the 1920s. What shop furnishings it must have enjoyed: all those off-cuts – snips of brocade for net curtains; plaid strips turned into rugs, taffeta ribbon drapes for the parlour, satin bedspreads. It was possible to buy a toy draper's shop complete with peg-doll assistant, a customer, miniature scissors and bolts of cloth, although no child who lived above a shop needed one to play with when the real thing was downstairs. When the draper's daughter outgrew the house and it transferred to my mum, it acquired a grand piano and became home to several film stars. Who would have thought that Shirley Temple, Tyrone Power and Alice Faye were among those who sat on its red velvet chairs?

I have only vague recollections of the interior before the doll's house came to me – I remember a twist of metallic paper which stood in for the flames of a fire and the delicate wire tracery of a pot holding ceramic flowers. A hand-painted Bakelite clock stood on the bureau and, along with a three-piece suite my grandma re-upholstered, is the only relic from those years. The double-fronted house was completely refurbished – its slate roof re-papered, its white walls repainted and its window surrounds transformed by a 1960s light, bright blue which, at that point, matched the paintwork of my childhood home. The re-upholstered red velvet suite came with a single lace floret pinned to each chair. That, too, resembled real life in the form of the three-piece suite with its own antimacassars in our lounge.

The doll's-house chimney pots were slender painted cotton reels; a strip of red-brick paper was pasted at the base of the house. The stairs were re-carpeted in red corduroy, probably using the same piece of fabric with which my grandma made my favourite doll a handsome fur-collared coat. A knitting needle formed a satisfying hand rail (and newel post). Unbeknown to the casual observer, the house has two attics, accessible from the rear. As a child of her time, the 1920s draper's daughter may have required maids to sleep in those rough-hewn rooms; I had no such thoughts, but was delighted that those secret spaces existed, tucked away out of sight.

I too was a child of my time and so I re-papered two of the walls with sticky-backed plastic: pale pink with bronze dots for the bathroom and yellow with abstract diamond shapes for one of the rooms downstairs. I was not the only hooligan, however, because some other walls had already been redecorated in lumpy

wood-chip. Many years later, the downstairs room shamed me
by giving up its no-longer-so-sticky-backed plastic to reveal a
pretty 1930s wallpaper reminiscent of vintage summer frocks but,
in the early 1960s, vintage florals meant nothing to me.

Like the different wallpapers, the doll's house furniture
expressed the different decades in which it was played with. My
mum's suggested a typical thirties interior: its dark wood dining
suite had a sideboard with nail-head handles and a pattern
carved on its cupboard doors; a dark wooden block with fake
drawers represented a bureau. Some thirty years later, my own
dining suite, composed of hard plastic and 'contemporary', as
the word was then, was equally of its moment. Mine was a
G-plan style suite with stick legs and coloured chairs, some
green, others orange (the kind of chairs that have come around
again and are found in open-plan kitchens). My mum's doll's-
house furniture came from a Sheffield toyshop dedicated to
doll's houses which was bombed during the Blitz – all those
diminutive houses blasted and shattered, just like real ones;
mine came from Redgates, Chesterfield's over-stuffed toyshop,
where doll's-house furniture was part of the general mish-mash
of toys on sale.

My mother's miniature Queen Anne tea service imitated the
silver Queen Anne-style service my grandma bought when setting
up home while my grandfather was fighting in the Great War.
My own doll's house tea set was a clunky metal one for everyday
use, a bright kitchen blue with poorly modelled cups and saucers.
I also bought a set of aluminium saucepans, the largest of which
held a life-like ceramic cabbage with crinkled edges; to further
tempt Beatrix Potter's Hunca Munca two unattractive lamb
chops sizzled in a frying pan. Thanks to its film-star tenants my
mum's version of the house held more glamour; mine more
mod-cons. These included a metal telephone and slender tele-

phone table, and a record cabinet similar to the real-life Dynatron downstairs.

The house in which I grew up was built for my parents and was a model of a different kind. A sign of the post-war New Jerusalem and of all the hope held out at the start of the New Elizabethan era, it gave my mum the chance to choose furniture again and on a much larger scale. After all, playing with dolls and playing house are steps along the way towards the real thing.

A wartime survey concluded that most people wanted security before wealth and, after putting their lives on hold for six long years, many of them were all the more determined to settle down. Naomi Mitchison's diary records a conversation with a young ATS officer: 'The girls all wanted to be married and have homes of their own rather than to have careers, that was what the army had done to them; when [the officer] told them it was possible they mightn't all get married, they tore her to pieces.' *Punch* made a characteristic dig at the accelerated speed of some post-war romancing. A young woman sends a telegram: 'Marvellous evening – met B. – show – supper – dance – asked marry – under consideration – writing.'

Katharine Whitehorn and her friends 'all yearned for love'; they read and re-read Nancy Mitford's best-selling novel *The Pursuit of Love*, a welcome shot of wit and upper-class shenanigans after all that gritty austerity. Its young characters 'talked of romance. These were most innocent talks, for to us, at that time, love and marriage were synonymous, we knew that they lasted for ever, to the grave and far, far beyond.' For my mum, the immediate post-war world also meant romancing. Her autograph book contained a rhyme that was doing the rounds back then, 'X is her name, single is her station. Happy the man who makes the alteration.' No mention of the woman's happiness – that was taken for granted. This was the generation who believed that a diamond engagement ring with three small stones represented love today, tomorrow and always.

My parents met at a New Year's dance; there were so many dances back then, occasions for old-fashioned romancing via waltzes and foxtrots. When they married in 1950, my grandma took the second bedroom and gave the main one over to them. (At that time, Eva was still living at the corner shop with my great-grandparents.) Before waving the young honeymooners off for a week in Torquay, the wedding guests trooped upstairs to look at the clusters of roses with which my mum had re-papered the walls and the dark new bedroom suite with its Utility label. Downstairs, the sitting room had a recently purchased dining table and leatherette sofa. Out with the old chaise longue: my mum wanted something new. So did Chesterfield Council who were busy ripping out old lead ranges and replacing them with fawn-tiled fireplaces. Nella Last acquired her tiled fireplace during the 1930s; my grandma had to wait until 1949.

In her wartime 'Letter from London', Mollie Panter-Downes reported that, despite the housing shortage, 'a poll taken of urban housewives showed an overwhelming preference for houses instead of flats. In the middle of a global war, the British dream is still of a little box behind a hedge.' My parents were no different: they too wanted their own home – and a house with a garden. For some years after the Second World War, however, demand for new housing considerably out-stripped supply. Three-quarters of a million houses had been destroyed or severely damaged and major cities were still soiled by Victorian slums. Between 1945 and September 1948, 750,000 new houses were built; permanent housing accounting for almost half the total, the rest pre-fabs; there was still a long way to go. 'We're two of the lucky ones,' an advertisement for the Westminster Bank declared, illustrating the statement with a happy family group, echoing those seen in post-1918 advertisements. 'We have home, a job and two children . . . Some day we're going to buy our own house.' Some day, but not yet.

When my parents approached the Council in 1952, they joined the Housing Waiting List at number 2,001. 'Why not build your own home?' a colleague suggested to my father, and so my parents took that unprecedented step. A meeting with the town architect to ratify their plans called for best clothes and so my mum's honeymoon suit got a fresh outing, as did her honeymoon hat. My parents sat quietly and dutifully before the architect, who, in response to some anodyne remark about being a recently married couple, informed them that marriage without children was licensed fornication. That made them sit up straight and was surely an old-fashioned view, even then.

In 1955 only 29 per cent of people owned their own home; my parents were among the new breed of home-owners taking the future in hand. Photographs show the young couple on their own plot of land and Annie and Eva standing on the same spot, the younger generation taking a decision the older ones would never have dreamed of. The rented shop where Annie and Eva spent many years stood on the corner of a terrace built to celebrate Queen Victoria's Jubilee, with no hot water, one cold tap and a privy in a communal block across the yard; electricity did not arrive until the mid-1930s. In Annie's married home, the council house in which my mum grew up, the neighbour's kitchen window faced theirs; Cora was used to standing before the window in her pyjamas to wave goodnight. The house my parents built took them into new territory in every sense.

The house was completed in the year of the Queen's Coronation. A family friend presented my parents with an embroidered tray cloth as a house-warming gift. The cloth was decorated with flowers and coronets, with the auspicious year, 1953, picked out in mauve silk thread, the personal and the regal combining. As a marker of her new role, Cora hand-stitched a set of bathroom curtains. To help her accomplish this Herculean task Eva gave her a cream Bakelite box with the word 'Pins' scrawled across its lid in silver lettering, one of Eva's many 'treasures' that had fascinated Cora as a child: a small homemaking gift for a young homemaker.

The post-war emphasis on homemaking was insistent. Those uncertain how to go about it (many of whom had spent their recent years saluting), could read magazines like *The Home Decorator* or *Practical Householder*, or purchase a set of Woolworth's 'Homemaker' pottery which, as if to help young couples acquire the knack, set out a visual itinerary including splayed-legged tables, plants, a corkscrew and a cheese knife. Even tea towels became pictorial advisers, displaying the accoutrements of contemporary living, and in vivid patterns too – brightening those brand-new kitchens with blocks of primary colour. Young women were no longer embroidering hollyhocks but buying cacti and spider plants, and converting raffia-covered wine bottles into lamps. Like other young homemakers of the period, my parents bought a Formica-topped kitchen table, the latest thing and wipe-clean too. There was also a kitchen stool, which was not only practical but suggested there was no time for relaxing on weekday mornings in the new fast-moving world.

The majority of the receipts for my parents' early furnishings have survived (put into a bureau and long since forgotten) and so it is possible for me to see my childhood home take shape: a coffee table, a bedspread, the walnut bureau . . . Like many other homemakers of the period, their tastes straddled the contemporary and the traditional, G-plan furniture mixing with the Regency style that was enjoying a revival. The dining furniture was ordered in readiness for completion but the lounge remained unfurnished for nine months (ideal for the house-warming party) and the stairs were uncarpeted for a further three. Many families acquired a television set to watch the Coronation (or the World Cup) but my parents needed their money for bricks and mortar; it was 1957 before they purchased an Ecko TV. In the meantime (and thereafter), they numbered among the estimated 50 per cent of adults who were weekly cinema-goers.

When I became a home-owner in miniature, my purchases reflected those in the family home to an uncanny degree. Sadly, I did not have an 'exquisite little amber lamp with a white globe . . . all ready for lighting', like the one in Katherine Mansfield's story 'The Doll's House', nor a lamp that actually glowed, like that which delighted writer Emma Smith as a child. But I bought, or was given, a standard lamp resembling the one my parents owned – even its lampshade was the same colour – and a Bush television set and television table. For all its accessories, my house was nothing like as crammed as those museum-quality Victorian doll's houses, brimful with cooking pots and needlework samplers, candlesticks and miniature paint-ings, many of which were contributed by adults, just as my grandma re-covered the velvet chairs for me. Sanderson included wallpaper for doll's houses among their products and may have been the source of my red brickwork; each generation replenishes doll's houses for the next.

Jocasta Innes described the fun she had as an adult redecorating a doll's house and what pleasure it gave her to transform a 'suburban villa with a glaring red roof, blue windows and paper bougainvillea creeping across its green walls'. When she had finished with this 'hideous modern' house (which sounds not unlike the one I loved so well), it looked like a 'neo-Georgian residence in one of the select parts of St John's Wood, very swanky and prosperous'. Few of us have her formidable skills. Nonetheless, many doll's houses, however humble, are labours of love, just like the one the 1920s draper made for his daughter.

Doll's house collector Faith Eaton owned two doll's houses, including a 1939 shop-bought house complete with sandbags and stirrup pump, wartime lessons in homemaking being more stringent than most. Its dolls dressed appropriately in siren suits and tin hats, and looked ready to do their bit. Unlike my larger dolls, my own doll's-house dolls were never satisfactory. I loved the house itself and its furnishings far more than the dolls who lived there. The house and its diminutive objects were my delight: opening those tiny drawers and lifting the lid on tiny saucepans. I wanted to shrink like Alice and step inside.

An Edwardian child, Gertrude Freeman, visited a toyshop with her grandmother as a Christmas treat. Tea at Fullers preceded their trip to a shop in Birmingham's Great Western Arcade which sold hundreds of doll's-house pieces, each costing one penny. (You could buy carefully crafted hand-made doll's-house furnishings for a penny in the 1900s.) Gertrude's grandmother told her to pick an item of furniture and, when she did, said, 'Now choose another . . . Now choose another . . .' Again and again. Twenty-four times. Gertrude's account takes me straight back to childhood. Imagine her joy at being invited to choose twenty-four doll's house treats.

Towards the end of my time with the doll's house I bought a new set of kitchen furniture: sturdy white wooden pieces, simple, rustic, fit for a shabby-chic kitchen today (though I doubt that the cooker would pass muster). I particularly liked the Victorian-style dresser, with its open shelves for plates, although it must have looked incongruous against those sticky-backed-plastic walls. Around this time, Alison Uttley described her love for the real dresser that had stood in her mother's kitchen. It was big enough to hide in and its shelves were full of jugs, each one with its own history. Uttley bemoaned the disappearance of a piece of furniture known to so many country children over the years but which future generations would not be able to enjoy. She thought she was describing a way of life that was vanishing and, in some respects, she was. However, the vogue for the past was already well underway – and was even making its presence felt in doll's houses.

21 **THE LADYBIRD BUTTON:** CHILDHOOD

The ladybird button dates from the 1960s and my childhood. Many button boxes have ladybirds of their own – the 'realistic' creatures, pencils or cartoon characters (hence the equivalent American term 'goofies') that came into vogue in the 1930s and by the 1960s were increasingly visible. The ladybird gave its name to a publishing phenomenon and to a range of conservative children's clothing, which, along with Start-Rite and the sensible Clark's shoes and sandals into which my own feet were regularly buckled, helped to reassure parents they were giving their children the best possible start in life.

I came into the world at a nursing home. According to *The Baby Book* supplied by the home beforehand, I was 'the happy event' my mother was expecting – and she was 'expecting', not 'pregnant', that word considered too graphic in the late 1950s. I am a second child, and so my mum *did* know what to expect but, like Elizabeth Jane Howard's account of her own experiences, had known 'absolutely nothing about what was going to happen' first time round. 'The Birth of a Baby', a series of photographs by *Picture Post* photojournalist Grace Robertson was 'killed' by that magazine because it 'feared [that] the real-istic shots of a young woman in labour would alarm too many readers!'

The Baby Book advised on such topics as 'Before Baby Arrives', 'Maternity Wear', 'Diet For the Expectant Mother', and 'Bringing up Baby' (although, for a child of the 1930s, schooled in the cinema, the latter was more likely to conjure up thoughts of leopards and Cary Grant). The book advised that 'the lady in waiting' should try to lie down for an hour each afternoon (at least half an hour was essential), and make a point of walking a couple of miles a day. The information on labour runs to only two pages, but there are several comfy pages of knitting patterns for the layette. This was where 'the oft-maligned maiden aunts . . . come in useful'.

Like other fifties women, my mum concealed her bump as much as possible. Maternity wear was much less widely available then and although *The Baby Book* did not approve, she wore colourful housecoats as maternity smocks. Mothers were advised to 'look [their] charming best [while] waiting for the stork to arrive', a feat she accomplished by wearing a scarlet Chinese-style satin jacket with a mandarin collar.

The stork was present on almost every one of the cards that greeted my arrival. At least they addressed both my parents by name, unlike the Edwardian convention whereby newspapers announced the birth of a daughter or son to merely 'the *wife* of Mr John Brown'. Mum and I spent a week cosseted by the nursing home. (Visiting Hours 3.30–4.30 daily; evenings, 7–8 p.m. Children not allowed.) Breast was best, though information was provided on 'artificial feeding'; this was an era of four-hourly feeds. My mum was reared on four-hourly feeds herself, although by the time I was born, Truby King's rigidity had been replaced by Dr Spock's more relaxed approach.

The Baby Book advised my mum to establish a timetable and stick to it (though not to make Baby or herself a martyr to it) and to put Baby outside in the pram all day 'winter or summer, rain or shine . . . the only really unsuitable weather . . . is fog.' She was not a martyr to that advice either. The book also advised her not to worry, which was at least less dictatorial than advice given around the time of my mum's own birth: 'You must remember that your moods do affect your child *through* you, and therefore for its sake, you must shun the ugly and depressing things of life and keep as cheery, as happy and as light-hearted as you possibly can.'

Some 1950s toddlers wore the all-in-one 'pixie' suit – 'mother's pride and joy'. My own recollections of early childhood clothing merge with evidence supplied by photographs and a couple of actual frocks, one with the smocking that was such a strong feature of children's clothing then, and a dress embroidered with umbrellas (perhaps for when Baby was outside all day in her pram?).

Memories of clothing occasionally form part of a child's early comprehension of the outside world. One of Alison Uttley's earliest memories was of being

> pressed against full striped skirts, with silver-buckled belts and pockets hidden in many folds at the back, or held to stout bosoms encased in hard whalebone stays . . . There was bead-trimming down many of these bosoms, which scratched my cheeks, or braid, in whorls and curls, twisting in fascinating spirals.

Emma Smith recalls a dress

> knitted by hand from a thick silk yarn . . . soft to touch, and slithery. But what teases the very edge of memory is its colour.

That colour! – the strong pure sugary pink – it ravishes my senses. Even after eighty years I can recall the shock of pleasure at the delicious pinkness of my miniature silk dress.

Other children remember bulky underwear, and layers and layers of clothing to keep out the cold. Diana Athill describes being so swaddled in clothing for a winter's drive in an open cart that she could barely move; Lesley Lewis struggled with gaiters with innumerable buttons that required buttonhooks. As a slightly older child, Emma Smith longed to wear blue, like her sister, but was always dressed in brown. The narrator of Barbara Comyns's autobiographical novel *Sisters by a River* suffered the same fate and, on one occasion, actually ran away because she hated the dress so much. The late-nineteenth-century M. V. Hughes was more biddable. She gave no thought to clothing and simply wore whatever her mother put out for her. Years later, as a young college student required to make her own choices, she had no idea what to wear.

Again and again, accounts describe the shame and humiliation of cast-off clothing, and of having too few clothes. Emmeline Pankhurst was appalled by the plight of the children she saw in the Manchester Workhouse:

little girls seven and eight years old on their knees, scrubbing the cold stones of the long corridors. These little girls were clad, summer and winter, in thin cotton frocks, low in the neck and short-sleeved. At night they wore nothing at all, nightdresses being considered too good for paupers.

This was the late nineteenth century but those judgements were echoed in my great-aunt's experiences of institutional life in the 1900s.

Before she was adopted, Eva had nothing to call her own.

One of the things she insisted upon when describing her adoption many years later was her surprise and delight at being given clothes of her own – clothes she could choose – and hair ribbons, changes of underwear, books and toys. We should not underestimate the meaning of clothes and nice things for those who have never had them. (And girls from Eva's children's home still had to scrub floors in the 1930s before setting out for church.)

Novelist Ethel Mannin, Eva's contemporary, recalled that at her school ragged girls who could not provide their own pinafores were given school pinafores and seated apart from the rest, the money for these collected beforehand in class. Girls with lice were similarly segregated and known as 'the dirty girls', a finger-pointing label used as readily by teachers as by fellow pupils. 'Sticks and stones will break my bones, but words will never hurt me' – except this playground mantra rings false.

I wonder what label attached itself to my great-aunt in the years before her adoption, and if she was called a 'dirty girl'. Eva and others from her home attended a nearby elementary school and the difference between them and their fellow pupils must have been obvious. A Galway school run by the Catholic Church as late as the 1960s was attended by children from the local children's home whose clogs set them apart, and where the threat, if you misbehaved, was that you would be seated next to one of these girls. Children from this home were good candidates for tormenting – being offered sweets whose coloured paper wrappers concealed stones. What a mean trick to play on girls with nothing remotely sweet in their lives. I wonder if someone offered Eva a sweet-like stone? All these lessons in having and having not; the stigmata of inequality and difference.

Angela Rodaway became a volunteer worker in a day nursery during the 1930s and observed how, like the impoverished adults described by that decade's Health Committee, the children were transformed by a change of clothing. During the day she and her colleagues

> washed dozens of little overalls and twice as many pairs of knickers. All the children were put into clean clothes as soon as they arrived . . . At night, just before they went home, they dressed again in their own clothes. This seemed completely to change their personality.

By the time my mum had children of her own, my grandma used her skills for our benefit. As a girl I fared particularly well: jumpers, cardigans, twinsets, blouses, pinafore dresses. A bought dress was a rare thing, a bought cardigan too – and not until around the age of eight, when it was likely to be a navy blue nautical number, with white edging and gilt anchor buttons, or one of those best-behaviour cardigans with ribbon facings and polite, characterless pearl buttons (See Chapter 19: The 'Perfect' Button). Home-sewn dresses were made of whatever fabric came to hand; pictorial designs for children were not then widely available and my grandma bought material from little draper's shops, not department stores. A dress I loved, an abstract blend of grey and fuchsia, would now seem an odd choice of pattern in which to dress a child. Coats were a different matter. Coats were always bought: a 'best' coat and one for school. The patterns for children's coats in a 1950s *Weldon's Journal* are formal and conservative, with little hats and gloves; double-breasted coats with velvet collars had changed little from those worn by the Princesses Elizabeth and Margaret Rose twenty years earlier.

I was fascinated from an early age by the clothes women wore. Cutting out 'ladies' was a delight, as were the paper dolls whose frocks fastened precariously with tabs. In what is surely a memory of her own childhood, Lettice Cooper describes the fictional Aunt

Ellen, who comes to stay with a box full of wonderful things to delight her niece Rhoda: 'dolls' hats of stiff yellow straw trimmed with ruches of ribbon, and sometimes paper dolls'. She came 'to the nursery to cut out ladies from magazines and make them stand up on the table with cardboard stands'. Angelica Garnett recalled how her aunt, Virginia Woolf, enjoyed cutting out paper dolls for her to play with and was as 'ready to fall for the temptations of coloured string and sealing-wax, notebooks and pencils' as any child.

Annie and Eva entered into my games too, and there were real dolls to dress, as well as paper ones. This was where my grandma came into her own. Relieved of the need to make clothes for adult customers, she adapted her skills to small silent ones and was just as willing to add details and flourishes. The best treat was waking to find all my dolls dressed in new outfits; she was constantly making dolls' clothes. My very first doll, who had nylon curls, blue eyes that closed, and said 'Ma-ma' when you rocked her, had a thick cowslip-yellow coat for cold weather, with a blue collar and imitation blue pockets. Lindy's coat had a double row of lemon buttons, a belted back and a tiny button to secure the coat beneath the collar, just like a real coat. In time, Lindy was superseded by other dolls, for whom Annie was always knitting – jumpers, trousers, little boots – but my favourite knitted garment was an edge-to-edge cardigan in bluebell wool which fastened with a single button. This cardigan had striped sleeves, lemon alternating with bluebell, which may have been because there was insufficient bluebell wool, but was far more pleasing than a single colour; and what effort involved in knitting all those tiny horizontal stripes.

Dressing dolls could be a charitable act. In the 1930s the *Derbyshire Times* invited its readers to dress dolls for the Christmas party it funded for poor children and the children of widows (my mum included). In a similar vein, Jenifer Wayne's school held a doll show each year for which each pupil was obliged to dress a doll for 'Johanna Street. This was a "poor" school indeed, as we were firmly and regularly told.' Goody-two-shoes pupils started their handicraft early and were knitting 'tiny pink bonnets and booties for weeks'; the most Jenifer remembered knitting was 'a vest that stood up by itself, with a huge pearl button on one shoulder'. This charitable knitting was compulsory, and so not exactly charity at all; the thank-you letter the school received may have been equally forced. 'We were given to understand that the effort put into this letter must have been great indeed; there was a kind, gravely-smiling implication that it was marvellous for such poor children to be able to write at all.'

Poor children could also read, although poorer schools struggled with insufficient funds. *Up to London to See the King: A Story for Six-Year-Olds* was awarded to my mum as an infants'-school prize in the mid-1930s but dates from 1904. The book has a helpful section at the back, listing 'the hard words'. Chapter by chapter, these are broken down and hyphenated to indicate pronunciation, but the last words listed, in a row of their own, are 'do not' and, in bold, its contraction 'don't', which some thought was all the elementary-schoolchild needed to know.

Things had moved on by the time I started school, thanks, in large part, to the 1944 Education Act which, the Festival of Britain's New Schools Pavilion reassured parents, 'gives to everyone a fair freedom of choice'. The pavilion showed the new trend for children to investigate subjects on their own and described the fresh equipment – the new desks, chairs, laboratories, libraries, and the physical education, art and drama placed at a child's disposal. One of my infant classrooms had Formica tables in different colours, a contemporary way of denoting status in class.

A reception-class English workbook, circa 1960, a series of

short illustrated exercises, explained that the 'keynote' in learning
to read is 'self-help'. The workbook taught other lessons too, its
first page showed Mrs Smith hanging out the washing, Mrs Brown
holding aloft a steaming pie and Miss Jones looking studiously
at her typewriter. A further reception-class primer featured short
exercises in arithmetic and composition, each illustrated by the
child's own crayoned drawing. One entry reads: 'Today is Tuesday
29th November. We have taken our Snowdrop bulbs out of the
cupboard.'

In a few years' time, children would be assisted by the Ladybird
Key Words Reading Scheme, issued in 1964, in which Jane helps
Mummy and Peter helps Daddy (although both help to wash up,
hang out the washing and polish the dining-room table). These
slim-backed books with their clean conformity, primary-coloured
illustrations and floribunda roses blooming in suburban gardens
with well-kept lawns opened the world of reading to generations
of children. For older children, like myself, Ladybird offered
gloriously colourful guides to history, wildlife, British birds and
much more, all illustrated with memorable drawings: in my mind's
eye, Elizabeth I still stands proud. These illustrations were as
informative as their text, but I remember smarting when, aged
eight, a school photographer, wanting to set the scene, placed an
illustrated book for a much younger reader before me.

As a very small child, my mum read the magazine *Chick's Own*,
bought each Wednesday, together with an ice-cream cornet, after
Annie delivered her takings to the Provident Office; she then
moved on to Enid Blyton's *Sunny Stories* and assorted schoolgirl
annuals. Winifred Foley, another thirties child, devoured *Bluebird*.
Week by week, she could be Lil of the Lighthouse, Wanda of the
Movies, the Heroine of St Katherine's and (even better for a poor
child), 'the Richest Girl in the School'. For me, there was *Bunty*
and *Judy*. Courtesy of my brother, I also read *Valiant* and the

Beano, which was hardly fair: I loved Lord Snooty and the Bash Street Kids but he had no interest in the Four Marys. I had the advantage with toys too, playing with Lego and toy cars as well as dolls, and a wonderful pedal car.

Sunday-afternoon reading belonged to my grandma, sinking into her deepening lap. Oh, the excitement of Jimmy Brown and his family, whisking off to join Mr Galliano's circus, and life in a gypsy caravan, without a single backward glance, the way only storybook characters can do. This was the 1930s, however, and Jimmy's father, a carpenter, was unemployed and so only too ready to make a fresh start. And who would not want to be spirited circus-girl Lotta, brave horse rider, pulling faces, evading lessons and not knowing how to sew. ('Can't you *really* sew? . . . I thought all girls could.') Reading may seem boring to a bare-back rider, but unless you can read the road signs, how can you hope to rescue a runaway chimpanzee? I delighted in *The Treasure Hunters* too, enjoying the little hidden house almost more than the discovery of the lost treasure; and *The Enchanted Wood* and *The Magic Faraway Tree*, a new world whirling round each Sunday, with the prospect of exploding sherbet biscuits (far more tempting than the angel dust that crackled in your mouth or the papery flying-saucer sweets you could buy in corner shops, four a penny). There was poetry too, especially *Now We Are Six*.

Reading alone meant the town library. I can still smell the combination of polished wood and books, and hear the purposeful silence. Paperbacks were found in a corner of the top floor of Boots, where for 2*s* 6*d* – what discoveries: pony stories, the Famous Five, Puffin paperbacks, Malory Towers. Some learn early how to carry a book for effect, a lesson I took longer to absorb. By the time I did, I was buying books from Brayshaw's, a town-centre shop which sold smart fountain pens along with black-spined Penguin Classics and Virginia Woolf. Thanks to the reinvention of youth and, from the late 1960s, the lines between childhood and adulthood blurring, I could re-visit children's books, discover all over again that King John was not a good man, and savour the making of one-and-twenty buttonholes in cherry-coloured twist at the same time as reading Hermann Hesse and *Soledad Brother*. Young women had long ceased to dress like their mothers; some dressed like children in lieu of becoming themselves, and buttons depicting illustrations by nineteenth-century children's writer Kate Greenaway were being sewn on to adult as well as children's clothing to complement the floor-length floaty dresses worn in the never-never land of that time.

22 **SUSPENDERS:** CORSETRY, SCANTIES (& SEX)

Those of us who came of age after the reign of the suspender belt cannot know the disaster of a broken suspender button, nor the need to speedily find a replacement – be it a tiny sew-through button – or an aspirin, as per Katharine Whitehorn's article 'Sluts'. Even a small piece of coal has held up stockings, in extremis. The suspender button introduces the delicate subject of underwear, skimpy and scanty, as well as voluminous, and in every colour from white to black, not forgetting shades of grey.

Until the 1880s, women were not depicted wearing corsets or any other item of the underwear advertised for sale in newspapers, catalogues and magazines. Heaven forfend that any female flesh be revealed; those garments stood alone (indeed literally so, thanks to their rigid construction). Given the delicacy of the subject and Victorian blushes, one wonders who was the intended beneficiary of the motto 'By Industry We Thrive', an aphorism embroidered along the tops of a pair of stockings shown at the 1851 Great Exhibition. Whose heart was meant to beat faster at the sight of those instructive words?

'Steel-bound and whalebone-lined' is how Irene Clephane

described the 'hideous' late-nineteenth-century fashions worn by her mother and the torture inflicted by the bustle or, rather, the tiny waist that rose above it. The seventeen-inch waists of the 1880s and '90s caused all manner of harm. Even working-class women were not immune from the fashion: my great-grandma's nipped-in waist could not have been achieved without tight lacing. Then came the extraordinary S-bend effect created by the 'straight-fronted' corset of the Edwardian era, popularised by the couturier Lucile, which found favour among women of more exalted status and, making it impossible for its wearers to stoop, required the service of a pair of 'lazy tongs' if a lace handkerchief were dropped. No wonder women were grateful when Paul Poiret's simple Directoire look came along.

In the nineteenth century, corsetry, even more than millinery, was regarded as indubitably female. Delicate advertisements re-assured women of the corsetier's discretion. In 1914, Chesterfield's Spirella agent, Mrs W. W. Bateman placed one to 'thank the many ladies who have called to inspect her Spirella show' during the town's Shopping Festival and invited them to call again. Her corsets were made to order and, what is more, 'unbreakable'. Before one wonders what the ladies of Chesterfield got up to in their underwear, it is worth remembering that boned corsets *meant* bone. 'The number of stays – bones – you had in your corset was a status symbol, so that a woman asked for "a 28-bone corset".' Most corsets were convent-made (as was many an Edwardian trousseau).

By the 1920s, advances in corsetry were such that there were even special corsets for dancing. In the thirties, boned corsets were out, though readers of *Miss Modern* were advised that 'the modern figure – however slight – must be corseted to be svelte. Be thankful that firmly woven elastic takes the place of old-fashioned whalebone.' The new 'foundation garments' could still exercise a degree of old-fashioned purgatory, however, as evidenced by this description:

> Struggling into a brand-new roll-on was a feat that demanded muscular power and invincible faith. There were always moments – they seemed like desperate ages – when one was trapped. The bottom edge of the surely hopelessly narrow tube of pink elastic had been prised to just above one's knees; the top edge had become welded, it seemed, to a place just below the buttocks that the whole thing was eventually supposed to redeem. For terrible, long, red-faced, almost tearful moments, one thought one's thighs were clamped together for ever . . . When at last the thing had been lugged and levered into position, and its suspenders tethered to lisle-topped stockings, one walked about feeling exhausted and strangely buoyant: legs and top half moving quite independently of the newly-rigid middle. It didn't stay rigid for long; after a few washes, the edges of the pink elastic tube began to splay out into thick waves, almost frills, that made one's waist bulkier than ever.'

During the 1940s corsets, like so much else, acquired a wartime flavour: Berlei promised they performed a 'secret service' – and for 'only four coupons!' By the 1950s, *Vogue* was advertising a two-way-stretch doll-size girdle, an interesting concept (and size), though there was nothing doll-like about the corset Fiona MacCarthy recalled wearing in 1958.

> Youthcraft Girdles were garments of horrible complexity, more like a suit of armour than mere underclothes, encasing our young bodies in what was advertised as a 'firm but flexible elastic net'. These panty girdles had detachable gussets and suspenders. Were they specially designed to discourage intercourse?

Amazingly, in the early 1960s, foundation garments were reported to be more popular than ever: 'The mere thirty million that women spent on corsets ten years ago is now sixty million: the estimate for next year is a gross figure of a quarter as much again,' Katharine Whitehorn wrote in *The Spectator*; over 100 corsetry firms were in business. Spirella, 'the oldest hands at the game', had revamped its Oxford Circus showroom and operated through a team of 6,000 Mrs Batemans, many of them part-time, a third of whom had worked for the company for more than twenty years, taking ten measurements for a girdle and six for a bra, before sending them on to the factory.

'We in our elasticised net and nylon girdles, our boneless wonders, should pity [Edwardian] ladies from our hearts,' Alison Adburgham wrote. Today, we pity her generation and sympathise with Mary Quant: 'I can't see any reason why foundation garments should not be sleek and modern and pretty and fit and move with the body at the same time.' Mary Quant was equally dismissive of suspenders. 'To me, they look like some sort of fearful surgical device.' To solve these problems Quant produced her own 'Youthlines' with its 'girl-loving Lycra': 'For living in. Happily. Like skin. Running, jumping, twisting.' They and Pretty Polly Stand Easies, advertised in magazines like *Nova*, were part of the 'underwear revolution', as designated in the mid-1960s by *Vogue*, which, like all other sixties revolutions, was primarily a symbol of youth.

Unlike corsets, the bra is a positive rite of passage, a proud symbol of womanhood; most women remember wearing their first bra. Mrs Smiling in *Cold Comfort Farm* regards brassieres with a collector's eye: 'She was reputed to have the largest and finest collection . . . in the world. It was hoped that on her death it would be left to the nation.' Growing up in the 1920s meant flattening the breasts; other eras accentuated them. For Lorna

Sage, 'even if you had hardly any breasts going bra-less [to the school dance in the 1950s] was unthinkable . . . a lack of elastic armour was a sign of moral idiocy'. In those days, a bust meant your school days were numbered. In Edna O'Brien's *The Country Girls*, 'big girl' Cynthia, has a bust, 'A thing no other girl in the convent dared have'. So desperate is Baba to have the same that she purloins some tubes of udder cream from her veterinarian father's surgery and applies it to her breasts. *Vogue*'s 1960s 'underwear revolution', included the 'no-bra bra', an interesting advance on the Floating Action Bra (£1 2s) of the previous decade. In a few years' time, not wearing a bra would become a feminist statement.

Modern women shed layers as earlier generations piled them on. Daisy Lansbury wrote in 1936, recalling her Edwardian childhood:

> I do not suppose there are *any* little girls who wear one knitted woollen vest, one curious garment in pink flannelette called a chemise, one red stay-belt, pink flannelette knickers, one red crocheted woollen petticoat, one pink flannelette petticoat, and on Sundays, a white embroidered cambric petticoat on top, as I did.

The Victorian Gwen Raverat could have trumped that with an even longer list. And although young girls of my grandma's generation struggled with layers of underclothing, how else could they have hoped to stop runaway trains, *Railway Children*-style, without their flannelette petticoats?

In the early nineteenth century only aristocratic women wore drawers. By the 1890s and the craze for cycling, America's Mrs Amelia Jenks Bloomer's invention acquired a necessary popularity. Harrods advertised 'Very Special' black serge knickers with a chamois leather seat for cycling, while at the Army and Navy

Stores women awheel could warm their derrières with knee- or ankle-length bloomers in cashmere or fancy mixtures. Those who favoured 'Sanitary Woollen Clothing', and could ignore its unattractive greyish-cream pallor, could strike a note for the Aesthetic Movement by choosing Jaeger's stockinette combinations. Equally ardent 1930s Woodcraft Folk affirmed their allegiance with green underwear, while the elderly ladies who had known better days and whom Jenifer Wayne's school entertained to a charitable lunch stuffed cakes into the legs of their baggy drawers; the poor but equally resourceful Angela Rodaway hid market vegetables in hers. Three cheers for resourcefulness and strong knicker elastic (which also gave rise to the phrase 'hand trappers', on a par with elastic armour).

Stout underwear can dampen the spirits, however. A character in a Barbara Pym novel despairs of hers: 'It was depressing the way the same old things turned up every week.' When a friend comes to stay, the kitchen is 'festooned with lines of depressing-looking underwear – fawn locknit knickers and petticoats of the same material. It was even drearier than mine.' But there is something to be said for 'spinsterish' underclothes: lumpy, grey underwear saves a Barbara Comyns heroine from a dastardly fate.

The independent young flapper striding into the future in her sheath-like dress wore fewer underclothes than her forebears. A dainty Princess Petticoat (8s 11d) and matching knickers (6s 11d) in delicate shades of artificial silk could be purchased from Gorringes for a ladylike 15s. 'The cami-knicker at its best is a thing of sheer delight,' a contemporary journalist swooned. The fictional Miss Pettigrew discovers that silk underclothes make her feel 'wicked, daring, ready for anything. She left her hesitations behind with her home-made woollens.'

Many women made their own underclothes – and by hand; even after the widespread use of sewing machines, a mystique persisted that hand-made underclothes were superior. A character in Barbara Comyns's *A Touch of Mistletoe*, who is intent on doing things properly, reassures her sister that 'real people feel almost ill if they have a machine stitch anywhere near them'. Wartime contriving demanded particular dexterity with a needle and scissors. 'Delia cuts out two brassieres for me from my old college blouse, and we proceed to sew,' May Smith wrote in 1941; two years later she made 'a nifty brassiere out of an old petticoat and embroider[ed] same'.

Dainty petticoats, camisoles and camiknickers in satin, silk or artificial silk were loved by young women even if older generations thought such skimpy clothing 'ridiculous'. However, a 1920s advertisement 'for those dainty undies that you always put on fresh' serves as a reminder that, while some flitted about in lace-edged drawers, in times gone by not all underwear was changed daily. Frothy confections notwithstanding, Agnes Miall advised hard-working bachelor girls to opt for sober woollen combinations.

By 1932, some were tempted by camiknickers in lace georgette with the new 'sunbathing' effect at the sides, or 'scanties', the new slim-fitting knickers designed to replace 'panties and belt' under shorts or beach dresses. Ruby Keeler sang of packing her scanties to 'Shuffle Off to Buffalo'. Before the kill-joy recommendations of the Hays Code, early 1930s Hollywood was remarkably upfront in its allusions: think Dick Powell with his giant can opener, all set to open Ruby Keeler's tin-can clothing in *Gold Diggers of 1933*.

Black underwear has long had racy connotations, as Caithleen explains in *The Country Girls*.

The black underwear was Baba's idea. She said that we wouldn't have to wash it so often; and that it was useful if we ever had a street accident, or if men were trying to strip us in the backs of cars. Baba thought of all these things. I got black nylons too. I read somewhere that they were 'literary'.

Black underwear was part of growing up and becoming a woman, as Baba tells her. 'We want to live. Drink gin . . . We want to go places.'

Skimpy underwear was not just a matter of clothing but also of modernity (and sex). Jenifer Wayne recalled 'a flighty, precocious, and to me incomprehensible type' who boarded her school bus. While Jenifer wore long oatmeal socks with elastic garters, 'Of course, *she* wore stockings; and there was a scandalous story that she had once been seen going up to the top deck of the bus in cami-knickers – satin, with lace and wide-open legs – instead of the regulation navy bloomers.'

By then young women could read Elinor Glyn's short-story collection *It*. Three years later, even *My Home* was advising its readers, via a short story 'Ticket to Heaven', that 'Men don't fall in love with a woman's sense of fairness or her sterling worth . . . They fall in love with that world-famous quality, "IT".' IT's moment was brief, however, and all too soon subsumed by romance. As Katharine Whitehorn recalled, it took years for women's magazine editors to be able to stop writing 'romance' when they meant 'sex'.

The man-made fabrics that became increasingly popular from the 1950s resulted in all sorts of gauzy nylon nightgowns, 'baby-dolls' among them. The 'Gifts She'll Adore' offered by Swallow's lingerie department in 1965 were all double-denier nylon and included, for those romantic occasions, 'Juliette' a 'delightfully feminine waltz-length double nightgown with a lace encrusted fitted bra and a fully circular swing skirt' in white/white, white/marshmallow or white/glazier blue (89*s* 6*d*). It would be hard to tell whether the subsequent frisson was caused by desire or static.

With an innocence we would today find touching, one late-nineteenth century couple sought full-length nightgowns for their honeymoon. Innocence is not far along the spectrum from desperate ignorance, however. Although she gave birth to five children, the Edwardian Kathleen Dayus never saw her husband naked; convent girls were not the only ones struggling to dress and undress beneath the shelter of their nightgowns. And even in the early 1960s the instruction to sales assistants was that the shop-window dummy should *never* be left unclothed.

When Joan Wyndham acquired a pair of peacock-blue Jaeger pyjamas (Jaeger had come a long way since that greyish-wool stockinette), her fellow WAAFs wanted to borrow them for dirty weekends. 'And some of them are virgins!' She and her closest friends wanted to know how to get more pleasure from sex. They invested in a thirty-bob tube of clitoris cream and were delighted to discover that, when rubbed on, the 'magic ointment' worked.

As reliable contraception became more widely available, fewer women needed to trust to hot baths, gin and doing the mending as ways of avoiding pregnancy. Though Marie Stopes published *Married Love* in 1918 and opened a family-planning clinic three years later, it was years before women had easy access to contraception and the knowledge they needed. Although the Family Planning Association began its work in 1930, it met with opposition in its early years; Naomi Mitchison helped found a North Kensington clinic, and in times of acute desperation, allowed abortions to be performed at her home to safeguard women's lives.

The FPA estimated that in 1951 the average age at which women first had sex was twenty-one. Though the Pill made a major breakthrough ten years later, it was only available to married women; it was 1970 before the Pill could be prescribed to single women nationwide. Fay Weldon put it pithily: 'Getting married and not pregnant? There's posh for you.' The women writers of the 1960s did much to break taboos. Nell Dunn's *Up the Junction* tackled back-street abortion with a candour unavailable to her literary forebears Rosamond Lehmann and Jean Rhys; Lynne Reid-Banks's *The L-Shaped Room* and Margaret Drabble's *The Millstone* showed that, contrary to expectations, sex was not always bartered for a wedding ring. In 1968 only 28 per cent of (predominantly middle-class) women used the contraceptive pill. By 1975 its use had increased to 75 per cent and spread to all social classes. 'Younger women don't realise what hell it was . . . The perpetual anxiety. It was a real revolution,' Mary Quant told the *Observer*'s Rachel Cooke.

The revolution in underwear was tights, which went into mass production in the mid-sixties. 'This Christmas should be fab – I'm hanging up my stretch tights!' a *Punch* cartoon joked in 1963, although a 1965 'Swallow's of Chesterfield' Christmas brochure featured gift-packed nylons, not tights. Twiggy Lawson recalls how expensive they were when they first became available. Nonetheless, tights meant freedom, along with the miniskirt, and no more schoolboys pinging schoolgirls' suspenders.

Tights were another revolution that passed my grandma's generation by. Annie never wore them. I remember her corsets, though: barricades of Germolene-pink elastic and shiny satin. Like Enid Bagnold's name tapes, my grandma's corsets came in handy in an unexpected way. In the early 1960s they transported a tiny fir tree, hidden within their folds, through customs: what customs officer enquired closely into a lady's underwear?

23 **THE APRON BUTTON:** DOMESTICITY

For many years, middle-class domesticity meant having a word with the cook and keeping an eye out for any dust the parlour-maid had overlooked. For women like my grandma it meant cooking and cleaning; drubbing clothes in the copper and squeezing the life out of wet sheets with a mangle – '*Don't* put your fingers in the mangle' was a constant refrain during my childhood when I visited my grandma on washdays; she never owned a washing machine. My mum had a Hoover twin tub (which, later, I acquired, she having long since graduated to an automatic washing machine). A twin tub meant hauling scalding wet clothes from the wash tub into the spinner and a certain amount of water sloshed overboard. Like countless women, before and since, the women of my family have washed, baked, cleaned and scrubbed, and all other domestic tasks in between. No wonder they have needed cheerfully patterned aprons and overalls with colourful buttons to fasten them and brighten their domestic load: long-sleeved overalls that button down the front; sleeveless tabards fastened with a button either side; pull-on aprons criss-crossed with fabric strings, tunics with a deep marsupial pocket.

Numerous styles certify domesticity – should you care to enquire. Key, though, is the task for which they are intended: something frilled and dainty for pouring tea, or something altogether more robust for the real graft of fettling and scouring, down on your hands and knees. My great-grandma and great-aunt, Betsy and Eva, had more aprons than most: a clean apron signifying the start of each day behind their shop counter.

By 1961 fewer than 5 per cent of households employed paid help and less than 1 per cent had a resident domestic servant. Ten years earlier there were only 178,000 resident servants in England and Wales, compared with some 700,000 in the early 1930s. An even larger exodus from domestic service had taken place after the Great War as young women who tasted the freedom and better pay of munitions work resisted the return to drudgery. At each World War, women who had formerly employed servants had to put on aprons themselves and learn to do without the 'anonymous caps and aprons who worked the strings'.

The servant problem was debated endlessly during the 1920s and '30s. According to *Woman's Life*, those who had acquired skills in the workplace could usefully translate them into the home. (Conversely, private secretary Daisy Lansbury said that it was her mother teaching her to think about the pie in the oven that might burn while she dusted upstairs that taught her to organise and plan her office work.) Readers of *The Lady* in 1919, some of whom were discovering their kitchens for the first time, could protect their clothes with the 'Frazerton Overall, made in good washing material with strong hand-made buttons and closely sewn buttonholes'. Available in blue, mauve, tourmaline or mignonette, colours whose very shades seem soothing, the overalls were individually named – 'Hilda', priced at 12s 6d; 'Emily' (13s 6d); 'Florence' (14s 6d), or the more expensive 'Julia' (15s 6d). Ten years later, in its own bid at reassurance, *The Needlewoman* promised frock overalls with blue-green bone buttons 'for the messiest of jobs . . . with an added degree of smartness', a contradictory assertion if ever there was one. Readers were provided with a pattern for 'a pretty apron' so that 'nowadays when we all have to take part in *the actual work* of our homes' (my italics) women could make their own: 'few garments are more becoming'. I doubt that anyone was fooled. This was the era when colourful saucepans made an appearance on kitchen shelves along with vividly decorated crockery. (One journalist joked that, for those fortunate enough to own a piece of *Clarice Cliff*, there might even be something *likeable* about doing the washing-up.) Now that the woman of the house was inhabiting her kitchen and doing her own housework, there was a greater desire for colour.

Whether women identified themselves as a Florence or a Julia, advertisers keen to put an attractive gloss on domesticity depicted them doing the housework in smart clothes. Hot on the heels of universal suffrage, Electrolux promised to confer not only leisure but the freedom of the house on the women who used their vacuum cleaners. The interwar woman left her brand-new gas cooker in sole command of dinner while she went upstairs to make the beds, or – better still – left the house altogether to 'shop or play'. Best of all, was the 'Atmos Mechanical Housemaid' which enabled a bespectacled woman (advertising's shortcut for intelligence) to read the newspaper while it washed, dried, ironed and did everything but cook the dinner. Yes please. (Its shout line: 'It sounds too good to be true!') And how quickly even more invidious messages crept in: 'The dirt you *can't* see is the worst,' one woman tells another in 1930.

Advances in household technology are always appealing. In January 1931, seventeen-year-old Celia Fitton noted one in her diary: 'In Afternoon, Mother, Auntie, Elsie and myself went to Corporation Electrical Department to see the electrical cooker demonstration . . . very interesting'; a later entry refers to the family's electric fire. Relatively few households were blessed with newfangled gadgets at this time and some were still without electricity. The following year Vera Brittain denounced domesticity, deploring the fact that, for all advertisers' claims, the majority of women lived in poky, dusty houses, with no labour-saving devices in sight. Cheerful aprons notwithstanding, the reality, then as now, was that cleaning requires effort, eats up time and can be filthy work. In 1924, some fifty years before campaigns for wages for housework, an article in *Good Housekeeping* asked, 'Should Wives have Wages?: Even in a coal mine, there are shifts.' In a similar spirit of rebellion some brides put their foot down and refused to have ornaments on the mantelpiece: no more dusting.

In 1922 the WI magazine *Home and Country* ran a series of 'Hints for the Busy Housewife', presumably designed to aid the post-war novice. The first of these, 'From 6.30 a.m.–9 a.m.', described housework in intricate detail. The result is exhausting to read, let alone accomplish. As if 6.30 a.m. were not early enough, the first jobs of the day begin the night before. Ten minutes before bed, chairs are turned upside down on the table, the fender and fire irons put beneath it and the rugs rolled. 'Then I bring in the ash box, shovel, black-lead box with its brushes, and the newspaper, small coal and about ten dry thin sticks, and leave matches by the side – all to hand for the next morning at 6.30 a.m. – not a second later!' The following morning, the writer has several jobs in hand before breakfast and her first cup of tea. 'After making the tea, I fill up the kettle at once and add a little coal to the fire; we do not want to wait for the washing-up water do we?'

Beds are aired, mattresses arched, windows thrown wide open, weather permitting; a white apron is worn when dealing with bedding, a black one for sweeping and dusting. A pause for a second cup of tea refreshes the writer sufficiently for her to tackle 'that bit of extra daily work': 'Monday, wash day; Tuesday, sitting room, ironing, airing clothes; Wed, bedroom; Thurs, upstairs passages, stairs and hall; Friday, flues and big baking day; Sat, kitchen and scullery, & clothes to soak for Monday's wash.'

Nancy Mitford's irreverent upper-class novel *The Pursuit of Love* comes to mind:

How dreadful it is, cooking, I mean. That oven . . . there is that awful hot blast hitting one in the face. I don't wonder people sometimes put their heads in and leave them in out of sheer misery. Oh, dear, and I wish you could have seen the Hoover running away with me . . . I think housework is far more tiring and frightening than hunting is, no comparison, and yet after hunting we had eggs for tea and were made to rest for hours, but after housework people expect one to go on just as if nothing special had happened.

'The trouble with housework,' as Monica Dickens and women before and since have discovered, 'is that whatever you do seems to lead to another job . . . or a mess to clear up.' My grandma disliked housework and was not one for titivating with a duster, but if a job needed doing, she was all for doing it properly. When my mother was a child, Friday was the day when Annie (and other working women who wanted things straight for the weekend) tackled the housework. Kitchen, living room and bathroom were given a thorough clean. Rugs were thrown outside and beaten and the kitchen lino scrubbed. The downstairs rooms acquired a complicated aroma of disinfectant, soap and polish. It was best to keep out of the way when this scourge of household dust descended on Racecourse Road. Down on her knees with a pail of water, stretching her arms to reach the dado; fettling, black-leading and silver polishing, a domestic dervish in cross-over pinny and beads. (Even when cleaning, Annie was never without a string of beads.)

Wartime bride Margaret Broughton wrote a lengthy list of 'things needed for marriage' – an enamel pan, egg whisk, mixing basin, Pyrex dishes, a flat iron . . . and ticked the items she succeeded in obtaining (a surprising number when women were being told that two flat irons could be made into four hand grenades and one nine-inch enamelled saucepan a bayonet). Hers is an inventory far greater than the actual sieves and spoons listed; a promissory note for happiness and a peaceful future.

Domesticity took on further new meanings during wartime: a 1941 cover of *Housewife* magazine showed a young mother clutching a saw. Julia Strachey's post-war diary echoed this with a glorious portrait of Anne Olivier Bell. Strachey, whose husband Laurence Gowing was teaching at Newcastle University, told herself 'I must avoid being the housewife full of shopping and food problems, to whom he returns every evening', and extolled her friend Anne who, with husband Quentin, had recently moved to the city three weeks after giving birth. Though initially exhausted and struggling with flu she had been 'MAGNIFICENT' and was now 'well and very chic and radiant in a cherry candy-striped apron, with a baby on one arm and a carpentry saw on the other. In between feeding the baby she has made marvellous carpentry miracles.'

'Your home is your factory', women were told, the word 'factory' making an appeal to all those recently engaged in building Spitfires. Women at the centre of the home, unpaid but essential workers, were crucial to William Beveridge's vision of post-war Britain. Advertisers were still busy providing reassurance. In 1947, a woman in evening dress, with the stiff curls, perfect lipstick and exaggerated femininity of the period, accepts a light for her cigarette at a white-tie event: 'It's hard to imagine that only this morning she was doing her own housework . . . The modern housewife desires to be a social success as well as a good house-keeper', Chemico cleanser informed women – a brand name contemporary readers would have found reassuring but which, along with Radiation refrigerators, is more unsettling today. Advertisers were also busy provoking anxiety with the proliferation of new soap powders – Daz, Surf, Tide etc. – giving rise to ever more competitive claims about washing whiter than white.

My mum's twin tub arrived in the mid-1950s; the Hoover Junior vacuum cleaner, which did sterling work for nearly sixty years, and which she was asked to demonstrate for friends, so novel was its purchase, arrived at around the same time. By 1955, the majority of householders were said to own vacuum cleaners, although only 18 per cent had washing machines and a tiny 8 per cent, refrigerators; in Wales, as late as 1960, only 5 per cent of households owned a fridge. Fridges were still on several shopping lists: my parents' Frigidaire (£72 12s 0d) appeared in May that year. My mum had two children before she had a fridge, something unthinkable for the vast majority in Britain today. I remember the jettisoned meat safe with its tightly meshed windows.

In the matter of post-war gadgetry, America was way ahead. In January 1955 *Modern Woman* introduced its new Home Editor, straight from New York, who told her readers: 'household equipment has practically taken over the American home. Its workings are so complicated that American housewives slave day and night saving their labour . . . Pretty soon . . . the American housewife will almost have to have an engineering degree.' By the 1960s, Britain was catching up. Towards the end of that decade my mum had a Kenwood mixer: 'The [Kenwood] Chef does everything but Cook – that's what wives are for!' was its snappy advertising line. On the occasions chips were on the menu, however, she wielded a sturdy aluminium slicer which produced perfect timbered chips but took considerable strength to slam the enamelled handle down on to the potato and propel it through the slicing grid.

Naomi Mitchison learned something of housework through working as a VAD nurse during the First World War – all those wheelchairs and lockers that needed polishing – but knew nothing whatsoever about cooking; that she left to the cook. However, ignorance of cookery was not just a question of social class. Nella Last worried about the younger generation's abilities, writing of a young newly married woman who could not prepare cabbage because she had never cooked one and was reduced to preparing eggs for lunch and tea most days. 'She cannot wash, bake, clean to any system.' However, Nella Last also criticised a near-contemporary: 'As I often tell her, if she made soup and porridge and baked more instead of tinned soups – for six of them – and didn't rely on cornflakes always and silly little bought cakes that were stale the next day, she could economise on her Co-op bill.' Some took a different view: 'I myself loathe cooking,' says Nell in Elizabeth Taylor's *The Wedding Group*, 'To me, it's like having a migraine. And all the fuss and nonsense that's written about it. I read [a woman's magazine article] . . . about pastry baskets filled with cherries. "Make angelica handles if desired" . . . Who on earth could desire an angelica handle?'

My grandma never owned a fridge (nor other labour-saving devices, apart from a mangle and that push-pull carpet sweeper, the Ewbank, if either can properly be described as labour-saving). During the years I knew them, my grandma and great-aunt's kitchen was sparsely furnished – a post-war cabinet with top and bottom cupboards and a pull-down counter; the sturdy mangle; a curtain across the sink and a pantry that was almost bare: like other women without refrigeration, Annie and Eva shopped daily. No wonder I sold imaginary goods as well as button 'sweets' in my childhood games: a loaf for Annie, a pound of tea for Eva; handing over buttons in exchange.

When cooking, my great-aunt Eva consulted *Home Management* (which advised boiling greens for at least twenty minutes). Years earlier she had tussled with an elementary-school teacher who thought that, as a shopkeeper's daughter, Eva could provide ingredients for other pupils as well as herself. According to a Plain Cookery book from 1917, the elementary-schoolgirl might be expected to tackle stuffed heart; fast forward to 1969–70, and I was learning to cook much simpler fare – cheese pie, raspberry buns and rock cakes. One day a week I swung my way to school with a satchel over one shoulder and a wicker basket over the other arm, with a day-glo plastic floral cover to keep the rain off the Christmas-biscuit-assortment tin in which I would carry my offerings home. First-year girls learned cookery (and sewing) as well as Latin, though in some schools a distinct line was drawn: Latin or cookery, not both; an echo, perhaps, of a remark made to M. V. Hughes and others at North London Collegiate school in the 1880s: 'Why did The Lord create Messrs Huntley and Palmer to make cakes for us, if not to give our clever girls a chance to do something better?'

In 1958, the year I was born, the first issue of *Woman's Realm* told its readers: 'Every woman finds happiness and fulfilment, as well as duty. This need never be a narrow domain, bounded though it is by kitchen, nursery and household chores. Indeed it can be the widest and most wonderful and most rewarding realm in the world.' Many women found that realm too narrow and confining. That year, Penelope Mortimer's novel *Daddy's Gone A-Hunting* provided a bleak portrait of the commuter-belt wife, trapped by biology and culture.

Thinking. Planning. Preparing. Twelve times every year your body becomes elaborately prepared, for nothing. Living is a perpetual preparation for nothing. Stick flags in the bridge rolls, check the store cupboard, empty the ash-trays; have everything in order, have a manicure, send little messages over short distances by telephone. When you move there is a rustle of old shopping lists, like dead leaves; when you sit still there is the terror of time slipping away. You must get on. You run about inside the high walls . . . But there's nothing there. It is all the same as it was before. You have been busy with handfuls of air, moving shadows, disciplining emptiness.

Five years later, in 1963, *The Feminine Mystique* jolted its readers and changed their lives when Betty Friedan posed the question many women were afraid to articulate: 'Is this all?'

One difficulty for housebound women was money – or their lack of it. Women like my mother who had worked before marriage, and even those who had not, were now entirely dependent on their husbands. Derbyshire schoolteacher May Smith, who vowed she would not become one of those 'Devoted, Docile Wives', quickly bemoaned this fact: 'hate the thought of being absolutely and utterly dependent on Freddie. Makes me feel both embarrassed and – well, too Dependent. Cherished my independence dearly . . . I mourn its going.' For Lorna Sage's mother, and many like her, money was 'a minefield'. Some women of that generation who were mistresses of thrift and nifty budgeting and who, by saving a shilling here and there, managed to conjure presents out of housekeeping funds, nonetheless believed that managing money was beyond them. This also afflicted women like the fictional Laura in Mollie Panter-Downes's *One Fine Day* who has been brought up to think that 'understanding about money was as much a give-away for a woman as hands,' (work-worn hands being a symbol of inferior social status) 'so she was stupid about money'.

By the 1960s, women had greater spending power than formerly, more married women were working and able to buy more of what they wanted in a world of rapidly expanding consumerism. But this was not the picture for everyone. In 1964, *Guardian* Woman's Editor Mary Stott was shocked to hear of women who did not have a personal allowance and assumed they must be in the minority. She was unprepared for the correspondence that followed, including a response by Margaret Wheeler who outlined her journey from independent and equal teacher to dependent wife and mother, step by sorry step. Some women still had no idea how much their husband earned, a situation that persisted way beyond the 1960s. Years of economic dependency after independence pulled the rug out from under marital bliss. Advertisers who infuriated women by suggesting there was nothing they wanted more for Christmas than a new kitchen gadget were all too aware that this was the only way some of them would get one. 'I'm giving my wife a Kenwood Chef,' was the other half of that sexist advertising tag. No money of their own meant little or no money for new clothes (let alone new aprons). Lorna Sage's mother embarked on a complicated dance with Mrs Smith, from whom she bought second-hand clothes, and her husband, from whom she hid their purchase until she could safely bring them forward as if she had owned them all along.

When I was busy discovering clothes and beaded purses at Annie and Eva's house, I came across two floral sleeveless overalls, circa 1950s, one pink, one green, each with a gathered waist and buttons from throat to hemline. I converted the green one into a smock and wore it to a music festival (though, alas, that did not end my washing-up). Soon, *Spare Rib* would produce a tea towel reminding women that 'You start by sinking into his arms and end up with your arms in his sink,' and Vivienne Westwood would make her own witty feminist statement, a knitted jacket in dish-cloth string with two enormous buttons – the metal lids of the domestic scourer Vim.

BUTTONHOLES STEP-BY-STEP

STITCHED BUTTONHOLES

Step 1. These should be made on fabrics that fray easily or on bulky fabrics such as tweed. First cut slits, the exact size required for buttons, through two thicknesses of material. Oversew edges to prevent fraying.
Step 2. Work round the edges of the slit in buttonhole-stitch, making a small bar of stitching across one end. The work should be done in thread which matches your fabric exactly.

BOUND BUTTONHOLES

Step 1. These are for fine, firm fabrics. Tack a crossway strip of fabric over position of buttonholes – right side face to face with right side of dress fabric. Surround each position with an oblong of stitching. Cut slit midway between the two lines of stitches, clip diagonally at each end.
Step 2. Draw strip through to wrong side and tack, forming a tiny inverted pleat at each end.
Step 3. Stitch through at seam-line on right side to hold the piping in place, using fine running stitches.
Step 4. Trim away surplus material at back and hem down round the slit very neatly.

'The ABC of Home Dressmaking, No. 2',
Woman's Illustrated (26 January 1957)

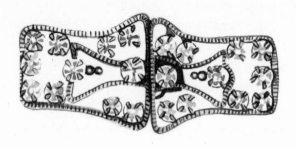

24 **THE DIAMANTÉ CLASP:** A LITTLE RAZZLE DAZZLE

Now a jewel in the button box, the diamanté clasp was once a glinting addition to a stage costume, an extravagance added to the short flared skirt of a pink taffeta dress that was one of several I wore when 'dressing up' at my grandma's. My mum wore the pink taffeta when performing as a pupil of the Miss Iliffe School of Dancing, something she did many times during the 1930s and '40s. A golden-yellow gown of hers had an emerald green sequined heart beating on its bodice; a scarlet and white blouse, drum majorette-style, fastened with large gilt buttons. Stage clothes catch the light and need to be seen from a distance. It is as well for them to sparkle now and then.

The short pink dress was made for 'Forget-Me-Not Lane', a lively troupe number, each girl dressed in the same style but a different colour, wartime expediency resulting in a vivid display. The dancers appeared from the wings in a line, arms linked round waists, low kicks rising higher and higher as they circled in formation, separating to make the spokes of a wheel and then coming together again in a Busby Berkeley kaleidoscope of pattern, kicks and colour. Anyone who has seen *42nd Street* knows the pleasurable slam of multiple taps striking the boards. 'Forget-Me-Not Lane' was designed to make the audience sit up. Even without a diamanté clasp, the pink dress was obviously meant for the stage.

Buckles or buttons set with brilliants are all about show – and always have been. Aristocrats of earlier centuries had buttons decorated with diamonds. The French court took elaboration to extremes: the Comte d'Artois wore diamond buttons set with miniature watches; Louis XV had his own button-maker. Marcasite was a cheaper mineral substitute; cut steel also glittered and flashed like the diamonds courtiers wore. Cut-steel buttons became extremely fashionable and made the fortunes of several Birmingham manufacturers, notably Matthew Boulton (who later worked with Josiah Wedgwood to produce ceramic buttons). By the late nineteenth century – by which time women were the ones doing the sparkling – lustre glass had replaced steel; the majority of Victorian and Edwardian dazzlers are made from this material. Their popularity for eveningwear led to millions being imported, mostly from France and Czechoslovakia. Where would evening dress be without a little razzle dazzle?

Shoes set with brilliants were among those on sale during Chesterfield's 1914 Shopping Festival. In 1929, *The Needlewoman* insisted, 'You must have a lamé evening wrap.' This was the era in which some lucky, unknown woman arrived for dinner wearing a metallic-studded shawl that later came to my great-aunt Eva (probably via one of the big-house sales my great-grandfather frequented). Rich, poor, middling: all ranks of society like to dress up. The 1920s and '30s, as well as liking beaded and jewelled frocks for eveningwear and the Charleston, were agog for fancy dress, Cleopatras glittering among the Pierrots and Pierrettes.

The 'brilliant' cut diamonds favoured today were introduced

during this period. By the 1950s, costume jewellery promised never-ending sparkle and even the most sedate matron wore a jewelled brooch on her lapel. Brilliance was itself subject to fashion: yellower diamonds found favour in the 1930s; fifties women preferred white diamonds in their necklaces and floral sprays.

Diamanté sparkle, long dresses, dinner dances. Those 1950s evening gowns were accessorised with little bags for the powder compact every woman carried (the powder compact was that era's go-to gift for women at works Christmas dos). Compacts also glittered and shimmered. A fifties compact given to me has a black surface with two silver jewelled palm trees and a gold Bambi (suggesting a designer who perhaps did not know when to stop). Dinner dances provided occasions for my mum to wear long black velvet gowns with tight bodices and halter necks. Annie made her a white bolero to soften those backless gowns, a silver lamé dress and a blue taffeta evening coat with a mandarin collar; a pink net skirt she transformed from stage- to eveningwear required hours of hand sewing to create an arc of black net bead-studded flowers which swept from calf to waistband. My mum completed her Coty L'Aimant evenings with elbow-length white (or black) cotton gloves.

Formal wear required appropriate jewellery: a necklace of graduated 'diamond' slabs, crystal beads twinkling rainbows, earrings dangling like chandeliers. An 'Instant Paris' addition recommended by *Vogue* included a glittering necklace, rhinestone earrings and bracelets, or a string of graduated pearls. This passion for all things sparkling suited the shiny new post-war world. (It even extended into home furnishings: chrome cake stands were popular wedding gifts). Make-up too had its own shimmer. In 1958, Elizabeth Arden promoted a new foundation, 'Veiled Radiance'; Goya advertised thirteen 'Golden Girl Cosmetics' in

1965 and 'a totally new lip finish that turns your lipstick shades into shimmer shades!' (for 6s 6d). Shimmery nail polish set the party-goer back 6s.

My parents were among the 5 million people who, by 1961, went to a dance each week; they also liked to invite friends back. For my parents' circle, after-hours socialising meant dancing ('Bobby's Girl', 'Move Over Darling', 'Fever'. . .), nibbles and drinks, which is where the cocktail cabinet came in. The cocktail cabinet arrived in 1959. It was described as a wine cabinet on the receipt, which sounds more restrained and decorous. It did not hold wine, however (which, back in the day, was mostly Mateus Rosé) but spirits and the mixes for whisky mac, gin and tonic, gin and French, gin and It. The mirrored interior held a heavy soda siphon, a goblet with a chrome lid for ice, and numerous glasses, some of which were so fine you hardly dared put them to your lips.

Three metal cocktail sticks with billiard-ball tops – red, yellow, green – slotted into a holder inside the left-hand door; the inside-right held a lemon squeezer. If it seems odd that integral cocktail sticks were supplied in traffic-light colours, this was before the breathalyser, in the days of 'one for the road'. With both cabinet doors open and a mirrored counter resting on an open drawer, the whole was an invitation to pleasure. A narrow drawer held coasters and rinky-dink cocktail stirrers picked up in one place or another: I remember a giraffe with an especially elongated neck and a slim swizzle-stick with a pineapple atop. There were toothpicks for piercing maraschino cherries and tiny forks for skewering cocktail onions. Later came Chiplets, paprika-sprinkled hard-boiled eggs, and grapefruits studded with cubes of cheese, or cheese alternating with pineapple and cocktail onions. How sophisticated it seemed to me, the mirrored interior giving the whole a glamorous sparkle capable of unsettling the tipsy drinker who, while leaning in for a top-up, could see their face in several planes at once. The cocktail cabinet belonged to an adult world of music, perfume, laughter and smart dresses, although the party clothes of my mum's that I remember best are the ones she wore to go out. They complete a memory of soft fur, intense wafts of newly applied scent, and long cold earrings brushing against me as she leaned in for a goodnight kiss.

Just as, years later, I uncovered treasures at Annie and Eva's, as a child I loved to explore my mum's wardrobe and look at her clothes. I also discovered the mysteries of her dressing table: the cigarette lighter shaped like a lipstick, the shimmery beaded purse which held sixpence for the ladies' cloakroom; the pan-cake make-up and the eyeliner with its slender toothbrush-like applicator that, when discarded, made a perfect doll's toothbrush; the lace-edged handkerchiefs for patting stray lipstick; and always the faint drift of face powder in the corner of a drawer. Like Kezia in Katherine Mansfield's 'Prelude' discovering a bead, needle and stay button caught between the floorboards of an empty room, I was fascinated by these small-scale intimations of a grown-up world. My mum had a little plastic cape to protect her shoulders from hair combings when she sat at her triple-mirrored dressing table. Who sits at a dressing table now?

Evening dresses were shorter, earrings and dress rings larger, and my parents made occasional forays to the Carlton, a nightclub with gaming tables and a floor show that attracted singers such as Jackie Trent and Nellie Lucker. This sophisticated venue was something I could only imagine, but its name intrigued me because of those scented goodnight kisses. Even now, the name has a certain allure and conjures up little lights on tables, red plush, dicky bows and twinkling earrings. This was the era in which my mum wore a slip of a dress in tangerine and the scarlet one in tiered chiffon that came to me when I was in my twenties. At that time I also shook out an old stage dress of hers and wore it to a party. White sateen, with a soft full skirt, it made me want to sway and swirl. The dance changes, but a taste for dressing up, once discovered, is rarely lost.

25 **THE TOGGLE:** GOD, THIS MODERN YOUTH!

During the 1950s, the duffel coat became a shorthand for middle-class disaffected youth, its signals vastly different from the uniform of working-class Teddy Boys. When coupled with a college scarf, the duffel was ideally suited to long walks with hands stuffed into pockets on marches. The Suez Crisis, Aldermaston Marches, the launch of the Campaign for Nuclear Disarmament – the post-war world provided ample opportunities for political engagement and the sense that the world needed re-making, with the younger generation the ones to achieve that. The young Sheila Rowbotham favoured the existentialist look, with 'black stockings, tight skirts from Leeds C & A cheaper separates, the largest black sweater I could find and black high heels', a less confrontational display of disaffection than punk two decades later, although shocking to some back then.

Wooden toggles like those in my button box fastened the duffel coat I wore to school in the mid-seventies, aged seventeen. Times had moved on, but I too wore opaque black tights and they and the coat still had a certain anti-style, equivalent to the Army greatcoat favoured by some sixth-form boys who would not have dreamed of joining up. I completed the look with a home-made khaki shoulder bag, transformed from an army-store cast-off.

It was harder to be rebellious before a youthful uniform existed. In the 1920s, riding pillion and wearing Kissproof lipstick came close – unless you were a Bright Young Thing with the means to kick over the traces. In those days, outrageousness relied on money, and parents. Later, as Jenifer Wayne observed, 'the first duty of the novitiate outrager [was] to repudiate both'. She recalled the stir two schoolgirl sisters caused with their high heels, silk stockings and plucked eyebrows. In the days before television, and the immediate distribution (and saturation) of new ideas, the sisters' sensationalism was all the greater: 'the legs and lashes to be seen in Blackheath Village on a Saturday morning meant more to us than all the bra-less kaftans and the kohl of Women's Lib.'

In between the two came the emergence of a teenage style, in which fashion took on a 'role as signal, armour and decoration'. Barbara Hulanicki, founder of Biba, described young women in Brighton, 1950. 'The young girls wore the latest polished dirndl skirts under which swished petticoats of paper nylon. They wore colours that rocked the grey pavements . . . their dark heads were feather cut in boyish style, ears weighed down by bright coloured giant button earrings.' Dirndl skirts needed broad belts or cummerbunds to complete them, like the double-buckled belt in bubblegum pink a friend gave me: an assertion of fifties teen spirit.

Dodgem-bright skirts, clip-on earrings that scabbed the ears; petticoats crackling with starch – however uncomfortable, it was a relief to assert yourself. Mary Quant who, as a child, had hated being forced to wear her cousin's cast-offs, lived in a state of perpetual embarrassment until, as art students, she and her future husband and business partner Alexander Plunket Greene, started to break the rules. On one occasion, they blew Alexander's allowance in the smart London restaurant Quaglino's, Quant dressed in a short gingham skirt, black poplin shirt, knee socks and sandals, Alexander wearing prune-coloured trousers and his mother's pyjama jacket. One of the incredulous remarks flung at them was 'God, this Modern Youth!'

The opening of Mary Quant's Bazaar on London's King's Road in 1955 met with further incredulity – and outrage on the part of the city gents whose pinstripes and bowler hats she re-interpreted. Eighteen-year-old Diana Melly got a Saturday job there.

It was where anyone young and interested in clothes had to be. It's hard to appreciate now quite how radically different Mary's clothes were from anything else available at the time. When I wasn't working in Bazaar, I would do modelling for magazines like *Woman's Own*, *Vogue* and *Queen* and there it was all tweed suits, pinched at the waist, finished off with hats and gloves. We were constantly being told to make ourselves look older because fashion was directed at women over 30 . . . Mary Quant changed all of that.

Much youthful dress was imported from America, along with rock 'n' roll. In 1957 the American magazine *Cosmopolitan* asked, 'Are Teenagers Taking Over?' Something was in the air and that something was Youth, asserting itself in new ways and in direct opposition to age. 'Their 1950s was a different place,' wrote Lorna Sage. Three years later, British teenage spending power was estimated to be worth £800 million. Britain was enjoying its highest standard of living for many years; full employment meant that young people had money in their pockets and a relaxed attitude to go with it: lose one job, get another; buy new clothes and a new record each week.

Sales of 45-rpm singles increased from 4 million units in 1955 to 61 million in 1963. Just owning a record was almost enough (as was carrying an album cover to display your affiliations). Twiggy Lawson recalls her sister Viv buying Paul Anka's single 'Diana', even though she had no record player: 'we would sit around the table and she would hand it round and let us look at it'. Innocent times. Some weeks later their father relented and bought a second-hand Dansette. Saturday nights revolved around the dance halls. The youthquake had its own soundtrack.

Nell Dunn's *Up The Junction* (1963) plunges straight into that zesty, exuberant moment.

We stand, the three of us, me, Sylvie and Rube, pressed up against the saloon door, brown ales clutched in our hands. Rube, neck stiff so as not to shake her beehive, stares sultrily round the packed pub. Sylvie eyes the boy hunched over the mike and shifts her gaze down to her breasts snug in her new pink jumper.

No one could doubt the era.

Before she burst on to the scene as 'The Face of '66' Twiggy made her own clothes, starting at the age of thirteen to create the Mod styles she could not find in mail-order catalogues. Fabric was cheap; she and her school friends pooled their money to buy *Vogue* patterns which 'although expensive, could easily be adapted if you knew how. And I knew how.' Monday to Friday Twiggy was a grammar-school girl. Come Saturday night, she was a Mod, complete with Woolworth's white lipstick and black mascara.

In 1963, Mary Quant opened a second branch of Bazaar, launched the Ginger Group (her wholesale manufacturing venture), was designated a 'Woman of the Year', and received a *Sunday Times* International Fashion Award for 'jolting England out of its conventional attitude towards clothes'. The following year, André Courrèges launched his controversial Space Age collection, with its white-booted, short-skirted models. Fashion was on the front pages again and could not move quickly enough.

Boutiques opened up, one after another. Though not the first – Schiaparelli's opened in Paris in 1935; and Hardy Amies' in London in 1950 – Bazaar launched a different kind of boutique. It was not just that young women were served by women their own age, who dressed like them as well (no more supercilious, intimidating shop assistants), and were spending more on clothes than ever before, fashion was changing week on week.

Miniskirts reached higher and higher, popularised by Quant and named after her favourite car, that zippy little engine for zooming about busy streets. The miniskirt required tights instead of stockings – that revolution in itself – and had some employers adding 'modesty boards' to office desks to cope with the ever shorter skirts worn by female staff; women also had to learn how to exit cars gracefully, the sixties version of perfect poise. Just as the raised hemlines of the 1920s cut a dash for modernity, so the 1960s took fashion to, literally, new heights. Shorter skirts in Mondrian colours symbolised the excitement of the freewheeling, fast-moving, man-made future.

Nineteen sixty-three also saw the birth of the Biba phenomenon, initially via its Postal Boutique. Mail order was a growing trend in the 1960s, 'outstripping all other forms of retailing' via companies such as Freemans, Littlewoods and Grattan, but Biba was something else. When in May 1964, the *Daily Mirror* featured Barbara Hulanicki's 25*s* sugar-pink gingham shift dress with a keyhole back and matching Bardot-like headscarf, 17,000 were sold. That year saw Biba move into the first of its four premises: 'There should be a plaque on 87 Abingdon Road,' Twiggy has written. 'It wasn't like any other shop I had ever seen.' Chelsea schoolgirl Alexandra Pringle was equally bowled over: 'Perhaps it was the greatest frivolity of the sixties, but to me it also seemed awesome.' The rise – and fall – of Biba is now the stuff of legend: assistants pointedly *not* offering help; shoppers browsing in half-lit surroundings (ideal for shoplifting) and changing in communal cubicles (a new trend in itself) or simply disrobing where they stood.

From the beginning, Biba attracted office workers and school-girls as well as the famous and infamous. Young women watching *Ready, Steady, Go* on Friday evenings clocked what Cathy McGowan was wearing and bought it from Biba the next day. 'Our Saturdays were always spectacular, whatever the weather,' Hulanicki recalls, 'It became a meeting place.' It also provided 'a uniform for an era'. London bank worker Chris Haley chose a scarlet high-necked Biba trouser suit for her engagement party.

Mary Quant defined 'the girl who is with-it' as 'lively . . . positive . . . opinionated'. She had advice for the 'intellectual' who disregarded fashion but needed to learn that 'fashion is not frivolous; it is a part of being alive today', and had words for the 'square' who 'is a little low on nerve' (and usually chose a little black dress instead of a white lace bell-bottomed trouser suit). 'Girls in their teens and twenties are busy people who have no time to switch clothes during the day,' Quant said. 'They want clothes they can put on first thing in the morning and feel right in at midnight; clothes that go happily to the office and equally happily out to dinner.' (Winifred Holtby would have cheered.)

There were further similarities with the 1920s. Just as more accessible clothing had led to remarks about the merging of social classes, so Quant insisted that class was no longer an issue. After the 1944 Education Act, with working-class young men and women no longer having to 'know their place' and show due deference, that claim was more convincing. 'There was a time when clothes were a sure sign of a woman's social position and income group,' Quant said. 'Not now. Snobbery has gone out of fashion, and in our shops you will find duchesses jostling with typists to buy the same dresses.' If class was no longer a barrier, neither was gender. 'Since the sexes live much the same sort of lives, they want the same sort of clothes to live them in.'

Youth had its own language, and if you had to ask – forget it. Clothes, and much more besides, could be 'dishy, grotty, geary, kinky, mod' or 'poove'; there was also a kooky look. For a while, youth was not merely youthful, it was childlike. In one way this became an expression of Play Power and an assertion of kids' rights but, in another, strikes a more jarring note. Models posed sucking their thumbs and turning in their toes; a pseudo-innocence prevailed, as if, in finally being allowed to express youthfulness, and enjoy a period of irresponsibility, young women had to go right back to childhood. Some aspects of youth culture were more equal than others: women were dollies, dolly birds, birds, and still, overwhelmingly, girls. The sexual revolution was only just beginning and had a long way to go.

Pinafore dresses, knickerbockers, keyhole frocks, black stockings, high boots, chain-handled bags; zips were not just functional, they were hip. Gloves had two-inch zips on metal ring-pulls; chains dangled from zips on breast pockets and were slung loosely around waists in the jingle-jangle world of then. Black was out unless mixed with white to form gyroscopic swirls or diluted in some way: one of Mary Quant's most successful early lines was a slim white plastic collar to brighten a black sweater or dress. 'We sold these at two-and-six each and we sold literally thousands and thousands.'

Affordability was key, but there were still gradations within the new: a Courrèges couture coat retailed at £230 (a third of the annual salary of a staff nurse in 1964); *Vogue* instituted a new column, 'More Dash than Cash' (reinstated in 2009), in which nothing cost more than 45 guineas, which was still an exorbitant sum. A Mary Quant dress advertised by the *Sunday Times* in 1962, priced £27, was also beyond the reach of many. 'Bazaar in the King's Road was for rich girls,' Twiggy recalls. 'Biba was for anyone . . . Not only did the clothes look amazing, you could afford to buy something every week.' Barbara Hulaniki's husband and business partner, Stephen Fitz-Simon (Fitz), calculated that, with an average weekly wage of £9, a young woman would spend £3 on rent, £3 on food and £3 on clothes (though some of them surely allocated a portion for singles and LPs). Hulanicki remembers: 'Dresses were around £3, blouses £2, and very few things – even coats – cost more than £8.'

Home-dressmakers were not left behind. They could send for 'The Mary Quant Spring Wardrobe Designed for the *Sunday Times*', a paper pattern illustrated by three leggy young women with marionette faces. This was one of many patterns bought by Chris Haley who, as well as shopping at Biba, followed fashion by making her own clothes, assisted by her Aunt Queenie, a rag-trade worker. Simplicity, Butterick, McCalls and Le Roy were also among those producing patterns for the miniskirts and shift dresses seen in the newly launched colour supplements and the glossy and teen magazines.

'Clothes were everything and there was money to be made,' said Twiggy. Some of the new boutiques were launched by established retailers capitalising on the youth brand: in 1965, Lewis Separates re-branded its seventy-store empire as Chelsea Girl; Miss Selfridge was launched the following year. However, the majority of mainstream manufacturers, middle-aged and schooled in different times, were slow to grasp the serious potential of this moving, grooving, surging mass with money in their pockets and a desire for instant gratification.

When, in April 1966, American *Time* magazine coined the

famous phrase 'Swinging London', London's youth scene achieved instant international renown. Twiggy's own rise from obscurity showed how rapidly some transformations were made. In a matter of days, aged sixteen, she was a full-time, feted model, and a 'Woman of the Year' just after her seventeenth birthday. When, three years later, Twiggy was the focus of ITV's *This Is Your Life*, Marjorie Proops was invited on to the programme to explain her appeal to those who had yet to catch on.

The youthquake even made its presence felt via a doll. Enter Sindy, 'the free, swinging grown-up girl who lives her own life and dresses the way she likes'. What could be more appealing than a doll with whom you could play at being a woman? I was six when I met her. The outfit came first, chosen by me in Redgates, the toyshop too small for all it contained, whose riches included cellophane-wrapped red plastic lipsticks as hard as the pink plastic tubes that encased them, sparkly powder compacts without powder, and other tiny accoutrements with which to ape adult life, among them a pair of pink plastic Cinderella shoes with glitter suspended in the heels which, in memory, tower several inches high, although that is unlikely.

The Sindy outfit I chose featured a brown suede boxy jacket, similar to those worn by Mods and, in an odd synchronicity, some country ladies. There were flat lace-ups, a brown tweed skirt and an olive green polo-necked sweater which fastened all the way down the back with tiny poppers that peeled open in an instant – hey presto (press-stud) – for the girl eager to undress her doll. The outfit worn by this 'free, swinging grown-up girl' was reminiscent of those worn by the stockbroker wives quietly seething in commuter-belt isolation in Penelope Mortimer's 1958 novel *Daddy's Gone A-Hunting*. It was July 1964 but the sixties were not yet happening in a big way in my home town (or, at least, not noticeably within my landscape). The Sindy clothes were an unexpected gift; I had to wait until Christmas for the doll that would wear them. And, after that – so many outfits, bought for Christmases and birthdays, and with pocket money I saved. Two or three stand out: a quilted blue ski jacket with a fur-trimmed hood (more people were taking foreign holidays); a nurse's uniform with separate elasticated cuffs, like miniature cotton puff balls, and an air hostess's navy blue suit with a tiny plastic BOAC bag. Nurse or air hostess were still standard fare for girls. (As Lorna Sage pointed out, before women realised that air hostessing was glorified waitressing, the job was seen to have prestige and even glamour.) I would like to think I remember Sindy's uniforms because I already felt affronted by the limited possibilities they held out, although I suspect I just enjoyed their accessories. I don't think Sindy was a teacher: *Vogue* pictured a young teacher in a 1960s fashion shoot wearing her buttoned-up cardigan (buttoned up to the throat, not worn back to front, which would have suggested something else altogether), shepherding her young class through the playground, cardigans and teaching for ever linked in a stereotype of teacher's clothing. Katharine Whitehorn affronted her early-sixties readership when, as *Observer* fashion editor, she spoke out against the cardigan.

Sindy wore low court shoes which were nothing like the stilettos Barbie tottered in, nor the white shoes Caithleen wears in Edna O'Brien's *Girl with Green Eyes*, whose long pointed toes require her to walk upstairs sideways. There were red wellingtons to go with Sindy's black PVC mac and her plastic scarlet bag. She had ski pants too, like the ski pants worn by my mum with stirrups underfoot, the kind that create a taut outline suggesting that women's legs do not bend. Though of their time, they were nothing like as hip as the pastel-coloured pedal pushers in mint green or pink worn by the Shangri-Las (and Mum). I think – or do I imagine? – that Sindy wore her ski pants with a baggy jumper of the kind known then as a Sloppy Joe. There was a Sloppy Joe bra too (though not in Sindy's wardrobe; that was reserved for readers of *Vogue*). And what did Sindy wear for winter walks? A duffel coat with six imitation wood toggles.

A later addition, Sindy's boyfriend Paul – 'the well-dressed young man whose clothes are designed for a free-wheeling life' – was the kind of young man any parent would be pleased to escort their daughter. Paul rode a scooter, not a motorbike, which suggested safe modernity to the adult mind (by now scooters had been tamed), though it was obvious to any contemporary child that he was one of those adults who try just a bit too hard. And his tagline gave the game away. What self-respecting groovy girl wanted a '*well-dressed young man*'? Patch, Sindy's younger sister, an even later addition, designed to woo playmates not yet ready to graduate to the grown-up doll, had freckles of the kind a child might draw – dot, dot, dot – and nylon hair shinier than anything that could be achieved with Silvikrin or Vosene. A tomboy (though more girly than George in *The Famous Five*), Patch wore dungarees with a requisite gingham patch. I played with all three dolls, though Paul was not my type, nor Patch, really. Such good clean fun. No Afghan coat or paisley-swirling dress, no tuning in or dropping out – although the sixties moved on and I with them, out of the Sindy landscape.

26 **THE TURQUOISE BUTTON:** THE NEW KIND OF WOMAN

In 1964 my mum bought a short-skirted turquoise suit. All but one of the jacket's dozen buttons survive, a testament to her fondness for this boxy suit with buttoned breast pockets and cuffs. Even the four large holes punched in each button for thread have the wide-eyed look of the day. These may be ordinary buttons but their style, 'zooming' colour and chunky shape speak to the graphic simplicity of the 1960s.

The sixties happened for everyone, but not necessarily at the same time; it took until the 1970s for some aspects of that decade to alter the provincial landscape and, even then, some people felt the sixties happened elsewhere. One clear way in which that decade lit up the provinces, however, was in the matter of dress. The switch from accented femininity and formality into something free and easy was a boon to every woman willing to adopt the look.

My mum knew the sixties had arrived when she paid her 3s 6d for the complete and unexpurgated *Lady Chatterley's Lover* though, this being Chesterfield, she wrapped her copy in brown paper in order to read undisturbed at the hairdresser's. A few years later, the male assistant in a local chemist's shop approached her with a perfume that had just come in, quoting its tagline: 'May I be Intimate with you?' (Revlon introduced Intimate in 1955, but no provincial chemist would have asked that question then.) The sixties definitely had landed.

Mums need not be mumsy any more, and mine was a modern mum. She took me to the park wearing a Sloppy Joe jumper, ski pants and slip-on pumps, and pushed me in my pushchair in a tightly belted trench coat. Youth was no longer confined to the young. Women of my mum's generation were only in their thirties when the sixties struck, and were just as ready to pull on short (if not quite so short) skirts and psychedelic-patterned dresses as the next woman.

Not everything happened at once, though. In the early 1960s I seemed to be forever trailing after Mum in the search for the gloves that matched the handbag that toned with the shoes. In the previous decade, Katharine Whitehorn appeared on the cover of *Whitehorn's Social Survival* doing the trick she had been 'taught by the charm school people – holding gloves, bag, plate, glass, cigarette and fork and still having a hand free to shake'. The search for complementary accessories seemed an equivalent balancing act, as well as a hangover from those years.

A 1965 fashion shoot, 'One Woman in Her Day Plays Many Parts . . .' divided a woman's day into eight acts: Working Girl, Handyman, Sportswoman, Wife, Mother (shown wearing the same clothes as her daughter), Girl turns Gardener, Hostess (dressed for a party in a 'printed voile harem dress') and Chauffeur. 'And the silly thing is that the more she does, the harder it is for her to get any notice taken of it all.' The editorial was a peg on which to hang a fashion shoot, but it nonetheless signalled a change in tone as well as a new approach. The magazine was *Nova*.

'A New Kind of Magazine for the New Kind of Woman', *Nova*

blasted on to the scene in March 1965, priced 3s. My mum bought the first issue and stayed with the magazine until its demise ten years later. Pitched at 'women who make up their own minds', *Nova* was impressive for its sheer heft even before you turned to the first of its 178 pages. '*Nova* is a magazine for women who cook, sew, like clothes and realise that these are not enough. They still have time to think.' Extraordinary though it may seem, the idea that women think still required some underlining. A 1968 *Sunday Times* advertisement announced that 'At the *Sunday Times* we like bright women. Some of our best friends are. So are some of our best writers . . .' The advert was headed 'Birdbrain'.

Nova was a magazine to keep and come back to. Cutting-edge design complemented lengthy interviews and articles expressing cutting-edge views. Features from 1966 included 'The New Spinsters' ('solitary but no confinement') and 'Walled-in Wives – Diagnose Your Neurosis', the latter tackling a subject making waves since Betty Friedan's *The Feminine Mystique* (1963). And there were audacious cover features such as that in March 1967: 'Yes, we are living in sin. No, we're not getting married. Why? It's out of date.' Picture that incendiary headline thumping on to suburban doormats.

Everything was being questioned and debated; everything seemed up for grabs. Angela Carter recalled, 'the relaxation of manners, the sense of intellectual excitement, even the way, oh, God, you didn't have to shave your *armpits* . . . hemlines, politics, music, movies.' The burgeoning second wave of feminism was a crucial part of that; Angela Carter again:

truly, it felt like Year One, when all that was holy was in the process of being profaned . . . I can date to that time . . . and to that sense of heightened awareness of the society around me in the summer of 1968, my own questioning of the nature of my reality as a *woman*. How that social fiction of my 'femininity' was created . . . and palmed off on me as the real thing.

Writers were tackling subjects with a new candour and explicitness. 'Our subject matter is enormous,' Margaret Drabble wrote a few years later. 'There are whole new patterns to create.' It was hip to be a paperback writer, but women were still on the receiving end of the usual mixed messages. Shena Mackay's opinion was 'sought on everything from the Beatles to reasons why a pretty girl should waste her time on writing novels'.

The ease with which fiction could be translated into film and television brought its messages to much broader audiences, and swiftly: Rita Tushingham looks out from my mum's copy of *Girl with Green Eyes*, Carol White from *Poor Cow*. All those slim-spined paperbacks – Edna O'Brien, Lynne Reid-Banks, Andrea Newman, Nell Dunn's *Talking to Women* . . . On Tuesday evenings, my mum and godmother disappeared into the lounge to paint their nails, sips of gin and tonic alternating with strokes of Revlon nail polish, with its long, sleek, white shakeable wand and tiny ball-bearings to stop the varnish sticking to the bottle. Theirs was adult talk: women talking. It seemed exciting to me. And all the while Pentangle's theme tune for *Take Three Girls* spooled through my head, suggesting that growing up was all about sharing a flat in London.

Television seemed to exist on several planes, not just the eventual transition from black and white to colour, but different gradations of black and white: the perfectly modulated tones of stiff-upper-lip Sunday-evening war films versus *The Loneliness of the Long-Distance Runner*, the Establishment and the youthful anti-Establishment playing it out on our TV screens, Kenneth Moore in one corner, Tom Courtenay in the other. Weekday evenings were transformed by plays like *Up the Junction* and *Cathy Come Home*, unmissable experiences, dark, gritty dramas which brought tough questions about abortion and homelessness into the sitting room and helped bring in new legislation as well as changing public opinion in a decade of radical change: the abolition of the death penalty, the legalisation of homosexuality, abortion and divorce law reform, the collapse of theatre censorship, the Race Relations Act. Debates about sex and contraception – the word 'sex' itself gaining currency post-Chatterley and Profumo – followed the introduction of the contraceptive pill.

The sixties saw ever more women in the workforce, and more married women among them. Women civil servants, local government workers and teachers were accorded equal pay in 1961, but it would take the now-legendary 1968 Dagenham strike by Ford machinists to enable Barbara Castle, Secretary of State for Employment, to secure the 1970 Equal Pay Act (if not equal pay). A 1967 'Report on Women and Top Jobs' showed that, within the workforce as a whole, there were two men to every woman and that among all PAYE incomes, men had an advantage of 20 to 1 in salaries of £2,000–£2,999. At levels of over £5,000, that advantage rose to 50 to 1. Joan Bakewell discovered that, in the early years of *Late Night Line-Up*, TV's nightly commentary, she was paid less than her male colleagues. As Virginia Woolf wrote thirty years earlier, when discussing similar discrepancies and the lack of professional opportunities for women, 'The cat is out of the bag; and it is a Tom.'

I was reading *Jackie* in 1967, with its picture-box love stories and advertisements for sanitary towels, blue eyeshadow, identity bracelets and spot cream. A May 1969 issue advertised two careers: with the Women's Royal Army Corps you could be a PT instructor, shorthand typist or a kennel maid ('not many girls get to be WRAC kennel maids and grooms . . . But you might be lucky!'); alternatively you could nurse with the Queen Alexander's Royal Army Nursing Corps. Men would land on the moon two months later but *Jackie*'s readers were not encouraged to reach too far.

The new ideas finding currency in fashion, as in so much else, were reflected in adolescent clothing as well as adult styles. As I moved out of Sindy's landscape I began to move away from home-made clothes though, when crochet dresses were the latest thing, my grandma made me a scarlet-edged black dress with a matching poncho. (A poncho!) A shop-bought Courtelle dress ('The New Generation Jersey') was followed circa 1967 by a flared trouser suit from Coles in Sheffield, the source of any classy, modern clothes. It is strange to relate that trouser suits were challenging when they first came in; when *SHE* magazine featured Biba's first trouser suit in October 1964 it reassured readers that the jacket came with 'a slim skirt for the timid'.

My mum bought a pair of Mary Quant shoes in Sheffield: chunky-heeled clover-pink suede with purple detailing. She and I 'tried' paper knickers which pouched oddly and unattractively and were rather like wearing an elasticated J-cloth. The experiment was short-lived. (They pouched, I presume, because, being made of a similar fabric, they could not be stretched without putting holes in them.) In 1968 with my older brother in the lead, as so often then, he and I bought vests from Wakefield's army stores, knotted them with string and generated psychedelic swirls by boiling them up on the cooker. The shop-bought tie-dyed grandad vest I wore was a haze of bruised colour, but do-it-yourself was far more satisfying.

If Sheffield was our place for classy, well-made clothes, Chesterfield Market was the source of cheap and cheerful grati-fication: skinny-ribbed sweaters, leather chokers and (eventually) all things glittery. My first smock, the first garment I bought, a bright checked plaid with an appliqué apple on the bodice and buttons all the way down the back, came courtesy of the market. By now, Chesterfield's Swallow's and John Turner's demonstrated a muted decorum increasingly at odds with the times. They attempted to keep abreast of fashion, but Swallow's 1965 Christmas catalogue, offering Paisley Viyella blouses, formal in style and with names like Aintree Gold, Newbury Red and Kempton Blue suggest they were backing the wrong horse. Its younger styles, depicted by well-scrubbed girls dancing in Tricel dresses, included a party dress in a bolder paisley pattern. 'This is the trend and you must get with it, at Swallow's'; but these were not aimed at young women but at schoolgirls shopping with their mothers.

The dance changed yet again, miniskirts skipping towards full-length dresses, via flower-power smocks, kaftans, Afghan coats, cheesecloth and crushed velvet. How proud I was of my plum-coloured crushed-velvet flares. Floral prints like those designed by Celia Birtwell had a zinging graphic intensity – 'graphic' was a new buzzword – and were nothing like the naturalistic flowers of earlier decades, nor even the stylised flowers of yore; the childlike blooms of the late sixties and early seventies had their own unreality. There was a general softening and lengthening of line similar to that which accompanied a return to femininity in the 1930s, but with a different meaning. Colours changed too. Everything was plum, cherry, dusty pink, purple or clover – like my mum's Mary Quant shoes. Farewell maroon, a colour that existed during my childhood but then disappeared, as did fawn – though few would grieve for fawn, the dying fall of the noun conveying the timidity of the actual shade. Colours do not disappear, of course, it is merely the names that change; each decade selecting its own. For me, Tango meant a fizzy orange drink, but in the 1920s 'a lovely affair of tango silk' conveyed a Valentino sophistication and a different kind of fizz altogether.

My own suede shoes were dusty pink with latticework straps. I also wore a midi-length clover-pink herringbone skirt which buttoned down the front. Cardi coats were in: mine was another shade along the pink-to-purple spectrum, with murky-pink and white woollen fringing; my mum's was purple, though we *never* wore them at the same time; Mum also wore a dark purple midi coat. Fashion still appealed across the generations, although tastes were soon to diverge. In 1971, we saw *The Boyfriend* and afterwards only just managed to resist tap dancing all the way back down the cinema steps. The 1920s were back.

27 **THE STATEMENT BUTTON:** BIBA AND THE HANKERING FOR VINTAGE

How could I resist the large marbled button I found in a vintage shop? The shop itself was irresistible. It had rails of desirable clothing, a wall of scraped-back wallpapers reminiscent of a host of summer frocks, and a tiny haberdashery section where this button lay in wait. A single button of this size made a statement when securing an aslant-line jacket or dress.

A liking for retro is commonplace now, but it felt new in the early 1970s. The speed with which, in the late 1960s and early '70s, a liking for art nouveau bled into a desire for the 1920s, jazz style and art deco and then back towards the Pre-Raphaelites and forward into deco again showed fashion keeping pace with major exhibitions and broader cultural reappraisals. From this point on, it became possible to buy new clothes in period styles as well as seeking out the originals. The most sophisticated way to do this was via Biba.

As fashion moved to mid-calf and full-length styles, Barbara Hulanicki's designs moved, tardis-like, through the decades. A 1970 Biba poster shows a woman in an Edwardian-style belted suit, her ankles just visible, her hat reminiscent of a bulky reticule.

Funnel-collared coats, buttoning from chin to floor, would not
have looked out of place in the wardrobe of a daredevil woman
driver (just the thing for Miss Levitt with her revolver); tapestry
coats were medieval in tone; a 1940s-style frock with button
detail was similar to a dress my grandma made using different-
coloured fabrics for bodice, skirt and sleeves. For those wanting
the Biba experience without stepping into the past, a flared pink
trouser suit brought things bang up to date. Obligatory long full
sleeves on Biba blouses, with their extra-long buttoned cuffs,
billowed and draped in rayon and satin and were far too glamorous to let trail in the washing-up. (Suffragette writer Elizabeth
Robins wrote that Edwardian women laughed behind their long
full sleeves at men's false chivalry; late-twentieth-century women
also found plenty of double standards to mock.)

My own recollections of Biba date from around the time the
store moved to its fourth and last incarnation at the revamped
Derry & Toms on Kensington High Street. I was only six when
Barbara Hulanicki opened her first shop in London's Abingdon
Road following the success of Biba's mail-order boutique, but I
remember the fashion shoot that appeared in the October 1973
issue of *19* as part of the 'Big Biba' launch: satin, faux fur and
metallic furnishings, chocolate suede boots and pillbox hats, as
befits an era of stacked heels and glam rock.

I fell in love with Biba from afar. This mood coincided with
drive-in Saturdays, 'blue sunsets and grey lagoons', and all those
Velvet Underground-inspired Sunday mornings, with Nico
intoning 'Femme Fatale'. Biba's gold-on-black insignia held out
a promise every bit as exciting as the music I was listening to.
For me, Biba was tall, slim black-and-gold cylinders of talcum
powder, heavy glass bottles of intensely perfumed cologne and,
above all, make-up – the chubby tubs of lip gloss and flat palettes
of the mulberry and terracotta eyeshadow that were redolent of

early-seventies glamour. I bought these from Miss Selfridge in Nottingham's Victoria Centre, an almost-brand-new shopping centre with a delicate Heath Robinson-like water feature and tinkling clock. In Miss Selfridge I also found a 1920s-style welted cardigan and a pair of clompy shoes to accompany the Biba look.

I cannot think of Biba and the Victoria Centre without immediately seeing the images from Sunday colour supplements, *Nova*, *19* and *Honey* that formed a collage on my bedroom wall. In black-and-white or sepia-tinted photographs young women with long flowing Crystal-Tips hair gaze at the camera in vintage-style frocks and berets; or pose, oh so casually, in blue satin cami-knickers edged with coffee-coloured lace, available from Antiquarius in the King's Road, while wearing mauve one-bar Anello & Davide shoes (priced £3.75). Three pounds seventy-five is nothing now, but was decidedly something then. When, aged sixteen, I bought myself a light blue pair, I felt I was splashing out; striding out too. I immediately had a use for my great-aunt Eva's buttonhooks.

Barbara Hulanicki recalled that when she and her husband and business partner Fitz took over the Derry & Toms building on Kensington High Street, theirs was the first department store to open in London since shortly after the Second World War. Hot, dark, crowded, sultry and exotic, with sofas to sink into, 'Big Biba' turned shopping into a seven-storeyed theatrical experience. Linda Grant has written of department stores as theatre, with their front-of-house and behind the scenes staff: 'all have their theatrical equivalents'. Biba made a play on the department store, as if shopping itself was one big fancy-dress party, with theatrically dressed characters, including a glam usherette in fishnet tights, to assist you. Biba offered women an adult dressing-up box and gave them permission to perform.

The store enacted the upstairs/downstairs aspects of the past

– a butler at your service, a 'below stairs' in the basement where you could purchase food and drink, plus a relatively new phenomenon, take-away meals. For a nation hooked on *Upstairs, Downstairs* (that period's *Downton Abbey* equivalent), the ready-made meal was a nice approximation of your own Mrs Bridges coming up with a menu for the day. Upstairs, its Rainbow Room restaurant was as glamorous as any seen on a 1930s film set; English country flowers were planned for the store's Roof Garden: 'it was going to look like a page from a Kate Greenaway book' (to go with those Kate Greenaway buttons).

The art-deco styled department store beloved of interwar women was being recreated – and was far more vampish than even a thirties vamp could wish. The young women who had moved and grooved in the 1960s now slouched and reclined, lounging on animal prints, satins and velvets. Fake ostrich feathers accentuated the outré look. There were Minnie Mouse shoes, and high heels with wispy swansdown pom-poms to tempt young office workers channelling their inner Jean Harlow when heading home after a long, drab day. Satin dresses swirled in homage to Vionnet's bias cuts, black floor-length evening gowns whispered Schiaparelli. The shop struck a pose and, by association, so did anyone who shopped there. Never had shopping been more knowing.

Biba's resplendent gold logo, calling to mind the gilded extravaganzas of art-deco cinema design, tagged everything in store (and out). The thick black plastic bags stamped with gold were desirable in themselves, especially the tiny ones designed to hold those black-and-gold pots of Biba make-up. In its 'Logo Shop' 1930s style met 1970s consumerism head on with nappies, diaries, chocolates, baked beans, ashtrays and even Biba plates on whose dense black discs a gold man and woman in evening dress were entwined. Not since Clarice Cliff had dining been so exotic. A casbah offered kohl for the eyes and henna for the hair; jewellery, flowers and a bookshop. Tights and sweaters came in twenty-four Biba colours, 'the winter colours of 1973', including army, copper, petrol, tobacco, navy, sand, plum, camel, midnight . . . Outside, the winter colours grew ever darker: from 1 January 1974 Britain went on to a three-day week. One year later Biba, no longer wholly owned by Hulanicki and Fitz-Simon, came to an end amid boardroom struggles; its luscious extravagance was no more.

I was a provincial schoolgirl. A chunky black-and-gold Biba postcard stood on the desk at which I did my homework. Each evening I saw its golden sketch of two childlike young women standing beneath a gold sliver of a moon, like the crescent moon on the 1920s *Vogue* poster Sellotaped to my bedroom wall next to my outsize Mucha postcards. Biba was a dream, a promise of possibilities. I kept my Biba make-up in a shell-pink-and-white 1920s beaded evening bag with a fine chain handle, the kind of fragile bag I would now keep in a drawer and look at from time to time. The bag was originally Annie's; this was when I developed a hankering for period clothes and made my discoveries at my grandma and great-aunt's house.

In 1976 Jocasta Innes described her own 'weak spot for really old clothes' –

> my favourite jacket is a most beautifully shaped and tailored black wool Victorian one with two rows of what I only recently discovered were real silver buttons, bought for 50p in a junk shop – you won't need to be told that one of the things that makes them so much more elegant and special is the lavish use of trimmings, and their superb quality: yards of fine lace insertion and edging on blouses and underwear . . . hand-made buttons covered with silk netting, silk fringing, braid . . .

Junk shops, market stalls, jumble sales . . . For some of us at least, the hunt for vintage was on. Reproduction clothing was good but it was far more exciting to find the real thing.

Although second-hand had become chic in some circles, second-hand chic was slow to reach the provinces. Such clothes still carried the baggage of earlier periods and the stigma of hand-me-downs. My mother's generation knew all about clothes being passed on from one child or one woman to the next. A character in Lettice Cooper's 1938 novel *National Provincial* insists, 'No woman ought to be dressed in another woman's leavings,' precisely because so many women were. Little would those women have guessed that their ordinary clothes would be sought years later, and rows of vividly patterned frocks become a standard feature of many a vintage shop. Those of us who chose to wear someone else's clothes were fortunate in having a choice our forebears lacked and were making an altogether different statement. Some clothes I wore until I could wear them no longer, but I blush at the carelessness with which I swapped, borrowed (and discarded) an apparent wealth of summer frocks. Unlike those fictional girls of slender means, however, I was never fortunate enough to wear a Schiaparelli evening gown. Some acquisitions of mine were serendipitous: my mum and I were amazed to discover that the black-and-white-striped dress with full skirt and broad lapels I bought in London was almost exactly the same as one she was photographed wearing in the North of England when I was a baby.

By the late seventies reproduction vintage clothing was available on every high street. A 1978 Miss Selfridge magazine featured crêpe-de-Chine blouses from £9.95 and a forties-style dress at £19.95 (a secondary-school teacher earned around £90 a week; a nurse £54). Floral-sprigged Edwardian-style dresses went with stripped floorboards and all those cast-iron fireplaces put back into houses whose original features were being restored. Where Biba had vamped and glammed, others kindled a romanticism that harked back to even earlier times. In 1979 Laura Ashley offered a 'sophisticated Victorian blouse' at £20.65, though many of the women buying it would have found themselves wearing caps and aprons and laundering someone else's blouse had they lived in the nineteenth century.

CLOTHING PRICES: 1970–79

Kendals, Manchester, autumn 1970

Wet-Look Boots	£10.50
Jaeger Military-Style Coat	£29.50
Frank Usher Evening Gown in Crimplene	£26.50

Kendals, Manchester, summer 1971

Shiny Wet-Look Raincoat in PVC	£15.00
Sundress in Terylene Voile by Peter Barron	£10.25
Gingham Dress by Polly Peck	£12.15

Miss Selfridge, 1978

Crêpe-de-Chine Blouses, from	£9.95
Indian Cotton Dress	£16.95
Forties-Style Dress	£19.95
Knitted Waistcoats	£7.95
Shawls	£4.25
Lacy Knit Jumper	£8.95

Laura Ashley, 1979

Short-Sleeved Romantic Blouse in Cotton Lawn	£11.40
Sophisticated Victorian Blouse in Cotton Lawn	£20.65
Short-Sleeved Spring Dress in Cotton Lawn	£18.90
Full-Length Victorian White Nightie	£14.65
Three-Tiered Gypsy Style Skirt	£14.65

NB: 1970 prices have been decimalised.
The Value of a Pound, Oksana Newman
and Allan Foster, eds. (1995)

28 **PEARL BUTTONS:** FULL CIRCLE

If one garment meant something special to me, it was a navy blue and white crêpe-de-Chine suit with pearl buttons. I would have loved this suit in any case, but I loved it all the more for what it represented. It was bought during a weekend my mother and I spent in Bath when I was seventeen. She and I regularly shopped in Sheffield; less frequently, we caught the train to Nottingham for those Biba moments, but a weekend away was something new. The suit came from Walcott Street, swisher then than now (and also the source of my Utility wrap-around dress). We spent the weekend shopping, though it was not our purchases that make the occasion memorable, but the very fact of our trip. The sun shone; I was in my eighteenth year; we talked and talked: women talking.

When first made, in the 1930s or '40s, the suit would have been called a two-piece, an old-fashioned word for this slinky skirt and short, belted jacket, the product of a little dressmaker or a woman proficient with a sewing machine. The straight skirt had kick pleats, the jacket a narrow fabric-covered belt and scalloped collar. I wore this suit until I could wear it no longer and, when it finally died a death, snipped off one of its pearl buttons as a keepsake.

The Walcott Street button is one of many pearl buttons in the button box. Mother-of-pearls outnumber all other types. There are plenty of small drabs, but no other beauties like these exist in quantity. Beauties to me at least: art-deco fish-eyes with bevelled edges; a flower incised with a star; a four-way button scored with diagonal lines; pearly geometrics designed to be decorative, not useful. There is a metal shank button to fasten a man's collar and a daintier one for a child. In size, they range from the tiniest button of fingertip size, to heavy, bold circles more than one inch in diameter. Most belonged to Annie; many are from a Pearly Queen stage outfit she made for my mum in 1946.

This was not among my childhood dressing-up clothes. It came to me after my grandma's death, part of the rag-bag mix of evocative this and that, along with the 1920s beaded panel and my great-grandma's black satin unfinished coat. The Pearly Queen costume was black velvet – a flared skirt and matching waistcoat on to which my grandma stitched a haberdasher's worth of buttons. I know what a considerable number there were because, many years later, I removed them. Annie may have had to beg and borrow some, but with rationing still in force, people tended to hold on to what they had, and cuff buttons, which formed the vast majority, always come in useful. They zig-zagged around the hem and shimmered in star patterns on the skirt and waistcoat.

'Fashion has little or nothing to do with pearl buttons,' *Household Words* observed in 1852. Their ubiquity means that many generations have them in common. In an early photograph of my great-grandma she is wearing a jacket on which a row of pearl buttons descends in a tight white line; perhaps one of these sits in the button box today. I wish I had seen the blouses and frocks decorated with my grandma's 3D shapes and squares, each one a declaration of 1930s modernity, but I remember other pearl buttons of hers from my childhood. Both she and my great-aunt Eva embellished the theme with mother-of-pearl necklaces I now wear: Annie's discs; Eva's pearlised leaves. When my mother married in 1950 she wore a floor-length taffeta dress with a sweetheart neckline (courtesy of Annie), a pearl-studded veil and a three-string pearl necklace (graduated pearls being 'in', as per *Vogue*); she wore a knotted string of pearls to my christening. My mum's pearls were costume jewellery, but when nineteenth-century button manufacturer Arthur Turner married a Miss Sheldon (a descendant of the Ralph Sheldon who introduced tapestry-making to England in 1569), special pearl buttons were handmade for her bridal gown.

Shell buttons had probably been made by hand since the Renaissance but, from the mid-nineteenth century on, their production was industrialised. *Household Words* described the journey shells made from the Pacific and Indian oceans. They arrived at the London docks in mahogany crates and were auctioned in the salesrooms of Mincing Lane before being trans-ported by rail to Birmingham, the heart of the button industry (coarser shells were destined for Sheffield to be made into knife handles). Thereafter, the shells were washed, cut, rasped, turned, engraved, ornamented, drilled and polished and their edges milled, before the finished buttons were finally sewn on to the pieces of card that were eventually delivered to department stores and draper's shops and taken home by women like Annie.

Looking closely at the pearl buttons passed down to me, I see how even seemingly uniform buttons have individual features that distinguish one from another, and how many different aspects of women's lives a mere handful of these buttons suggests. My grandma's buttons record a lifetime of domestic sewing but they also hark back to her professional days, a reminder of all those backroom seamstresses and little dressmakers to whom women turned for their fabric roses and Ginger Rogers frocks. Smart buttons shout best-dress occasions or the touch of cinematic glamour women wanted in the everyday. Utilitarian buttons are reminders of kitchen-table lives and the piles of darning, making over and making good which our forebears faced week on week – among them buttons for children's clothes and early lessons in sewing. (Though some, like M. V. Hughes who learned to sew a buttonhole in the 1880s, found in sewing a passport to education and independence. Ever one to puncture notions of prescribed femininity, she later entered into a competition with her sister-in-law to see who could spend the least on clothes.) The quantities of cuff and blouse buttons speak for a century of women striding forward in working hours, whether pupil-teachers, white-blouse workers, bachelor girls, or the young women whose miniskirts required 'modesty boards' to save them from the unwanted attentions of male colleagues.

The days of having a best dress and one for everyday are long gone, so too are the years when keeping up appearances required careful management and what you wore said where you stood in the social spectrum. We have access to ever cheaper clothing and a new fund of second-hand clothes is visible in charity shops on every high street; vintage clothes, beloved of yesteryear, now fetch eye-watering prices. Plain and fancy sewing have ceased to define and confine; women are free to indulge a passion for dressmaking or never cross the threshold of Haberdashery.

Reading autobiographies and memoirs I am struck by how often women describe the clothes they wore on special occasions or the ache they felt – even as children – in not having the right clothes, especially those at the poorer end of the scale, whether 'dirty girls' without pinafores of their own or the women who, like Carolyn Steedman's mother, wanting twenty yards of cloth for a New Look skirt, knew that clothes are 'the best boundary between you and a cold world'. Fashions come and go but women's memories endure of the clothes they have loved, longed for and been denied. Those young women who, in decades past, yearned for the long dress which together with Betty Grable curls and Kissproof lipstick signified their becoming a woman, were no different from me, years later, delighting in my crêpe-de-Chine suit. As journalist Alison Adburgham observed, 'the social occasions of different generations vary, but the heart that beats beneath stomacher or camisole is the same, as are its reasons for laying away a dress in lavender, for treasuring a handkerchief, a glove, and a red silk rose'.

The buttons have come full circle – bought and worn by Annie, stitched by her on to clothes she made for my mum, and later worn by me: Betsy's jacket from the 1890s, Annie's geometric shapes, my mum's Pearly Queen stage dress, my much-loved suit, not forgetting the buttons that for Annie were the most important of all, the ones she stitched on to the dress when my mother was first brought home. These buttons criss-cross the generations: emblems of our braided lives.

NOTES

For more information on individual publications see the Bibliography

Preface: Family Buttons and Vintage Finds

'epitome of family history', *The Times*, 30 March 1964
'They change', Virginia Woolf, *Orlando*, p.131

1 The Jet Button: From Mourning to Glamour

'shining like', Alison Uttley, *The Button-Box and Other Essays*, p.186
'the correct scale', Irene Clephane, *Our Mothers*, p.195
'agents for', R. H. Langbridge, ed., *Edwardian Shopping*
'Watered', Alison Adburgham, *Shops and Shopping 1800–1914*, p.68
'like small picture-frames', Margaret Hunter, 'Mourning Jewellery: A Collector's
    Account', *Costume*, Vol 27, Issue 1, January 1993, p.11
'opportunities', *Manchester Guardian*, 26 October 1914
'Black, black, black', Mary Brough-Robertson quoted by Max Arthur, ed., in
    Forgotten Voices of the Great War, p.172
'quite a strong', Agnes M. Miall, *The Bachelor Girl's Guide to Everything*, p.112
'not a shred', Barbara Comyns, *Sisters by a River*, p.146
'an ample severity', Rosamond Lehmann, *The Weather in the Streets*, p.68
'They walked', Alice Wilson and Irene Burton, 25 March 1999, *Millenium
    Memory Bank*, British Library Archive, Disc 1 ICDR0007571
'Black is right', 'Christian Dior's Pictorial Fashion Guide for Every Woman',
    Woman's Illustrated, 4 December 1954
'a good background', H. D. Willcock, ed., *Browns and Chester*, p.207
'Sloane Street', E. M. Delafield, *The Diary of a Provincial Lady*, p.191–2

2 **The Blackcurrant Button:** Elementary Sewing and the White-Blouse Revolution

'slower and more dignified', Angela Rodaway, *A London Childhood*, p.15

'All the remains', *A London Childhood*, p.26

'The Cameron', *The Lady*, 12 June 1919. Women workers were more visible after the Great War, hence this advertisement, but by 1919 their roles had changed little.

'Artisan', Stavely Netherthorpe School Admission Register, Derbyshire Records Office, Matlock, D6935/2/2

'If she carries', Testimonial, Teachers' Application Form, author's own, 31 July 1912

'herring-bone', quoted by Carol Dyhouse in *Girls Growing up in Late Victorian and Edwardian England*, p.87

'directly to', *Girls Growing up in Late Victorian and Edwardian England*, p.89

'Now, dear', M. V. Hughes, *A London Girl of the 1880s*, p.10

'who sometimes', *Sisters by a River*, p.96

'It was', *A London Girl of the 1880s*, p.11

'crowning glory', 'The Home: Special Notes on Many Subjects by "Domestica"', 'Care of the Hair', *Derbyshire Times*, 5 October 1910

'Do Men', *The Lady*, 7 July 1910

'Arthur's Education Fund', Virginia Woolf, *Three Guineas*, pp. 7–8

'the stuck-up', unsourced article, Annie's commonplace book, author's own

'the type-writing', John Harrison, 'A Manual of the Type-writer' quoted in 'The Cultural Work of the Type-writer Girl' from Victorian Studies, Vol 40, number 3, 'Women Workers Timeline/Office/Politics/Women in the Workplace 1860–2004', Women's Library exhibition, 2004

'one example of', *Fashions For All*, February 1910, quoted Barbara Burman, 'Home Sewing and *"Fashions for All"* 1908-37', *Costume*, Vol 28, Issue 1, 1994, p.79

'To some', 'The Importance of Home Dressmaking', *Home Notes*, 2 February 1895

'a necessary reel', Clementina Black, ed., *Married Women's Work*, p.32

'very hard for it', Lady Adele Meyer and Clementina Black, *Makers of Our Clothes*, p.97

'scattered over London', *Makers of Our Clothes*, pp.99–100

'Four apprentices', Alison Uttley, *A Ten O'Clock Scholar & Other Essays*, p.124–5

3 **Girls Rule OK:** The Purple, White and Green

'Purple . . . ', quoted by Diane Atkinson, *Suffragettes in the Purple, White & Green*, p.15

'almost every draper', 'Some hints about dress', *Votes for Women*, 2 July 1909
'Militant Jam', *Suffragettes in the Purple, White & Green*, p.31
'ranks with', *Votes for Women*, 4 February 1909
'not merely', *Votes for Women*, 2 July 1909
'Wanted a good', *Votes for Women*, 2 February 1907
'Defiance', advert, *Votes for Women*, 4 February 1909
'patented invention', advert, *Votes for Women*, 4 February 1909
'faced death', Holloway Prison Banner, Museum of London
'dreadful women', 'like nothing', Evelyn Sharp, *Unfinished Adventure*, p.138
'From every part', quoted by Emmeline Pankhurst, *My Own Story*, p.217
'only admiring', Erika Diane Rappaport, *Shopping for Pleasure*, p.217
'The Suffragette', *Shopping for Pleasure*, p.217
'those whose windows', *Shopping for Pleasure*, p.220
'travelled the road', *Unfinished Adventure*, p.127

4 **The Silver Thimble:** The First World War and Munitionettes

'a great circle of women', Rebecca West, 'Hands That War: The Night Shift',
   Daily Chronicle, 1916, quoted in Jane Marcus, ed., *The Young Rebecca*, p.388
'Say, young Doll', Naomi Loughman, 'Munition Work', Joyce Marlow, ed.,
   The Virago Book of Women and the Great War, p.167
'educated women', 'Women Munition Workers', *The Times*, 16 July 1915
'short skirts', Sylvia Townsend Warner, 'Behind the Firing Line: Some
   Experiences in a Munition Factory by a Lady Worker', *Blackwells*, 1916,
   p.191
'The Miaows', 'Behind the Firing Line', p.199
'who have been at work', 'Hands That War: The Night Shift', *The Young Rebecca*,
   p.387
'£1 1s and something', 'Behind the Firing Line', p.204
'friend's sister's niece', *The Virago Book of Women and the Great War*, p.168
'Years back', Madeline Ida Bedford, 'Munition Wages', Catherine Reilly, ed.,
   Scars Upon My Heart, p.7
'put out to service', Kathleen Gilbert, *Out of the Doll's House* Archive, 80DH/02/,
   The Women's Library, London School of Economics
'The caps', Elizabeth Gore, 'Woolwich Arsenal', *The Virago Book of Women and
   the Great War*, p.165
'The first fashion touch', *The Virago Book of Women and the Great War*, p.165
'No one else', 'Behind the Firing Line', p.195
'to look like glass', *Out of the Doll's House* Archive
'a sweet night smell', 'Hands That War: The Night Shift', *The Young Rebecca*, p.388
'very young', 'Hands That War: The Cordite Makers', *The Young Rebecca*, p.382

'passionate diligence', 'Hands That War: The Night Shift', *The Young Rebecca*, p.387
'[we] were just about', 'Mary Brough-Robertson, Munitions Worker', *Forgotten Voices of the Great War*, p.171
'You make us shells', Siegfried Sassoon, *Glory of Women*, in Jon Silkin, ed., *The Penguin Book of First World War Poetry*, second edition (Harmondsworth: Penguin, 1981), p.132

5 **The Shoe Button:** Bachelor Girls Stride Ahead

'How narrow', Virginia Woolf, *Orlando*, p.205–6
'picture dresses', Lucy Duff-Gordon, *Discretions and Indiscretions*, p.259
'boyish woman', *Discretions and Indiscretions*, p.259
'little hats', *Discretions and Indiscretions*, p.81
'whatever current trend', Eileen Whiteing, *Anyone for Tennis*, p.58
'If painting' ('Si la peinture est entrée dans la vie, c'est que les femmes la portaient sur elles!'), quoted by Isabelle Anscombe, *A Woman's Touch: Women in Design from 1860 to the Present Day* (London: Virago, 1984), p.120
'wore light stockings', *A London Childhood*, p.53
'rollocking young', *My Weekly*, 10 January 1920
'"Why call them"', Millicent Fawcett, *Evening Standard*, 4 October 1927
'Miss Infatuation', advert, *Illustrated London News*, 4 May 1929
'flying squad'; 'girls who', *Daily Mail*, 31 May 1929
'we are on', Brian Braithwaite, Noëlle Walsh and Glyn Davies, eds., *Ragtime to Wartime*, p.11
'There is still', Margaret Cole, ed., *The Road to Success*, p.vi
'Business, if accepted', *Woman's Life*, August 1931, Museum of Domestic Design & Architecture (MoDA), MJ144
'but let her first', Florence Sangster, 'Advertising', *The Road to Success*, p.211
'a business girl', Catherine Horwood, *Keeping Up Appearances*, p.47
'not to smell,' Frances Donaldson, *Child of the Twenties*, p.139
'simple designs', *Woman's Life*, 21 September 1929, MoDA, MJ144
'one-piece', Margaret Story, *How to Dress Well*, 1924, MoDA, BADDA 4035
'Remember that', *Miss Modern*, October 1930, quoted in *Keeping Up Appearances*, p.46
'Pity the Pretty', *Miss Modern*, October 1930
'Our ambitious', *Miss Modern*, November 1930
'the comforts', *Modern Home*, March 1930
'relentless in its realism', *London Illustrated News*, 7 May 1932
'For the Women of Today', May Edgington, 'Reckless Cinderella', *My Home*, December 1930

'Jazz reigns supreme', *Ladies Field*, 24 January 1920
'The dance craze', *Ladies Field*, 10 January 1920
'a demi-turban', *Daily Mail*, 1 January 1920
'Why, why', Vera Brittain, quoted by Carol Dyhouse in *Glamour: Women, History, Feminism*, p.93
'line after line', Winifred Holtby, 'Fashions and Feminism' (1927), Mary Stott, ed., *Women Talking*, p.112–4

6 The Mackintosh Button: Derring-Do and Fantasy Photographs

'If you are to drive', Alison Adburgham, 'Veteran Ladies', *View of Fashion*, p.51
'Pillion Girls', *Daily Mail*, 2 November 1927
'Free and Independent', *Punch*, 27 June 1928
'I envied those pilots', Amy Johnson in Margot Asquith, ed., *Myself When Young*, p.153–4; 'drawn irresistibly', p.154; 'Two pounds', p.155
'Looping the Loop', 'Chesterfield Shopping Festival', *Derbyshire Times*, 25 April 1914
'In England', *Lady's Pictorial*, 5 June 1920
'Clothes for the Airwoman', *Lady's Pictorial*, 3 May 1919
'waving paws', *The Lady*, 23 August 1928
'Could one fly', Mrs Victor Bruce, *The Bluebird's Flight* (London: Chapman and Hall, 1931), p.2
'the first solo flight', *London Illustrated News*, 23 June 1928
'Penny Plain', Tom Phillips, *Women and Hats*, p.110

7 The Linen Button: Small Miracles on Small Means

'Will not break', carded buttons, author's own
'the wife of a working man', 'Details of Expenditure of a Housekeeping Allowance of £2 5s 0d a week', *For Home and Country*, p.17
'feckless, filthy', Winifred Foley, *A Child in the Forest*, p.14; 'in the poorer', p.62
'Clothing [was] frankly', Maud Pember-Reeves, *Round About a Pound a Week*, p.61
'I want to go', Rebecca West, 'Much worse than Gaby Deslys', *The Young Rebecca*, p.230
'clothes that today', *A Child in the Forest*, p.17
'She had no vanities', Rose Gamble, *Chelsea Child*, p.33
'helped to set', Flora Thompson, *Lark Rise to Candleford*, p.101–3
'the astonishing difference', *Round About a Pound a Week*, p.64
'Olive's personal', Lettice Cooper, *National Provincial*, p.210
'How Violet', *National Provincial*, p.380

8 **The Baby's Button:** 'Pray Let partiuclare care be taken'en off this Child'

'pray Let partiuclare Care', 'Threads of Feeling' exhibition, London Foundling Museum, 14 October 2010–6 March 2011
'it must be jolly', National Children Adoption Association, Annual Report 1927–8, author's own
'The heart was made whole', John Styles, *Threads of Feeling*, p.70

9 **Eva's Glove Button:** Model Gowns and Inexpensive Dress

'At the moment', 'Through the Eyes of a Needlewoman: Notes from my Diary', *The Needlewoman*, July 1929
'Grand Shopping Week', *Derbyshire Times*, 4 April 1914
'unique and artistic windows', *Derbyshire Times*, 18 April 1914
'The Fashion House', *Derbyshire Times*, 15 October 1910
'if you had a maid', Lesley Lewis, *The Private Life of a Country House 1912–1939*, p.176
'Gloves must', Margaret Story, *How To Dress Well*, p.421, MoDA, BADDA 4035
'Gloves with a Reputation'; 'Costumes of Distinction', *Chesterfield at Swallow's*, 1923, Local Studies, Chesterfield Library
'One can always be certain', *How To Dress Well*, p.429
'the effort to persuade', Virginia Woolf, 'The London Scene 2, Oxford Street Tide', 1932, *Ragtime to Wartime*, p.139
'sealing-wax red'; 'bronze-faced round'; 'the east of one's dreams'; Elizabeth Montizambert, *London Discoveries in Shops and Restaurants*, p.7–9
'quality, something necessary', Alison Settle, *A Family of Shops*, p.11
'Well, Master Tom', 2 June 1877, *A Family of Shops*, endpapers
'The warm air', Lettice Cooper, *The New House*, p.164
'Sometimes, after school', *A London Child of the 1930s*, p.124
'The air', Dodie Smith, *I Capture the Castle*, p.81
'If I could buy this', Jean Rhys, *Voyage in the Dark*, p.111
'read fashion magazines', Asa Briggs, *Friends of the People*, p.189
'our kind of people', *National Provincial*, p.86
'Green patterned silk', *Woman's Weekly*, 8 February 1936
'universal game', René Cutforth, *Later Than We Thought*, p.34
'most forward-looking', Pauline Rushton, *Mrs Tinne's Wardrobe*, p.22
'Modom wanted'; 'Inexpensive Small Ladies', *Punch* 1920s quoted in *The Literary Companion to Fashion*, p.190
'rigid social hierarchy', T. J. Rendell, 'Millinery Techniques in the 1920s', *Costume*, Vol 12, Issue 1, January 1978, p.86; 'All the saleswomen', p.93
'If a small alteration', Naomi Mitchison, *You May Well Ask*, p.47

'adding a fashionable', 'In Fine Style: The Art of Tudor and Stuart Fashion', The Royal Collection exhibition, 2013
All details relating to Mrs Pennyman's expenditure are from Katina Bill, 'Clothing Expenditure by a Woman in the Early 1920s', *Costume*, Vol 27, Issue 1, January 1993, pp.57–60

10 The Interwar Fashion Button: Tennis and Afternoon Tea

'unbelievably enclosed', *Anyone for Tennis?*, p.57
'I think you', *Home Chat*, 12 September 1925
'vogue for colour', *Illustrated London News*, 30 April 1927
'eye shades', *Illustrated London News*, 30 April 1927
'Men who might', *Pottery Gazette*, September 1928
'la plage du soleil', advert, *Illustrated London News*, 4 June 1927
'vintage period of sunshine', *Illustrated London News*, 20 August 1932
'for those who really', 'Fashion Parades on the Beach', *The Needlewoman*, July 1929
'If your job is sedentary', *Woman's Life*, 22 September 1928, MoDA, MJ144
'Quite a large number', Victoria Glendinning, *Elizabeth Bowen*, p.118
'Fashion Parades', *The Needlewoman*, July 1929
'The All Conquering', *The Needlewoman*, January 1929
'We hope you', M. V. Hughes, *A London Family Between the Wars* (Oxford edition, 1979), p.13
'Books!', *A London Family Between the Wars*, p.16
'on demand', Nicola Beauman, *A Very Great Profession*, p.10
'swing daily', Winifred Holtby, 'The Wearer and the Shoe', *Testament of a Generation*, p.65
'while you can', advert, *Fancy Needlework Illustrated*, Vol 7, Number 73
'a scarlet portable', Elizabeth Bowen, *The Death of the Heart*, p.134
'orange curtains', Rosamond Lehmann, *Invitation to the Waltz*, p.64
'wash up the lunch things', Jenifer Wayne, *Brown Bread and Butter in the Basement*, p.61

11 The Edge-to-Edge Clasp: Kissprufe Lipstick and Ginger Rogers Frocks

'the joy of saving', *Anyone for Tennis?*, p.51
'Celanese goes from', advert, *The Vogue Guide to Practical Dressmaking*, MoDA, BADDA 3263
'cut out for chic', *The Vogue Guide to Practical Dressmaking*
'noted for', *The Vogue Guide to Practical Dressmaking*
'Mme Elsa', *Time*, 13 August 1934
'the long caterpillar', *The Times*, 4 March 1929

'that would make me', Joyce Storey, *Our Joyce*, p.84

'solid purple', Jenifer Wayne, *The Purple Dress*, p.8

'our lives were narrower', *Brown Bread and Butter*, p.165

'a hoarded rustle', *The Purple Dress*, p.8

'Olivia considered', Rosamond Lehmann, *Invitation to the Waltz*, p.46

'This then is a ball', Nancy Mitford, *The Pursuit of Love*, p.51

'and there was a queer place', *Invitation to the Waltz*, p.133

'the wives of men', May Bell talking to Virginia Heath, 'The Way We Were', *Staffordshire Sentinel*, April 2001

'15s for', Rachel Brewis, 'Reminiscences', *Costume*, Vol 16, Issue 1, January 1982, p.91

'Dressmakers at this time', Ann Wise, 'Dressmakers in Worthing 1920–50', *Costume*, Vol 32, Issue 1, 1 January 1998, p.83

'my wages', 'Dressmakers in Worthing', p.86

'looked at [Olivia]', *Invitation to the Waltz*, pp.47–9

'greatly admired', *Anyone for Tennis?*, p.58

'Men ask', advert, *Good Housekeeping*, 1926

'The films have', *Ragtime to Wartime*, p.153

'What Price Beauty?', *Ragtime to Wartime*, pp.152–3

'Powder, thundered', Winifred Watson, *Miss Pettigrew Lives For a Day*, p.73

'Although bright nails', *Miss Modern*, 18 February 1935, quoted in *Keeping Up Appearances*, p.49

'if you say to yourself', *How to Dress Well*, p.365, MoDA, BADDA 4035

12 **The Twinkling Button:** Stitch in the Chic

'noise beyond', quoted by Alan Richards in *The Extraordinary Adventures of Benjamin Sanders*, p.102

'all the bright', *Household Words*, 17 April 1852

'one of the most', *Household* Words, 17 April 1852

'beautiful buttons', 'Fashion from Paris', *Home Notes*, 9 February 1895

'full of bits', *The New House*, pp.79–80

'We are not able to stand', quoted in *Shops and Shopping, 1800–1914*, p.235

'We left Wellingborough', unpublished family memoir, courtesy of the late Judith Clark

'highly respectable draper', Oxford English Dictionary, 1989

'Decided to pop off', 29 March 1940, *These Wonderful Rumours!*, p.95

'A business girl', *Miss Modern*, October 1930, quoted in *Keeping Up Appearances*, p.46

'Ladies of Gentle Birth' and 'delicate shining materials', Amy Johnson, *Myself When Young*, p.152

'Most Exquisite Embroidery', advert, *Home Notes*, 9 February 1895

'No longer need you "make do"', *Things My Mother Should Have Told Me*, p.110

'made for just those women', MoDA, BADDA 3263

'Do you make your own frocks?', *Modern Home*, March 1930

'I made all these clothes', *Things My Mother Should Have Told Me*, p.91

'all the little tricks and arts', *Things My Mother Should Have Told Me*, p.91

'At this time of year', quoted in *Keeping Up Appearances*, p.22

'attractive designs', *How to Dress Well*, p.477, MoDA, BADDA 4035

'the village dressmaker', 'Country Crafts and Trades' in *A Ten O'Clock Scholar and Other Essays*, p.124

'I would bring', *A London Family Between the Wars*, p.58

'a new kind of open-work', *A London Home in the 1890s*, p.128

'The Other Woman Never Knits', Alison Adburgham, *View of Fashion*, p.36

'Mab Says Stitch', *Home Chat*, April 1930

'brings daily blessings', quoted by Rozsika Parker in *The Subversive Stitch*, pp.154–5

'a room did not feel very liveable', and 'must have enjoyed', 'The Lure of the Needle', *Guardian*, 10 April 1926

'Kotex says', *The Drapers Record*, 5 July 1930

'I was wild with excitement', Enid Bagnold, *Autobiography*, quoted in *The Literary Companion to Fashion*, p.185

13 The Blue Slide Buckle: A Paintbox of Summer Colour

'How lovely', *You May Well Ask*, p.46

'I noticed', 15 May, 1920, Virginia Woolf, *Diaries*

'try for me', quoted by Keren Protheroe in *Petal Power*, p.13

'The Flowers', Virginia Woolf, *The Years*, p.290

'for cruising and holidays', *Good Housekeeping*, June 1933

14 The Silver-and-Blue Button: Good Little Suits in Wartime

'Once the family budget', *Woman and Home Good Needlework Magazine*, December 1940

'No woman', *A Family of Shops*, p.35

'I believe everyone', Naomi Mitchison, *Among You Taking Notes*, p.144

'Mother remarked', May 1941, Joan Strange, *Despatches from the Home Front*, p.66

'ideal shelter suit', *Woman and Home*, December 1940

'slacks suit', *Ragtime to Wartime*, p.185

'It's the maddest', 12 September 1940, *Nella Last's War*, p.65

'Should women wear trousers?', Housewife, January 1940, MoDA, MJ75
'I know why', 1 August 1943, Nella Last's War, p.246–7
'NOW', Penny Kitchen, ed., For Home and Country, p.54
'Make one of your old coats', Woman and Home, December 1940
'Rationing has been introduced', 'Rationing of Clothing, Cloth, Footwear from June 1 1941', issued by Board of Trade, in Through the Looking-Glass, p.117
'[we] started to assess', 1 June 1941, Nella Last's War, p.148
'treasured silks', 'Renovating Clothes', For Home and Country, p.41
'must last longer', Board of Trade, Imperial War Museum
'how to patch an overall . . . boys can do', Board of Trade, Imperial War Museum
'bright new look', MoDA, BADDA 3488
'some classic pattern', Mollie Panter-Downes, One Fine Day (Virago edition, 1985), p.112
'one obvious occasion', 'Utility Clothing', The Times, 4 March 1942
'one of Ernie's Girlies', 21 March 1941, These Wonderful Rumours!; 'Oh dear', 1 June 1941; 'Oh monstrous!', 4 December 1941; 'a startling affair', 25 October 1941; 'I'll be glad', 12 October 1940; 'measly lunch', 10 May 1941; 'Awful feeling', 29 May 1940
'owing to the outbreak of hostilities', Cavendish School Logbook, Derbyshire Record Office, Matlock, 2 October 1939, D5031/FK

15 **The Land Army Button:** Uniforms not Uniformity

'already mentally clothed', Shirley Joseph, If Their Mothers Only Knew, p.8; 'khaki breeched', p.9; 'from an office calendar', p.137
'Nobody sees her', Vita Sackville-West, The Women's Land Army, p.23
'the appearance of uniform', 28 November 1939, These Wonderful Rumours!, p.57
'Your finest clothes', Three Guineas, p.25
'you cannot look fashionable', The Women's Land Army, p.25
'it was enough', If Their Mothers Only Knew, p.106
'no longer decide', 31 January 1943, Mollie Panter-Downes, London War Notes 1939–45, p.266
'Efficient, neat', Raynes Minns, Bombers and Mash, p.47
'only joined for the hat', Christian Lamb, quoted by Virginia Nicholson in Millions like Us, p.144
'lovely, every bit as fetching', 20 July 1943, Barbara Pym, A Very Private Eye, p.149
'AWFUL . . . fit beautifully', 11 September 1942, Eva Figes, ed., Letters in Wartime, p.272

'dinginess', Hilary Wayne, *Two Odd Soldiers*, p.12
'of the underwear', 30 December 1942, *These Wonderful Rumours!*, p.313
'To people feeling', *Two Odd Soldiers*, p.10
'some cleaning rags', 11 September 1942, *Letters in Wartime*, p.272; 'I've never known', 14 September 1942, p.273; 'in future', 11 September 1942, p.271–2
'the sight of', Sylvia Townsend-Warner, letter to Bea Howe, 4 December 1941, *Letters*, p.75
'lunch at Claridges', 1942, *Letters in Wartime*, p.274
'felt funny', 21 July 1943, *A Very Private Eye*, p.149
'there is no doubt', *Two Odd Soldiers*, p.11
'the astonishing effect', Betty Miller, quoted by Jonathan Miller in *On the Side of the Angels*, p.xiii
'War is a strange thing', *If Their Mothers Only Knew*, p.106
'a flowery frock', *The Women's Land Army*, p.25
'there is not much', 26 April 1941, Joan Wyndham, *Love is Blue*, p.10; 'not to mention', 'I have been given', 1 June 1943, p.103
'burnt sugar', 12 November 1939, *London War Notes 1939–45*, p.25
'any form of militarism', *The Purple Dress*, p.77; 'the faint smell', p.85; 'we were', p.81
'was this woman', Zelma Katin, *Clippie*, p.28; 'it's extraordinary', p.15
'the young woman teacher', Margaret Jolly, ed., *Dear Laughing Motorbyke*, p.10
'pretty frocks', Emma Smith, *As Green as Grass*, p.191
'a war profiteer', 'while [her] girlfriends', Valerie Grove, *So Much to Tell*, p.51
'In the rhythm', 28 August 1941, *Nella Last's War*, p.160
'All firms', 7 September 1941, Vere Hodgson, *Few Eggs and No Oranges*, p.180
'the regulation roll', *The Purple Dress*, p.85
'the woman who can look', *Housewife*, June 1941, MoDA, MJ75
'we have every reason', 'the BBC', 'Engineered by War', Mavis Nicolson, *What Did You Do in the War, Mummy?*, p.205
'When You're Off Duty', pattern for a jumper, *Woman's Weekly*, Victoria & Albert Museum
'Give up men . . . ', 12 September 1944, *Love is Blue*, p.155
'most people', 8 May 1945, *Among You Taking Notes*, p.321
'girls in their thin', 7 May 1945, *London War Notes*
'to be grown up', 21 March 1945, *Among You Taking Notes*, p.277
'Already I am scared', 27 March 1945, *Letters in Wartime*, p.283
'a symbolic gesture', *As Green as Grass*, p.219
'the temple of Janus', Sylvia Townsend Warner, letter to Paul Nordoff, 5 January 1946, *Letters*, p.91

16 **The Velvet Flowers:** Hats

'if you are going to wear a hat', Alison Adburgham, 'Nothing to Lose But Your Head', *Guardian* 25 October 1961, *View of Fashion*, p.38
'have a new winter hat', *The New House*, p.115
'extreme nor conspicuous', advert, *Derbyshire Times*, 25 April 1914
'quite exquisite', *Anyone For Tennis*, p.52
'diplomatic mission', *How to Dress Well*, MoDA, BADDA 4035, p.168
'exquisite millinery', advert quoted in Marjorie Gardiner, *On the Other Side of the Counter*, p.12
'was insufficient', T. J. Rendell, 'Millinery Techniques in the 1920s', *Costume*, Vol 12, Issue 1, January 1978, p.86
'call in tomorrow', 'The Tiredness of Rosabel', *The Collected Stories of Katherine Mansfield*, p.515
'the oddest little shapes', *The New House*, p.167
'Darling! It's perfect', Alison Adburgham, *A Punch History of Manners and Modes*, p.342
'introduced to felt hat', *The Diary of a Provincial Lady*, p.187
'there was a particular kind', Barbara Pym, *Jane and Prudence*, p.143
'garbed myself', 8 October 1939, *Those Wonderful Rumours!*, p.46
'A wonderful year', Alison Adburgham, 'Our Hats', *View of Fashion*, p.26
'transparent . . . glinting', Bill Lancaster, *The Department Store*, p.175

17 **The Coat Button:** Post-War and the New Look

'I think we all feel', 15 January 1944, *Among You Taking Notes*, p.266
'a smart forest green', Joan Wyndham, *Anything Once*, p.6
'when we could not', Katharine Whitehorn, *Selective Memory*, p.34
'Just arriving', *Good Housekeeping*, May 1946
'Smart frock', *Modern Woman*, April 1947, MoDA, MJ97
'explain to Tom Harrison', 9 October 1946, *Nella Last's Peace*, p.125
'Food for the Fed-up', *Modern Woman*, April 1947, MoDA, MJ97
'a remarkable vindication', Audrey Withers, *Lifespan*, p.63
'The skirt may be full', quoted by David Kynaston in *Austerity Britain*, p.257
'can be had', *The Times*, 27 February 1948
'the ridiculous whim', Rachel Cooke, *Her Brilliant Career*, p.xix
'Women today', *Austerity Britain*, p.257-8
'variety and change', Janet Hobson, letter to *The Times*, 12 February 1948
'bullied, cajoled', 'deplorably ugly', Blanche Branston, letter to *The Times*, 9 February 1948
'Suddenly I found', Audrey Withers quoted in Angela Holdsworth, *Out of the Doll's House*, p.170

'A crowd had gathered', *Her Brilliant Career*, p.xix

'the biggest skirt', Joanne Brogden quoted in Angela Holdsworth, *Out of the Doll's House*, p.170

'among the first', 'Jo', Charmian Cannon, ed., *Our Grandmothers, Our Mothers, Ourselves*, p.78

'For one post-war', *The Purple Dress*, p.142

'to enhance the new look', 19 January 1948, Selfridges' advert, *The Times*, 19 January 1948

'bought a good pattern', Margaret M. Trump, 'When I was at Marshall and Snelgrove', *Costume*, Vol 22, Issue 1, 1 January 1988, p.85; 'saved up', p.88

'The "New Look"'; 'One enterprising shop'; 'lacked the coupons', *Derbyshire Times*, 9 January 1948

'minor sensation'; 'startling vivid'; 'She pounded the pavements'; 'Note for the ladies', Chesterfield is too drab'; '"New Look" - Bad Luck', *Derbyshire Times*, 14 May 1948

'a memorable fuss'; 'the very stuff', Lorna Sage, *Bad Blood*, p.90

'tearing up the ration books', Carolyn Steedman, 'Landscape for a Good Woman', Liz Heron, ed., *Truth, Dare or Promise*, p.105; 'no New Look', p.109

18 The Small, Drab Button: Office Life in the 1950s

'Terylene - the wonder fabric', quoted by Keren Protheroe, 'Quality Stitch by Stitch: Clothing and Associated Publications Held in Marks and Spencer Company Archives', *Costume*, Vol 39, Issue 1, January 2005, p.100

'Jiffy Dress', *Woman's Illustrated*, 23 March 1957

'received a sackful', Joan Holloway, Jo Stanley, ed., *To Make Ends Meet: Women Over 60 Write About Their Working Lives*, p.74

'endured and survived', Gail Lewis, 'From Deepest Kilburn', *Truth, Dare or Promise*, p.218

'Lucy's a bright girl', advert, *Picture Post*, 13 December 1952

'There is nothing healthier', 'Happy and Healthy – the Family Guide to Better Living', a 'booklet to pull out and keep', *Woman's Illustrated*, 26 January 1957

'had no awareness', Carolyn Steedman, 'Landscape for a Good Woman', *Truth, Dare or Promise*, p.109

'Young Success: The Sparkling Stories of Girls with Glamorous Jobs', Rhona Churchill, *Woman*, 29 September 1956

'agent for an American', *Woman*, 14 July 1956

'Miss Manchester', *Woman*, 7 July 1956

'backroom girl', *Woman*, 23 June 1956

'parachuted into romance', *Woman*, 1 September 1956

Millie Levine: in conversation with Elizabeth Silkin, 7 December 2013, on behalf of the author

'I remember', Ella Bland, 'Behind the Counter', *Costume*, Vol 17, Issue 1, 1 January 1983, p.113

'understandably anxious', Margaret M. Trump, 'When I was at Marshall and Snelgrove', *Costume*, Vol 22, Issue 1, 1 January 1988, p.90

'The Rise of', *In Vogue*, p.227

'There was much', quoted by Ann Wise, 'Dressmakers in Worthing 1920–50', *Costume*, Vol 32, Issue 1, 1 January 1998, p.83–4

'When you're really', *Woman's Illustrated*, 23 March 1957

'no "bare legs"', Joyce Weston in 'Challenges and Triumphs', Jessica Campbell, *Barclays Magazine*, Issue 17, May 2003, 'Women Workers Timeline/Office/ Politics /Women in the Workplace 1860–2004', Women's Library Exhibition, 2004

'rich variety', *Bad Blood*, p.139

'Her originality', *The Purple Dress*, p.148–9

19 **The 'Perfect' Button:** The Etiquette of Dress

'The appearance', *Etiquette for Ladies*, undated, author's own

'I'm not too forward', *Ta-ra-ra Boom-de-ay*, music hall song

'if . . . introduced', *Home Management*, p.596

'We talk about', *The Provincial Lady Goes Further*, pp.190–1

'read avidly'; 'how to behave', *Last Curtsey*, p.75

'life was like', Rose Macaulay, *Crewe Train*, (Leipzig: Bernhard Tauchnitz, 1926), p.47–8

'her first serious', 'for oh these men', 'The New Dress', Virginia Woolf, *Mrs Dalloway's Party*, p.42–3

'love of clothes', 14 May 1925, Virginia Woolf, *Diaries*; 'clothes complex', 16 February 1940; 'idiotic anguish', 5 July 1940; 'great joy', 29 April 1935

'suburban', *Julia*, p.111

'I'm not sure', Barbara Pym, *Excellent Women*, p.97

'being persuaded', 16 February 1940, Virginia Woolf, *Diaries*

'In Narky', 18 May 1940, *These Wonderful Rumours!*, p.115

'Mrs Form's position', 'Delicate Monster', *Women Against Men*, p.11

'They counted up', *The Sleeping Beauty*, p.33; 'We look discarded . . . I'm sure', p.77–8

'shrunken miserably', *Good Behaviour*, p.183–5

'It was tough', Angela Carter, 'Truly, It Felt Like Year One', *Very Heaven*, p.210

'discreet mouse make-up', *Bad Blood*, p.211
'Sluts', Katharine Whitehorn, *Observer*, 29 December 1963

20 **The Doll's-House Doorknob:** Homemaking Large and Small

'the girls all wanted', 21 March 1944, *Among You Taking Notes*, p.277
'Marvellous evening', advert, *Punch*, 24 July 1946
'all yearned for love', *Selective Memory*, p.63
'talked of romance', *The Pursuit of Love*, p.41
'a poll taken', 7 November 1943, *London War Notes 1939–45*, p.298
'We're two of the lucky ones', advert, National Westminster Bank, *Good Housekeeping*, January 1949
'exquisite little' from 'The Doll's House', *The Collected Stories of Katherine Mansfield*, p.384
'suburban villa' etc, *The Pauper's Homemaking Book*, p.347
'Now choose another', Gertrude D. Freeman, 'Recollections of My Childhood and Later Days', John Burnett archive, Brunel University, WR127DQ

21 **The Ladybird Button:** Childhood

'the happy event', E. M. Newman, ed., 'Maternity Wear', *The Baby Book* (London: Newbourne Publications Ltd, 1954), p.9
'absolutely nothing', Elizabeth Jane Howard, *Slipstream*, p.134
'Birth of a Baby', Val Williams, *Women Photographers*, p.138
'look their charming best', *The Baby Book*, p.9–10
'the wife', Elizabeth Sloan Chesser quoted in *Myself When Young*, p.77
'You must remember', 'Nursery Routine: The Threshold of Motherhood', *Home Management*, p.499
'the pixie suit', *The Baby Book*, p.46
'knitted by hand', Emma Smith, *The Great Western Beach*, p.5
'pressed against', Alison Uttley, *Country World*, p.37
'little girls', *My Own Story*, p.25
'the dirty girls', Ethel Mannin, *Confessions and Impressions*, p.34
'a Galway school', Amelia Gentleman, interview with Catherine Corless, 'I Want To Know Who's Down There', *Guardian*, 14 June 2014
'washed dozens', *A London Childhood*, p.131
'doll's hats', 'came to the nursery', *The New House*, p.79
'ready to fall', Joan Russell Noble, ed., *Recollections of Virginia Woolf* (Harmondsworth: Penguin, 1975), p.106
'Johanna Street', 'tiny pink bonnets', 'a vest', 'We were given', *The Purple Dress*, p.15

'gives to everyone', Festival of Britain catalogue, 1951, p.74
'keynote', Ronald Ridout, *Second Introductory English Workbook*, author's own
'Today is Tuesday', infant school exercise book, author's own
'Lil of the Lighthouse', 'the Richest Girl in the School', *A Child of the Forest*, p.52
'Can't you *really* sew?', Enid Blyton, *Mr Galliano's Circus* (London: George Newnes, 1938), p.101

22 Suspenders: Corsetry, Scanties (& Sex)

'Sluts', Katharine Whitehorn, *Observer*, 29 December 1963
'By Industry We Thrive', *View of Fashion*, p.255
'Steel-bound and whalebone-lined', Irene Clephane, *Our Mothers*, p.191–220
'thank the many ladies', Shopping Festival advert, *Derbyshire Times*, 25 April 1914
'The number of stays', Katharine Whitehorn, *Roundabout*, p.83
'the modern figure', 'Dressing for Success', *Miss Modern*, October 1930
'Struggling into', *The Purple Dress*, p.12–3
'secret service', quoted in *Dear Laughing Motorbyke*, p.13
'Youthcraft Girdles,' Fiona MacCarthy, *Last Curtsey*, p.57–8
'The mere thirty million', 'the oldest hands', *Roundabout*, p.83
'We in our elasticised', 'All Our Yesterdays' from *Punch*, 2 May 1956, quoted in *View of Fashion*, p.243
I can't see', Mary Quant, *Quant by Quant*, p.148
'Youthlines', advert, *Nova*, March 1965
'To me', *Quant by Quant*, p.148
'She was reputed', Stella Gibbons, *Cold Comfort Farm*, p.11
'even if you had', *Bad Blood*, p.211
'a thing no other girl', Edna O'Brien, *The Country Girls*, p.81
'underwear revolution', 'no-bra bra', Sandy Boler, 'Beatrix Miller editor British *Vogue* 1964–1986', *Vogue*, May 2014
'I do not suppose', Daisy Lansbury, 'The Private Secretary', *The Road to Success*, p.74
'Very Special'; 'Sanitary Woollen Clothing', *Shops and Shopping*, p.184
'It was depressing'; 'festooned with', *Excellent Women*, p.81
'the cami-knicker', C.W. Cunnington, *English Women's Clothing in the Present Day*, p.198
'wicked daring', *Miss Pettigrew Lives for a Day*, p.92
'Delia cuts out', 4 August 1941, *These Wonderful Rumours!*; 'a nifty brassière', 25 June 1943
'for those dainty undies', *Woman's Life*, 25 June 1941, MoDA, MJ144

'sunbathing'; 'scanties', *English Women's Clothing in the Present Day*, p.225
'the black underwear', *The Country Girls*, p.151; 'We want to live', p.154
'a flighty, precocious', *Brown Bread and Butter in the Basement*, pp.138–9
'Ticket to Heaven', Mary Badger Wilson, *My Home*, April 1930
'Gifts She'll Adore', Swallow's of Chesterfield, Christmas catalogue, 1965, Chesterfield Library, Local Studies
'and some', 5 January 1944, *Love is Blue*, p.134
'Getting married', Fay Weldon, *Down Among the Women*, p.96
'Younger women', Rachel Cooke, 'Fifty Years of the Pill', *Observer*, 6 June 2010
'This Christmas', *Punch*, 18 December 1963

23 **The Apron Button:** Domesticity

'anonymous caps', *One Fine Day*, p.174
'Frazerton overall', *The Lady*, 12 June 1919
'for the messiest of jobs', *The Needlewoman*, July 1929
'The dirt you can't', advert for Goblin vacuum cleaner, *Modern Home*, March 1930
'In Afternoon', unpublished diary, author's own
'Should Wives Have Wages?', *Ragtime to Wartime*, pp.34–5
'From 6.30 am to 9 am', Women's Institute, *Home and Country*, June 1922
'that bit of extra daily work', 'Daily Routine – the Bedroom', *Home and Country*, August 1922
'How dreadful', *The Pursuit of Love*, pp.111–2
'the trouble with housework', Monica Dickens, *One Pair of Hands*, p.21
'things needed for marriage', unpublished notebook, courtesy of Kathryn Hartley
'I must avoid', *Julia*, p.231; 'MAGNIFICENT', p.230
'It's hard to imagine', 'Your Home', *Modern Homes Illustrated*, 1947
'The [Kenwood] chef', reproduced in the *Guardian*, Women's Page, 17 September 1998
'She cannot wash', 15 March 1950, *Nella Last in the 1950s*
'As I often tell her', 6 December 1950, *Nella Last in the 1950s*
'I myself loathe', Elizabeth Taylor, *The Wedding Group*, p.47
'Why did The Lord?', *A London Girl of the 1880s*, p.81
'Every woman', quoted by Robert Opie, *The 1950s Scrapbook* (London: New Cavendish, 1998), p.27
'Thinking, Planning', Penelope Mortimer, *Daddy's Gone A-Hunting*, p.67
'Devoted Docile Wives', 13 August 1945, *These Wonderful Rumours!*
' hate the thought', 1 October 1945, *These Wonderful Rumours!*
'a minefield', *Bad Blood*, p.160

'understanding about money', *One Fine Day*, p.83
'You Start by Sinking', *Spare Rib* tea towel

24 **The Diamanté Clasp:** A Little Razzle Dazzle

'You must have', *The Needlewoman*, June 1929
'Instant Paris', *In Vogue*, p.227
'Veiled Radiance' advert, quoted in *View of Fashion*, p.115
'Golden Girl Cosmetics', advert, *Nova*, June 1965

25 **The Toggle:** God, This Modern Youth!

'black stockings', Sheila Rowbotham, 'Revolt in Roundhay', quoted in *Truth, Dare or Promise*, p.189
'the first duty', 'the legs and lashes', *Brown Bread and Butter in the Basement*, p.172
'role as signal', *In Vogue*, p.203
'The young girls', Barbara Hulanicki, *A to Biba*, pp.30–1
'God! This Modern Youth!', *Quant by Quant*, p.27
'It was where', Diana Melly, 'Beyond the Fringe', *Independent on Sunday*, 30 October 2005
'Are Teenagers Taking Over?' quoted by Arthur Marwick in *The Sixties*, p.60
'Their 1950s', *Bad Blood*, p.174
'we would sit', Twiggy Lawson, *Twiggy in Black and White*, p.40; 'although expensive', p.34
'modesty boards', 'Office/Politics/Women in the Workplace, 1860–2004', Women's Library Exhibition, 2004
'outstripping', Barbara Hulanicki and Martin Pel, *The Biba Years*, p.24
'There should be', *Twiggy in Black and White*, pp.43–3
'Perhaps it was', Alexandra Pringle, 'Chelsea Girl' in *Very Heaven*, p.39
'the girl who is with-it', *Quant by Quant*, p.83; 'intelligent', p.82; 'they want clothes', p.99; 'there was a time', p.67; 'Since the sexes', p.68; 'dishy grotty', p.66; 'we sold these', p.53
'Bazaar in the Kings Road', *Twiggy in Black and White*, p.42
'Dresses were', *A to Biba*, p.106
'Clothes were everything', *Twiggy in Black and White*, p.54
'the free, swinging', Cindy strapline quoted by Robert Opie in *The 1960s Scrapbook* (London: New Cavendish, 2000), p.23
'the well-dressed young man', *The 1960s Scrapbook*, p.23

26 **The Turquoise Button:** The New Kind of Woman

'taught by', Katharine Whitehorn, *Observer*, 7 December 1997
'One Woman in Her Day', *Nova*, May 1965
'Women who make up', *Nova*, March 1965
'Nova is a magazine', advertisement, *New Statesman*, 10 September 1965
'At The Sunday Times', Women's Library Handling Collection, 1968
'the relaxation of manners', Angela Carter, 'Truly, It Felt Like Year One', Sara
    Maitland, ed., *Very Heaven*, p.213
'Truly, It Felt Like Year One', Angela Carter, quoted by Sara Maitland in *Very
    Heaven*, p.4
'Our subject matter', Margaret Drabble, 'A Woman Writer', *Books on Women*,
    Spring 1973, National Book League
'sought on everything', Shena Mackay interviewed by Ian Hamilton, *Guardian*,
    10 July 1999
'Report on Women', from 'Outlook for the Future', *Votes for Women 1918–1968*,
    Golden Jubilee Celebration, Women's Library, 5MWA9/1
'The cat is out', *Three Guineas*, p.60
'The New Generation Jersey', *Swallow's of Chesterfield*, November catalogue
    1965, Chesterfield Library, Local Studies
'This is the trend', *Swallow's of Chesterfield*
'a slim skirt', *The Biba Years*, p.39
'a lovely affair', advert for Gorringe's, *The Lady*, 8 October 1925

27 **The Statement Button:** Biba and the Hankering for Vintage

'There should be', *Twiggy in Black and White*, p.42
'Our Saturdays', *A to Biba*, p.78
'a uniform for an era', *A to Biba*, p.79
'all have', Linda Grant, 'The Ladies' Paradise', *Guardian*, 27 June 1998
'full of mysterious goodies', Biba, 1973 promotional newspaper, author's own
'It was going', *A to Biba*, p.146
'the winter colours', 1973 Biba promotional newspaper
'weak spot', *The Pauper's Homemaking Book*, p.282
'No woman', *National Provincial*, p.291

28 **Pearl Buttons:** Full Circle

'fashion has little', *Household Words*, 17 April 1852
'the best boundary', Carolyn Steedman, *Landscape for a Good Woman*, p.38
'Only these survive', *View of Fashion*, p.254

SELECT BIBLIOGRAPHY

Adam, Ruth, *A Woman's Place, 1910–1975* (London: Chatto & Windus, 1975)

Adburgham, Alison, *View of Fashion; drawings by Haro* (London: Allen & Unwin, 1966)

—, *Liberty's: A Biography of a Shop* (London: Allen & Unwin, 1975)

—, *Shops and Shopping 1800–1914: Where, and in What Manner the Well-Dressed Englishwoman Bought Her Clothes* (London: Allen & Unwin, 1981; London: Barrie & Jenkins, 1989)

—, *A Punch History of Manner and Modes, 1841–1940* (London: Hutchinson, 1961)

Alexander, Sally, *Becoming a Woman and Other Essays in Nineteenth and Twentieth Century Feminist History* (London: Virago, 1994)

Anderson, Gregory, ed., *The White-Blouse Revolution: Female Officer Workers Since 1870* (Manchester: Manchester University Press, 1988)

Arthur, Max, *Forgotten Voices of the Great War* (London: Ebury, 2002)

—, *Lost Voices of the Edwardians* (London: Harper Press, 2006)

Asquith, Margot, ed., *Myself When Young* (London: Frederick Muller, 1938)

Athill, Diana, *Yesterday Morning: A Very English Childhood* (London: Granta, 2002)

Atkinson, Diana, *Suffragettes in the Purple White & Green: London 1906–14* (London: Museum of London, 1992)

Bagnold, Enid, *Autobiography* (London: Heinemann, 1969)

Bakewell, Joan, *The Centre of the Bed* (London: Hodder & Stoughton, 2003)

Barber, Lynn, *An Education* (London: Penguin, 2009)

Barret-Ducrocq, Françoise, *Love in the Time of Victoria: Sexuality, Class and Gender in Nineteenth-Century London*, trans. John Howe (London: Verso, 1991)

Beaton, Cecil, *The Glass of Fashion* (London: Weidenfeld & Nicholson, 1954)

Beauman, Nicola, *A Very Great Profession: The Woman's Novel 1914–39* (London: Virago, 1983)

Beddoe, Deirdre, *Back to Home and Duty: Women Between the Wars, 1919–1939* (London: Pandora, 1989)

Berriman, Hazel, *Crysède: The Unique Textile Designs of Alec Walker* (Truro: Royal Institution of Cornwall, 1993)

Berry, Paul, and Alan Bishop, eds., *Testament of a Generation: The Journalism of Vera Brittain and Winifred Holtby* (London: Virago, 1985)

Black, Clementina, ed., *Married Women's Work* (London: G. Bell & Sons, 1915; London: Virago, 1983)

Blum, Dilys, *Shocking!: The Art and Fashion of Elsa Schiaparelli* (London: Philadelphia Museum of Art, 2003)

Bowen, Elizabeth, *The Death of the Heart* (London: Jonathan Cape, 1938; London: Vintage Classics, 1998)

—, *The Heat of the Day* (London: Jonathan Cape, 1949)

Braithwaite, Brian, Noëlle Walsh, and Glyn Davies, eds., *Ragtime to Wartime: The Best of Good Housekeeping, 1922–40* (London: Ebury, 1991)

Briggs, Asa, *Friends of the People: The Centenary History of Lewis's* (London: Batsford, 1956)

Bright, Janette, and Gillian Clark, *An Introduction to the Tokens at the Foundling Museum* (London: The Foundling Museum, 2011)

—, *Fate, Hope & Charity* (London: The Foundling Museum, 2013)

Brittain, Vera, *Testament of Youth: An Autobiographical Story of the Years 1900–1925* (London: Gollancz, 1934)

Broad, Richard, and Suzie Fleming, eds., *Nella Last's War: The Second World War Diaries of Housewife 49* (London: Falling Wall Press, 1981; London: Profile, 2006)

Broadley, Rosie, *Laura Knight Portraits* (London: National Portrait Gallery, 2013)

Brown, Mike, *CC41 Utility Clothing: The Label That Transformed British Fashion* (Sevenoaks: Sabrestorm, 2014)

Bullock, John, *Fast Women: The Drivers Who Changed the Face of Motor Racing* (London: Robson, 2002)

Burnett, John, ed., *Useful Toil: Autobiographies of Working People from the 1820s–1920s* (London: Allen Lane, 1974)

—, *Destiny Obscure: Autobiographies of Childhood, Education and Family from the 1820s–1920s* (London: Allen Lane, 1982)

Cannon, Charmian, ed., *Our Grandmothers, Our Mothers, Ourselves: A Century of Women's Lives* (London: Ogomos, 2000)

Clarke, Gill, *Evelyn Dunbar: War and Country* (Clifton: Simson & Co., 2006)

Clephane, Irene, *Our Mothers: A Cavalcade in Pictures, Quotations & Description of Late Victorian Women, 1870–1900*, ed., Alan Bott (London: Gollancz, 1932)

—, *Ourselves, 1900–1930* (London: John Lane, 1933)

Cole, Margaret I., ed., *The Road to Success: Twenty Essays on the Choice of a Career for Women* (London: Methuen, 1936)

Cooke, Rachel, *Her Brilliant Career: Ten Extraordinary Women of the Fifties* (London: Virago, 2013)

Comyns, Barbara, *Sisters By A River* (London: Eyre & Spottiswoode, 1947; London: Virago, 1985)

—, *A Touch of Mistletoe* (London: Heinemann, 1967; London: Virago, 1989)

—, *Our Spoons Came From Woolworths* (London: Eyre & Spottiswoode, 1950)

Cooper, Lettice U., *The New House* (London: Gollancz, 1936; London: Virago, 1987)

—, *National Provincial* (London: Gollancz, 1938; London: Gollancz, 1987)

Cunnington, C. W., *Englishwomen's Clothing in the Present Century* (London: Faber, 1952)

Cutforth, René, *Later Than We Thought* (Newton Abbott: David & Charles, 1976)

Davidoff, Leonore, and Belinda Westover, *Our Work, Our Lives, Our Words: Women's History and Women's Work* (Basingstoke: Macmillan Education, 1986)

Davies, Margaret Llewelyn, ed., *Life As We Have Known It* (London: Hogarth Press, 1931)

Dayus, Kathleen, *Her People* (London: Virago, 1982)

Delafield, E. M., *The Diary of a Provincial Lady* (London: Macmillan & Co., 1947; London: Virago, 1984)

Dickens, Monica, *One Pair of Hands* (Harmondsworth: Penguin, 1978)

Donaldson, Frances, *Child of the Twenties* (London: Rupert Hart-Davis, 1959; London: Weidenfeld & Nicolson, 1986)

Duff-Gordon, Lucy, *Discretions and Indiscretions* (London: Jarrolds, 1932)

Dunn, Nell, *Up the Junction* (London: MacGibbon & Kee, 1963; London: Virago, 1988)

—, *Talking to Women* (London: MacGibbon & Kee, 1965)

—, *Poor Cow* (London: MacGibbon & Kee, 1967)

Dyhouse, Carol, *Girls Growing Up in Late Victorian and Edwardian England* (London: Routledge & Kegan Paul, 1981)

—, *Glamour: Women, History, Feminism* (London: Zed, 2010)

Eaton, Faith, *The Ultimate Dolls' House Book* (London: Dorling Kindersley, 1994)

Edwards, Nina, *On the Button: The Significance of an Ordinary Item* (London: I. B. Tauris, 2012)

Epstein Diana, and Millicent Safro, *Buttons* (New York: H. N. Abrams, 1991)

Figes, Eva, ed., *Women's Letters in Wartime, 1450–1945* (London: Pandora, 1993)

Foley, Winifred, *A Child in the Forest* (London: British Broadcasting Corporation, 1974; London: Futura, 1977)

Forrester, Helen, *Twopence to Cross the Mersey* (London: Jonathan Cape, 1974)

—, *Liverpool Miss* (London: The Bodley Head, 1979)

Forster, Margaret, *Hidden Lives: A Family Memoir* (London: Viking, 1995)

Gamble, Rose, *Chelsea Child* (London: British Broadcasting Corporation, 1979)

Gardiner, Marjorie, *On the Other Side of the Counter: The Life of a Shop Girl 1925–1945* (Brighton: QueenSpark, 1985)

Gardiner, Juliet, ed., *The New Woman* (London: Collins & Brown, 1993)

—, *Wartime: Britain 1939–1945* (London: Headline, 2004)

—, *The Thirties: An Intimate History* (London: HarperPress, 2010)

Garfield, Simon, *Our Hidden Lives: The Remarkable Diaries of Post-War Britain* (London: Ebury, 2005)

—, *We Are At War: The Diaries of Five Ordinary People in Extraordinary Times* (London: Ebury, 2006)

Garth, Margaret, and Mrs Stanley Wrench, eds., *Home Management* (London: Daily Express, 1934)

Gibbons, Stella, *Cold Comfort Farm* (London: Longmans & Co., 1932; London: Penguin, 2000)

Glancey, Jonathan, *A Very British Revolution: 150 Years of John Lewis* (London: Laurence King, 2014)

Glendinning, Victoria, *Elizabeth Bowen: Portrait of a Writer* (London: Weidenfeld & Nicolson, 1977)

Grant, Linda, *The Thoughtful Dresser* (London: Virago, 2009)

Graves, Robert, and Alan Hodge, *The Long Week-End: A Social History of Great Britain, 1918–1939* (London: Faber, 1940)

Grove, Valerie, *So Much to Tell: The Biography of Kaye Webb* (London: Viking, 2010)

Hartley, Jenny, ed., *Hearts Undefeated: Women's Writing of the Second World War* (London: Virago, 1994)

Heron, Liz, ed., *Truth, Dare or Promise: Girls Growing Up in the 50s* (London: Virago, 1985)

Holdsworth, Angela, *Out of the Dolls House: The Story of Women in the Twentieth Century* (London: BBC Books, 1988)

Hoskins, Lesley, *Fiftiestyle: Home Decoration and Furnishings from the 1950s* (Enfield: Middlesex University Press, 2004)

Howard, Elizabeth Jane, *Slipstream: A Memoir* (London: Macmillan, 2002)

Hodgson, Vere, *Few Eggs and No Oranges: A diary showing how unimportant people in London and Birmingham lived through the war years, 1940–1945, written in the Notting Hill area of London* (London: Dobson, 1976)

Horwood, Catherine, *Keeping Up Appearances: Fashion and Class Between the Wars* (Stroud: Sutton, 2005)

Houart, Victor, *Buttons: A Collector's Guide* (New York: Scribner, 1977)

Howell, Georgina, ed., *In Vogue: Six Decades of Fashion* (London: Allen Lane, 1975)

Hughes, M. V., *A London Family Between the Wars* (Oxford: Oxford University Press, 1940; 1979)

—, *A London Girl of the 1880s* (Oxford: Oxford University Press, 1946; 1978)

—, *A London Home in the 1890s* (Oxford: Oxford University Press, 1946; 1978)

Hulanicki, Barbara, *From A to Biba: The Autobiography of Barbara Hulanicki* (London: Hutchinson, 1983; London: V&A, 2007)

—, and Martin Pel, *The Biba Years 1963–1975* (London: V&A, 2014)

Innes, Jocasta, *The Pauper's Homemaking Book* (Harmondsworth: Penguin, 1976)

Jameson, Storm, *Women Against Men* (Leipzig: Tauchnitz, 1933; London: Virago, 1982)

Jesse, F. Tennyson, *A Pin to see the Peepshow* (London: Heinemann, 1934)

Jolly, Margarita, ed., *Dear Laughing Motorbyke: Letters from Women Welders of the Second World War* (London: Scarlet, 1997)

John, Angela V., ed., *Unequal Opportunities: Women's Employment in England, 1800–1918* (Oxford: Blackwell, 1986)

Joseph, Shirley, *If Their Mothers Only Knew: An Unofficial Account of Life in the Women's Land Army* (London: Faber, 1946)

Katin, Zelma, in collaboration with Louis Katin, *'Clippie': The Autobiography of a Wartime Conductress* (London: John Gifford, 1944)

Keane, Molly, *Good Behaviour* (London: Deutsch, 1981)

Kennard, Mrs Edward, *The Golfing Lunatic and His Cycling Wife* (London: Hutchinson, 1902)

Kitchen, Penny, ed., *For Home & Country: War, Peace and Rural Life As Seen Through the Pages of the W. I. Magazine, 1919–1959* (London: Ebury, 1990)

Kynaston, David, *Austerity Britain, 1945–51* (London: Bloomsbury, 2007)

—, *A Family Britain, 1955–57* (London: Bloomsbury, 2010)

Lancaster, Bill, *The Department Store: A Social History* (London: Leicester University Press, 1995)

Langbridge, R. H., ed., *Edwardian Shopping: A Selection from the Army and Navy Stores Catalogues 1893–1913* (Newton Abbot: David & Charles, 1975)

Laver, James, *Costume and Fashions: A Concise History* (London: Thames and Hudson, 1995)

Lawson, Twiggy, with Penelope Dening, *Twiggy in Black and White: An Autobiography* (London: Pocket, 1998)

Rosamond Lehmann, *Invitation to the Waltz* (London: Chatto & Windus, 1932; London: Virago, 1981)

—, *The Weather in the Streets* (London: Collins, 1936; London: Virago, 1981)

—, *The Echoing Grove* (London: Collins, 1953)

Levy, Shawn, *Ready, Steady Go!: Swinging London and the Invention of Cool* (London: Fourth Estate, 2002)

Lewis, Lesley, *The Private Life of A Country House 1912–1939* (Newton Abbot: David & Charles, 1980)

Longmate, Norman, *How We Lived Then: A History of Everyday Life During the Second World War* (London: Hutchinson, 1971)

Lurie, Alison, *The Language of Clothes*, with illustrations assembled by Doris Palca (London: Heinemann, 1981)

MacCarthy, Fiona, *Last Curtsey: The End of the Debutantes* (London: Faber, 2006)

Mackenzie, Midge, ed., *Shoulder to Shoulder: A Documentary* (London: Allen Lane, 1975)

MacKenzie, Norman and Jeanne, eds., *The Diaries of Beatrice Webb*, abridged by Lynn Knight (London: Virago, 2000)

McDowell, Colin, *The Literary Companion to Fashion* (London: Sinclair-Stevenson, 1995)

Mackenzie, Tom H., *The Last Foundling* (London: Pan Books, 2014)

McKibbin, Ross, *Classes and Cultures: England 1918–1951* (Oxford: Oxford University Press, 2000)

Macqueen-Pope, M., *Twenty Shillings in the Pound* (London: Hutchinson, 1948)

Maitland, Sara, ed., *Very Heaven: Looking Back at the 1960s* (London: Virago, 1988)

Malcolmson, Patricia and Robert, eds., *Nella's Last Peace: The Post-War Diaries of Housewife 49* (London: Profile, 2008)

—, eds., *Nella Last in the 1950s: Further Diaries of Houewife 49* (London: Profile, 2010)

Mannin, Ethel, *Confessions and Impressions* (London: Penguin, 1937)

Mansfield, Katherine, *The Collected Short Stories of Katherine Mansfield* (Harmondsworth: Penguin, 1981)

Marlow, Joyce, ed., *The Virago Book of Women and the Great War, 1914–18* (London: Virago, 1998)

Marwick, Arthur, *The Sixties: Cultural Revolution in Britain, France, Italy and the United States, c.1958–c.1974* (Oxford: Oxford University Press, 1998)

Marcus, Jane, ed., *The Young Rebecca: Writings of Rebecca West 1911–1917* (London: Virago Press, 1983)

Meredith, Alan and Gillian, and Michael J. Cuddeford, *Identifying Buttons* (Chelmsford: Mount Publications, 1997)

Meredith, Alan and Gillian, *Buttons* (Princes Risborough: Shire, 2000)

—, *Buckles* (Oxford: Shire Publications, 2008)

Meyer, Adele, and Clementina Black, *Makers of our Clothes: A Case for Trade Boards. Being the result of a year's investigation into the work of women in London in the tailoring, dressmaking, and underclothing trades* (London: Duckworth, 1909)

Miall, Agnes M., *The Bachelor Girl's Guide to Everything; or, The Girl on Her Own* (London: S. W. Partridge, 1916; Oxford: Oneworld Publications, 2008)

Miller, Betty, *On the Side of the Angels* (London: Hale, 1945; London: Virago, 1985)

Minns, Raynes, *Bombers and Mash: The Domestic Front, 1939–45* (London: Virago, 1980)

Mitchison, Naomi, *Small Talk: Memories of an Edwardian Childhood* (London: The Bodley Head, 1973)

—, *All Change Here: Girlhood and Marriage* (London: The Bodley Head, 1975)

—, *You May Well Ask: A Memoir, 1920–1940* (London: Gollancz, 1979; London: Fontana, 1986)

—, *Among You Taking Notes…: The Wartime Diary of Naomi Mitchison 1939–1945*, ed. Dorothy Sheridan (London: Gollancz, 1985; Oxford: OUP, 1986)

Mitford, Nancy, *The Pursuit of Love* (London: Hamish Hamilton, 1945)

Montizambert, Elizabeth, *London Discoveries in Shops & Restaurants* (London: Women Publishers, 1924)

Mortimer, Penelope, *Daddy's Gone A-Hunting* (London: Michael Joseph, 1958; London: Persephone, 2012)

—, *About Time Too: 1940–1978* (London: Weidenfeld & Nicolson, 1993)

Newby, Eric, *Something Wholesale: My Life and Times in the Rag Trade* (London: Picador, 1985)

Newman, Oksana, and Allan Foster, eds., *The Value of a Pound: Prices and Incomes in Britain, 1900–1993* (London: Gale Research International, 1995)

Nicholson, Mavis, *What Did You Do in the War, Mummy?: Women in World War II* (London: Chatto & Windus, 1995)

Nicholson, Virginia, *Singled Out: How Two Million Women Survived Without Men After the First World War* (London: Viking, 2007)

—, *Millions Like Us: Women's Lives in War and Peace, 1939–1949* (London: Viking, 2011)

Nield Chew, Doris, ed., *The Life and Writings of Ada Nield Chew* (London: Virago, 1982)

O'Brien, Edna, *The Country Girls* (London: Hutchinson, 1960; Harmondsworth: Penguin, 1963)

—, *Girl with Green Eyes* (Harmondsworth: Penguin, 1964)

Owen, Elizabeth, *Fashion in Photographs, 1920–1940*, in association with the National Portrait Gallery (London: Batsford, 1993)

Pankhurst, Emmeline, *My Own Story* (London: Eveleigh Nash, 1914; London: Virago, 1979)

Parker, Rozsika, *The Subversive Stitch: Embroidery and the Making of the Feminine* (London: Women's Press, 1983; London: I. B. Tauris, 2012)

Panter-Downes, Mollie, *One Fine Day* (London: Hamish Hamilton, 1947; London: Virago, 1985)

—, *London War Notes 1939–45*, ed. William Shawn (New York: Farrar, Straus and Giroux, 1971)

Partridge, Frances, *A Pacifist's War* (London: The Hogarth Press, 1978)

Peacock, Primrose, *Buttons for the Collector* (Newton Abbott: David & Charles, 1972)

Pember-Reeves, Maud, *Round About a Pound a Week* (London: G. Bell & Sons, 1913; London: Virago, 1979)

Penn, Margaret, *Manchester Fourteen Miles* (Cambridge: CUP, 1947)

Phillips, Tom, *We Are the People: Postcards from the Collection of Tom Phillips* (London: National Portrait Gallery, 2004)

—, *Women & Hats: Vintage People on Photo Postcards* (Oxford: The Bodleian Library, 2010)

Protheroe, Keren, *Petal Power: Floral Fashion and Women Designers at the Silver Studio, 1910–1940* (London: Museum of Domestic Design & Architecture, 2011)

Pym, Barbara, *Excellent Women* (London: Jonathan Cape, 1952; Harmondsworth: Penguin, 1980)

—, *Jane and Prudence* (London: Jonathan Cape, 1953; London: Virago, 2007)

—, *A Very Private Eye: The Diaries, Letters and Notebooks of Barbara Pym*, eds. Hazel Holt and Hilary Pym (London: Macmillan, 1984)

Quant, Mary, *Quant by Quant* (London: V & A Publishing, 2012)

Rappaport, Erika Diane, *Shopping for Pleasure: Women in the Making of London's West End* (Princeton, N. J.: Princeton University Press, 2000)

Reilly, Catherine, ed., *Scars Upon My Heart: Women's Poetry & Verse of the First World War* (London: Virago, 1981)

Rhys, Jean, *Voyage in the Dark* (London: Constable, 1934; Harmondsworth: Penguin, 1969)

Rice, Margery Spring, *Working-Class Wives: Their Health and Conditions* (Harmondsworth: Penguin, 1939; London: Virago, 1981)

Richards, Alan, *The Extraordinary Adventures of Benjamin Sanders, Button Maker of Bromsgrove* (Bromsgrove: The Bromsgrove Society, 1984)

Roberts, Elizabeth, *A Woman's Place: An Oral History of Working-Class Women 1890–1940* (Oxford: Basil Blackwell, 1984)

Roberts, Robert, *The Classic Slum: Salford Life in the First Quarter of the Century* (Harmondsworth: Penguin, 1971)

Robins, Elizabeth, *The Convert* (New York: Macmillan, 1907; London: The Women's Pess, 1980)

Rodaway, Angela, *A London Childhood* (London: Batsford, 1960)

Rolley, Katrina, and Caroline Aish, *Fashion in Photographs, 1900–1920*, in association with the National Portrait Gallery (London: Batsford, 1992)

Rowbotham, Sheila, *A Century of Women: The History of Women in Britain and the United States* (London: Viking, 1997)

Rushton, Pauline, *Mrs Tinne's Wardrobe: A Liverpool Lady's Clothes, 1900–1940* (Liverpool: National Museums Liverpool, 2012)

Sackville-West, Vita, *The Women's Land Army* (London: Michael Joseph, 1944)

Sage, Lorna, *Bad Blood* (London: Fourth Estate, 2000)

Settle, Alison, *A Family of Shops: Marshall & Snelgrove* (Margate: Thanet Press, 1950)

Sharp, Evelyn, *Rebel Women* (London: A. C. Field, 1910)

—, *Unfinished Adventure: Selected Reminiscences from an Englishwoman's Life* (London: John Lane, 1933)

Sheridan, Dorothy, ed., *Wartime Women: A Mass-Observation Anthology, 1937–45* (London: Mandarin, 1990)

Shulman, Nicola, *Fashion and Gardens* (London: Garden Museum, 2014)

The Silver Studio Collection, foreword by John Brandon-Jones, introduction by Mark Turner, with a contribution by William Ruddick (London: Lund Humphries [for Middlesex Polytechnic], 1980)

Smallshaw, Kay, *How to Run Your Home Without Help* (London: John Lehmann, 1949)

Smith, Dodie, *The Hundred and One Dalmatians* (London: Heinemann, 1956)

—, *I Capture the Castle* (London: Heinemann, 1949)

Smith, Emma, *The Great Western Beach: A Memoir of a Cornish Childhood Between the Wars* (London: Bloomsbury, 1998)

—, *Maiden's Trip* (London: MacGibbon & Kee, 1948)

—, *As Green as Grass: Growing Up Before, During and After the Second World War* (London: Bloomsbury, 2013)

Smith, May, *These Wonderful Rumours!: A Young School Teacher's Wartime Diaries 1939–1945*, ed. Duncan Marlor (London: Virago, 2012)

Spalding, Frances, *Virginia Woolf: Art, Life and Vision* (London: National Portrait Gallery, 2014)

Stanley, Jo, ed., *To Make Ends Meet: Women Over 60 Write About Their Working Lives, Memories Collected by the Older Women's Project* (London: Older Women's Project, 1989)

Steedman, Carolyn, *Landscape for a Good Woman: A Story of Two Lives* (London: Virago, 1986)

Storey, Joyce, *Our Joyce* (Bristol: Bristol Broadsides, 1987)

Story, Margaret, *How to Dress Well, etc.* (New York & London: Funk & Wagnalls, 1924)

Stott, Mary, ed., *Women Talking: An Anthology from the Guardian Women's Page, 1922–35, 1957–71* (London: Pandora, 1987)

Strange, Joan, *Despatches from the Home Front: The War Diaries of Joan Strange, 1939–1945*, ed. Chris McCooey (Eastbourne: Monarch, 1989)

Strachey, Julia, *Julia: A Portrait by Herself and Frances Partridge* (London: Gollancz, 1983)

Strachey, Ray, *The Cause: A Short History of the Women's Movement in Great Britain* (London: G. Bell & Sons, 1928)

Styles, John, *Threads of Feeling: The London Foundling Hospital Textile Tokens, 1740–1770* (London: The Foundling Museum, 2010)

Taylor, Elizabeth, *At Mrs Lippincote's* (London: Peter Davies, 1945; London: Virago, 1988)

—, *The Sleeping Beauty* (London: Peter Davies, 1953; London: Virago, 1982)

—, *The Wedding Group* (London: Chatto & Windus, 1968; London: Virago, 1985)

Thompson, Flora, *Lark Rise to Candleford* (Oxford: Oxford University Press, 1954)

Thompson, Thea, ed., *Edwardian Childhoods* (London: Routledge & Kegan Paul, 1981)

Tickner, Lisa, *The Spectacle of Women: Imagery of the Suffrage Campaign, 1907–14* (London: Chatto & Windus, 1987)

Tomalin, Claire, *Several Strangers: Writing from Three Decades* (London: Viking, 1999)

Tyrer, Nicola, *They Fought in the Fields: The Women's Land Army: The Story of a Forgotten Army* (London: Sinclair-Stevenson, 1996)

Uglow, Jenny, *The Lunar Men: The Friends Who Made the Future, 1730–1810* (London: Faber, 2002)

Uttley, Alison, *The Button-Box & Other Essays* (London: Faber, 1968)

—, *Country World: Memories of Childhood*, selected by Lucy Meredith (London: Faber, 1984)

—, *A Ten O'Clock Scholar and Other Essays* (London: Faber, 1970)

Warner, Sylvia Townsend, *Letters*, ed. William Maxwell (London: Chatto & Windus, 1982)

Vicinus, Martha, *Independent Women: Work and Community for Single Women, 1850–1920* (London: Virago, 1985)

Watson, Winifred, *Miss Pettigrew Lives For a Day* (London: Methuen, 1938; London: Persephone, 2000)

Wayne, Hilary, *Two Odd Soldiers* (London: Allen & Unwin, 1946)

Wayne, Jenifer, *Brown Bread and Butter in the Basement: A 'Twenties Childhood* (London: Gollancz, 1973)

—, *The Purple Dress: Growing Up in the 30s* (London: Gollancz, 1979)

Weldon, Fay, *Down Among the Women* (London: Heinemann, 1971)

Whipple, Dorothy, *High Wages* (London: John Murray, 1930)

Whitehorn, Katharine, *Roundabout* (London: Methuen, 1962)

—, *Selective Memory* (London: Virago, 2007)

Whiteing, Eileen, *Anyone for Tennis?: Growing Up in Wallington Between the Wars* (Sutton: London Borough of Sutton Libraries and Arts Services, 1979)

Willcock, H. D., ed., *Browns and Chester: Portrait of a Shop, 1780–1946* (London: Lindsay Drummond [for Mass-Observation], 1947)

Williams, Val, *The Other Observers: Women Photographers in Britain, 1900 to the Present* (London: Virago, 1986)

Wilsher, P., *The Pound in your Pocket 1870–1970* (London: Cassell & Co. Ltd, 1970)

Wilson, Elizabeth, *Only Halfway to Paradise: Women in Postwar Britain, 1945–1968* (London: Tavistock, 1980)

—, *Adorned in Dreams: Fashion and Modernity* (London: Virago, 1985)

—, and Lou Taylor, *Through the Looking Glass: A History of Dress from 1860 to the Present Day* (London: BBC Books, 1989)

Withers, Audrey, *Lifespan: An* Autobiography (London: P. Owen, 1994)

Woodhead, Lindy, *Shopping, Seduction & Mr Selfridge* (London: Profile, 2007)

Woolf, Virginia, *Orlando* (London: The Hogarth Press, 1928)

—, *A Room of One's Own* (London: The Hogarth Press, 1929; Harmondsworth: Penguin, 1945)

—, *The Years* (London: the Hogarth Press, 1957; Oxford: Oxford World Classics, 1992)

—, *Three Guineas* (London: The Hogarth Press, 1938; Harmondsworth: Penguin, 1977)

—, *Mrs Dalloway's Party* (London: The Hogarth Press, 1973)

—, *The Diary of Virginia Woolf*, ed. Anne Olivier Bell, Volumes I—V (London: The Hogarth Press, 1977; 1978; 1980; 1982; 1984)

Wyndham, Joan, *Love is Blue* (London: Heinemann, 1986)

—, *Anything Once* (London: Sinclair-Stevenson, 1992)

Yerbury, F. R., ed., *Modern Homes Illustrated* (London: Odhams Press, 1947)

ARCHIVES AND WEBSITES

Chesterfield Library, Local Studies

Collection of Working-class Autobiographies, Brunel University

Derbyshire County Archives, Matlock

The Hodson Shop, Walsall Museum, Walsall Council, Libraries Museums and Arts

The Imperial War Museum online

Millennium Milestones Archive, the British Library

Museum of Brands, Packaging & Advertising

The Museum of Domestic Design and Architecture (MoDA)
The Oxford Dictionary of National Biography online
The Primrose Peacock Collection, Somerset County Council, Heritage and
    Libraries Service
The Victoria and Albert Museum online
Visual Arts Data Service – vads.ac.uk
The Women's Library, London School of Economics

NEWSPAPERS AND MAGAZINES
*Button Lines, Costume, Daily Express, Daily Mail, Derbyshire Times, Guardian,
Good Housekeeping, Home and Country, Home Chat, Jackie, Observer, The Ladies
Pictorial, The Lady, Miss Modern, Modern Home, Nova, Picture Post, Punch, The
Times, Votes for Women, Woman's Life, Woman's Illustrated, Woman's Weekly*

ACKNOWLEDGEMENTS

Immense thanks go to my agent, Clare Alexander, who set me thinking about using family buttons as my starting point for this book; and to Juliet Brooke, my editor at Chatto & Windus, and all her colleagues who have worked so hard on its behalf.

I am indebted to the many writers whose work I have consulted. Some of my research was an indulgence, enabling me to read and re-read many mamoirs, autobiographies and much period fiction, in addition to historical and academic accounts. Some stand out: Alison Adburgham's work is a joy as well as an inspiration; Jenifer Wayne's memoirs are brimful of details. I found *Costume* magazine equally invaluable and am especially grateful to Katina Bill's acticle, 'Clothing Expenditure by a Woman in the 1920s'. I was pleased to discover Agnes M. Miall through Virginia Nicholson's work, and to read of Eileen Power via Catherine Horwood.

Various individuals have been generous with their time, and helped with information of one kind or another. My thanks to Janette Bright, the late Judith Clark and her daughter Rachel, Chris Haley, Kathryn Hartley, Kate Kellaway, Elizabeth Silkin and her grandmother Millie Levine, Katrina Webster and Euronwen Wood; also to Maggie Wood of MoDA, Catherine Lister of the Hodson Shop Collection and the staff of the Local Studies department of Chesterfield Library. I am grateful to the staff of the London Library and to the Carlyle Membership which assisted my researches there.

In addition to family buttons and some of the clothes they fastened, I have referred to notebooks, photographs, household receipts and family objects. My mother's generosity in allowing me to write about her life remains unstinting.

Lynn Knight was born in Derbyshire and lives in London. The women of her family, who have passed on many stories along with beaded bags and buttoned gauntlets, fostered her interest in the texture and narratives of women's lives. She is also the author of the biography *Clarice Cliff* (2005), and a memoir, *Lemon Sherbet and Dolly Blue: The Story of an Accidental Family* (2011).

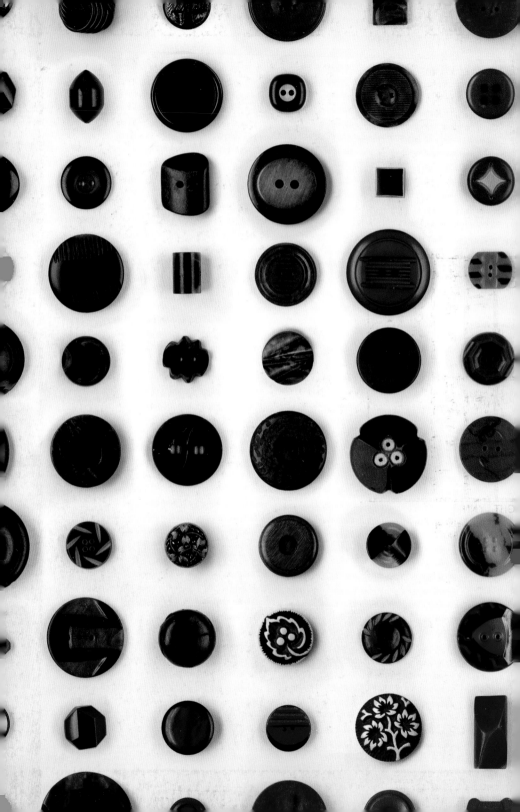